Novelists in their Youth

By the Same Author
The Language of Meditation
Egoism and Self-Discovery in the Victorian Novel
Trollope and Politics
Gissing: A Life in Books
C. P. Snow: An Oral Biography
The Life of Jane Austen
Jane Austen's Lovers (selected essays)

Editor
The Theory of the Novel
Jane Austen: Bicentenary Essays
Trollope Centenary Essays
Proust

Works Edited
George Gissing, *Denzil Quarrier*
George Gissing, *The Emancipated*
George Gissing, *Will Warburton*
George Gissing, *In the Year of Jubilee*
Henry James, *The Golden Bowl*
George Meredith, *The Ordeal of Richard Feverel*
Anthony Trollope, *Lord Palmerston*
Anthony Trollope, *Sir Harry Hotspur of Humblethwaite*
Anthony Trollope, *Dr. Wortle's School*
Anthony Trollope, *The Belton Estate*
Anthony Trollope, *The American Senator*

Novelists in their Youth

JOHN HALPERIN

Chatto & Windus
LONDON

Published in 1990 by
Chatto & Windus Ltd
20 Vauxhall Bridge Road
London SW1V 2SA

A CIP catalogue record for this book is available
from the British Library.

ISBN 0 7011 2937 9

Typeset by Opus, Oxford

Printed in Great Britain by
Mackays of Chatham, Chatham, Kent

For
Ann and John Whalley

The writing of this book
was generously supported by a fellowship grant
from the John Simon Guggenheim Memorial Foundation

Contents

Acknowledgements

For real rather than indirect help, useful and valuable advice, and sustaining support at various stages of writing this book, it is a pleasure to thank Nicholas Avery, Carmen Callil, Pierre Coustillas, Arthur Crook, Anthony Curtis, the Hon. Mrs Honor Earl, Leon Edel, the late Clarissa Farrell, Melvin J. Friedman, Michael Gilbert, Lady Glendevon, David M. Halperin, Elaine P. Halperin, Alexander R. James, Richard Lansdown, Jeremy Lewis, the Hon. Mrs Diana Marr-Johnson, Carolyn Levinson, Alberta Martin, Florence Muncy, the late Gordon N. Ray, Virginia Schaefer, Max F. Schulz, Norman Sherry, Gillian Tindall and William R. Tyler.

Needless to say, any errors in fact or judgement are my responsibility alone.

For generous grants which helped to bring this book into being, I am indebted once again to the John Simon Guggenheim Memorial Foundation, and also to the Vanderbilt University Research Council and its chair, Russell Hamilton.

I am indebted to the Oxford University Press for permission to reprint, in altered form, sections of Chapter Three which appeared in my *Gissing: A Life in Books* (Oxford and New York, 1982; reprinted 1987, 1988). A part of Chapter Four appeared in *Essays by Divers Hands* (Proceedings of the Royal Society of Literature, Vol. 46), Winter 1990.

J. H.
La Jolla, California, July 1989

Illustrations

Introduction

Nothing ever repeats itself exactly, and the most
analogous lives which, thanks to kinship of
character and similarity of circumstances, we
may select in order to represent them as
symmetrical, remain in many respects
contrasting.

> Proust, *Albertine disparue*

I thought how markedly . . . these works partake
of that quality of being – albeit marvellously –
always incomplete, which is the characteristic of
all the great works of the nineteenth century,
that century whose greatest writers somehow
botched their books, but, watching themselves
work as though they were at once workman and
judge, derived from this self-contemplation a
new form of beauty, exterior and superior to the
work itself, imposing on it a retroactive unity, a
grandeur which it does not possess.

> Proust, *La prisonnière*

Yet it happens to many writers that after a
certain age, when more mysterious truths no
longer emerge from their innermost being, they
write only with their intellect, which has grown
steadily in strength, and then the books of their
riper years will have, for this reason, greater

force than those of their youth but not the same
bloom.

Proust, Le temps retrouvé

People foolishly imagine that the broad
generalities of social phenomena afford an
excellent opportunity to penetrate further into
the human soul; they ought, on the contrary, to
realise that it is by plumbing the depths of a
single personality that they might have a chance
of understanding those phenomena.

Proust, Le côté de Guermantes I

For out of ourselves we can never pass, nor can
there be in creation what in the creator was not.

Wilde, The Critic as Artist

I

What is the relation between art and life? Is there any? If so, can it be
measured, or understood? Are there connections between literature
and the historical, cultural, and biographical moments at which it is
composed? Is literature in any way moulded by these connections,
and if so can we actually catch it, sometimes, in the act of being
'moulded,' of coming into being?

Perhaps foolishly, this book attempts to answer some of these
questions. I do assume that the tasks of the literary critic, the literary
historian, and the literary biographer are often the same tasks; and I
believe that criticism today might not be the worse for a more
spacious concern with these matters.

In his biography of Joyce, the late Richard Ellmann wrote:

The life of an artist . . . differs from the lives of other persons in
that its events are becoming artistic sources even as they
command his present attention. Instead of allowing each day,
pushed back by the next, to lapse into imprecise memory, he
shapes again the experiences which have shaped him. He is at
once the captive and the liberator. In turn the process of

reshaping experience becomes a part of his life, another of its recurrent events like rising or sleeping. The biographer must measure in each moment this participation of the artist in two simultaneous processes.

One might say this another way: 'Everything we think of as great has come to us from neurotics. It is they and they alone who found religions and create great works of art . . . without nervous disorder there can be no great artist.' That is Proust speaking, and on the subject of neurosis (as on so many others) he knew what he was talking about. Proust means, of course, that we must study the artist in order to know the work. His biographer, George D. Painter, acknowledges this readily enough:

> The biographer's task . . . is to . . . discover, beneath the mask of the artist's every-day, objective life, the secret life from which he extracted his work; show how, in the apparently sterile persons and places of that external life, he found the hidden, universal meanings which are the themes of his books; and reveal the drama of the contrast and interaction between his daily existence and his immeasurably deeper life as a creator.

Why do people so often progress, one after another, through the works of an author, once discovered? The answer seems clear. It is because his books are like no one else's; they appeal to the reader in such a way as to give him unique enjoyment. We search out the works of some authors rather than those of others not so much because of the works themselves but rather because of the name on the title page. When someone goes into a bookshop for the latest le Carré or the latest Updike, or inquires if yet another novel by Trollope is in paperback, he or she is asking, of course, for the author, a known quantity, rather than for the text, which until actually read is unknown to him except indirectly – through other works with the same name on the title page. The reader opens the book assuming that he or she will read on to the end because he or she has enjoyed the author's other books. This, after all, is the way in which the vast majority of people who read *do* read. To talk about a text without talking about its author, as today's (rapidly disappearing) 'decon-structionists' like to do, is to omit this crucial aspect of one's experience in reading novels: the *personality* of the novelist.

Wayne Booth reminds us in *The Rhetoric of Fiction* that the reader knows – indeed, cannot help knowing – that a story is being told by someone. Who the author is determines what is written and how the story is told, and so also determines in large measure the way in which the reader is likely to react to the story. Could we possibly discuss our response to *The Good Soldier*, for example, without also discussing the way in which Ford has chosen to tell his story? Inevitably we are led to ask: Why has Ford chosen to tell the story in *this* way? How can we separate Ford Madox Ford from *The Good Soldier*?

These questions steer us to an undeniable truth about all novels. They are told, as Mr Booth argues, by an implied author, who is created by the biographical author and is necessarily part of the formal experience of reading the novel. You cannot talk about form without talking about authors, just as you cannot talk about Euripides without talking about Athens. You cannot, after all, tell the dancer from the dance. All fiction is fiction; it is created by a biographical author who can be studied, analysed, and even, sometimes, understood.

In letters, diaries, notebooks, in any conscious form of autobiography, there will be some holding back. An autobiography can distort; facts can be realigned or omitted. But, as V. S. Naipaul has said, 'fiction never lies; it reveals the writer totally.' In *The Critic as Artist*, Wilde reminds us that 'Man is least himself when he talks in his own person. Give him a mask, and he will tell you the truth.' Samuel Butler admits this readily enough in *The Way of All Flesh*. 'Every man's work, whether it be literature or music or pictures or architecture or anything else,' Butler declares, 'is always a portrait of himself, and the more he tries to conceal himself the more clearly will his character appear in spite of him.'

So the role of the authorial personality in the work must be strictly observed and never forgotten. Anything in real life can be used in a novel, but its significance will often be found in its relationship to the authorial personality telling the story. All fiction emerges from the consciousness of the writer and is therefore shaped in the way that consciousness perceives. Seen in this light, novelists, perhaps, are the only people who tell the truth. Furthermore, the writer's perceptions and consciousness necessarily will be deeply involved in the shared assumptions of the culture, even if the writer rejects them. Wilde's famous assertion that Life imitates Art rather than *vice versa* reflects his understanding that art is always a product of the artist, and a reflection of his personality.

For even the most ferocious 'realist' does not merely 'copy' life: the artist arranges it to suit a purpose, whatever that may be. A man or a woman who writes a great work is nonetheless a man or a woman. 'I do not believe that they are right who say that the defects of famous [writers] should be ignored,' Somerset Maugham has written. 'I think it is better that we should know them [that is, the defects]. Then, though we are conscious of having faults as glaring as theirs, we can believe that that is no hindrance to our achieving also something of their virtues.'

Maugham suggests that biography can be as great an instrument for the achievement of what the Victorians called 'moral realism' as any novel by George Eliot or Trollope, and I am inclined to agree with him. Henry James actually thought of his novels as 'biographies', as the 'true histories' of 'real' men and women. Our knowledge that Beethoven was a nasty character cannot diminish our appreciation of his music; on the contrary, it may teach us that even those who, like ourselves, are flawed, can achieve something – in spite of, or perhaps because of, our flaws. In this way biography can make art more accessible, more comprehensible, to wider audiences. Insofar as the origins of art may ever be understood, biography may help us to understand them. The artist produces what he produces for the liberation of his soul, as Maugham puts it in *Ten Novels and Their Authors*. It is his nature to create, and it is the role of biography to illuminate his nature and thus that which is created. If the artist is a novelist he or she uses experience of people and places, apprehension of the self, loves and hates, deepest thoughts, passing fancies, to draw, in one work after another, a picture of life. It can never be more than a partial one, but if the artist is honest he or she cannot help, in the end, doing something else as well: 'he will draw a picture of himself.'

Hardy defines art as the pattern in things perceived by the artist. Just as the painter thinks with brush and colours, the novelist thinks with story and characters; the artist's view of life, though he or she may be unconscious of it – the artist's personality – exists as a series of invented human actions.

There is no such thing as being impervious to history. Erich Auerbach has demonstrated this convincingly in his great book

Mimesis; so has E. H. Gombrich in an equally great study, *Art and Illusion*. We live in the midst of our own historical moment, of course; our values, our thoughts, our prejudices, our perceptions, are products of that historical moment and of the accumulated wisdom of social history, as inevitably as they are products of our unique psyche. Whatever a person may choose to do, two of the reasons for that choice must always be found in the personality and in the moment. The personality and the moment permit and encourage certain responses to certain situations while discouraging others; a person's actions are seen by others as either appropriate or inappropriate depending upon the values and the taste of the present day – nor can the person help responding to the approval or the disapproval received. Every age reasons from different premises. Alexander the Great is considered by some historians today a vicious barbarian; in his own day the acquisition of as much land as possible, by whatever means necessary, was the prime measure of a great leader. Every person deserves to be judged by the standards of his or her day. We cannot help being conditioned by our milieu; and so it follows that the more we study history the more likely we are to be able to assess wisely the actions of the dead.

History used to be studied as a mirror of the present, a glass in which one could see reflected the meaning of the past and the probable course of the future. One can study it still for the same reasons. The trappings of our lives – our houses, our books, our means of communication and travel – may change, but our essential natures remain conditioned by the forces of the age we live in. This is always true. What is worked upon is always changing, as a direct result of what is working on it; human nature itself is an artifact of history, and can be studied that way.

II

The six authors treated in this book were born between the years 1840 (Hardy) and 1874 (Maugham), and died between the years 1903 (Gissing) and 1965 (Maugham). Their work appeared in the latter decades of the nineteenth century and the early decades of the twentieth. Hardy and James began to publish in the 1860s, Gissing in the 1880s, Conrad, Wharton, and Maugham in the 1890s. During the

1890s all of these authors were publishing fiction; during the 1920s all of them except James and Gissing were still writing.

Hardy and Gissing were good friends. James knew Gissing, was respected by Hardy, and worshipped by Conrad and Wharton. Gissing was read and admired by James, Wharton, and Maugham. Conrad knew Gissing and praised his work; Gissing thought Conrad the best of the generation of writers following his. Maugham was influenced by Conrad and Gissing, and wrote a novel about Hardy. Hardy, Conrad, Maugham and Wharton reached the height of their fame, prestige, and popularity in the first two decades of the twentieth century. Five of the six writers discussed here – Hardy is the only exception – expatriated themselves. Four died outside the country of their birth; three died in France.

Rather than choosing the subjects of this study by a throw of the dice, I have attempted to give some unity to the volume by concentrating on writers who shared a community of interests as well as a chronological period – one which may be defined, roughly, as that between the 1860s and the 1920s. More to the point – I have found something in each of my subjects that made him or her feel marginal or isolated or in some way anomalous, and I have tried to link that psychic wound, whatever its nature, to creative power, arguing that the one cannot be understood apart from the other, that the wound which never heals both allows and explains, insofar as anything so complicated can be explained, the creative process, or at the very least the desire to cry out, to be heard, to express oneself. In every case it is the impossible early wound that shapes the individual and gives form to what, as an artist, he or she produced.

I hope to show here what biographical criticism can do during a time of some radical departures from what, a generation ago, would have been considered conventional literary criticism. I think that we can understand a text well enough without having to 'deconstruct' it. Give me the first twenty or thirty years of an author's life, and I think I can explain, through examination of them and of the various influences (historical, psychological, geographical, familial, social, or whatever) exerted upon them, some of the reasons why the texts produced during the author's maturity came into being. Familiarity with an artist's formative years can help us to interpret and understand what he produces throughout his career – more reliably, I believe, than whatever we may think we learn from 'deconstructing' the work.

So I don't need to follow Hardy into old age to reach some conclusions about the themes of *The Well-Beloved* or *Jude the Obscure*; the author's first thirty years give us some of the answers. I don't need to follow James step by step until, at sixty, he produced *The Ambassadors*; the first twenty-five years of his life help explain the direction his novels were to take. I can draw a number of conclusions about *The Age of Innocence*, written by Edith Wharton in her fifties, by assessing the years leading up to the beginning of her career as a novelist. And so with the others. Some judgements can be made about a text without actually reaching it, chronologically, in the study of an author's life.

Biographical and historical study can also dispose of and dispense with some of the myths that have grown up around an author's life. Look at the facts; see, by the time adulthood has been reached, what interests or obsesses the writer, for reasons explainable at least in part as a result of his or her early years; and the rest may follow naturally and logically. An understanding of the truth – rather than the lies, which are legion – about Hardy's early years can help show why all of his novels are concerned in one way or another with class conscious-ness and class hostility. Knowing the nature of Conrad's youth can help us to gloss, in his fiction, a lifelong obsession with the lonely and the solitary. Edith Wharton's ambivalence about the city of her birth creeps into almost everything she wrote during a long career as a novelist. Familiarity with the horrors of Gissing's adolescence and Maugham's childhood can give us insight into much of the fiction they produced. And so with many other great men and women. In this instance I have had to limit myself to a set of six.

Some people, though probably not many, will already know the stories I am going to tell here; to most these stories will be unfamiliar. This book has been written with the common reader in mind – the reader who is interested in fiction, in history, in biography. The specialist may or may not find in these pages a new way of considering or approaching the work of my six authors; that he or she must decide individually.

Each of these biographical essays comes to an end at about the time the author begins to write. I draw some conclusions about the novelist's earliest work in order to point the direction upon which he or she has embarked. And I comment briefly on the rest of the career based on the influences that have informed the writer's impressionable

8

years and in this way inspired in the writer interests he or she will never entirely abandon. By the time an author begins to write, I believe, the themes and concerns to be addressed throughout the remainder of the creative life, *because of who the author is*, have already been set, and – relatively unsophisticated though they may be – remain largely unchanged, though often deepened and disguised.

Henry James, aged twenty, in Newport in 1863 (*Houghton Library*)

CHAPTER ONE

Inside Henry James

Was it not, surely, in order to concern myself
with them that I was going to live apart from
these people who would complain that they did
not see me, to concern myself with them in a
more fundamental fashion than would have been
possible in their presence, to seek to reveal
themselves to themselves, to realise their
potentialities?

> Proust, *Le temps retrouvé*

It was their good fortune, or else their misery, to
belong to a generation in which every individual
would be given a chance to discover and expose
his worth, down to the final ounce of strength
and nerve . . . All men were to be weighed in
this time.

> Shelby Foote, *The Civil War: A Narrative*

I think that to be an American is an excellent
preparation for culture.

> Henry James in 1867

It has been said that neither Henry James nor T. S. Eliot could ever
have been a child – that it's impossible to imagine them as anything
other than elderly sages. Tom Eliot in shorts? Henry James in
bell-bottoms? But of course they were young, once.

Near the end of his life, the expatriate James told Hamlin Garland that he – James – ought to have stayed in America. 'The mixture of Europe and America which you see in me has proved disastrous,' he is reported to have said. 'It has made of me a man who is neither American nor European. I have lost touch with my own people, and live here [in England] alone.' While on a visit to his brother in London in 1889, the philosopher William James told their sister Alice that the novelist was neither English nor American, 'but a native of the James family, and [he] has no other family.'

Henry James declares in one of his essays:

> I have not the least hesitation in saying that I aspire to write in such a way that it would be impossible to an outsider to say whether I am at a given moment an American writing about England or an Englishman writing about America (dealing as I do with both countries), and so far from being ashamed of such an ambiguity I should be exceedingly proud of it, for it would be highly civilized.

Perhaps what was unsettling for the man stimulated his art; once he had settled in England he produced as much great fiction as anyone who has ever written.

As we shall see, James was a 'divided' man, divided in several ways. As late as 1875, when he was thirty-two, he published an allegorical tale, 'Benvolio', about a character so split – so divided – 'it was as if the souls of two different men had been placed together to make the voyage of life in the same boat,' James writes here, 'and had agreed for convenience' sake to take the helm in alternation.'

If, as some believe, England's greatest novelist was a Pole – Conrad – could it be that America's greatest novelist was an Englishman? The answer to this question is complicated, revealing, and important. Throughout his early years, and indeed well beyond them, James found it difficult to decide – culturally, philosophically, geographically, and sexually – what he was. Many of these questions he never resolved. His mind was nourished on antitheses: past and present, experience and innocence, power and passiveness, masculine and feminine, Europe and America, tradition and experimentation. Whenever he managed, temporarily at least, to solve some of his dilemmas, this was accomplished by his living vicariously – in the lives of others, either in real life or in his fiction. The indecisiveness, the failure to become, as a young man, anything in particular, led him eventually to art, in which he could bury his divided soul. Art has often enough been a haven for neurotics. James's case is perhaps a genuine instance of what Keats, thinking of Shakespeare, called negative capability: the capacity of the artist to expunge or deny *self*, to make self, speaking figuratively, cease to exist; becoming a blank himself, the artist can then enter into, 'become', other people, and describe them from the inside. Someone capable of this sort of self-negation is perhaps never wholly himself, but rather always part of others – thus what has sometimes been called the 'androgyny' of art. James could perform this psychic magic.

One explanation for his ability to do it – apart from sheer genius, which cannot be adequately explained – may lie in the fact that he never satisfactorily charted out a persona for himself to inhabit. His remark to Hamlin Garland, made late in life, suggests this. 'I am that queer monster, the artist, an obstinate finality, an inexhaustible sensibility,' James declared two years before his death in 1916. He lived largely within his own mind, which was capable, in its creative energy, of taking him virtually anywhere. It could not take him, however, towards any vision of satisfactory human relationships: there aren't any in his novels. The only happily married couple in Shakespeare's plays is the Macbeths. So while this is an interesting aspect of James's vision, it would hardly seem to disqualify him as an acute observer and interpreter of humanity. He saw things in a certain way.

And perhaps in part because of his detachment from most of the usual paraphernalia of life, such as home and family, he became the most 'complete' artist America has ever produced. Nor is it surprising that he was the first great theorist of the art which he practised with, arguably, greater distinction than anyone else. But his thought was not by nature theoretical or abstract. He could be both broad and narrow, seeing great implications of Western society in the small facts of its polite routines. For him the subject of comparative cultures was crucially important: what he called the 'adventure' of culture could serve as an index to the greatnesses and failings of men, the fate of entire societies. James saw that one of the great and continuing stories of the West was the New World's rediscovery of the Old, and the Old's discovery of the New. The telling of this story required both action and inaction, movement and quiescence – for the subject was manners. James was the perfect conduit; in him the reaching out was forever balanced by the reaching in.

In the beginning it was his family rather than his imagination that took him almost everywhere. Born in New York on 15 April 1843, James was transported to Europe for the first time at the age of six months. Initially the family home was in Washington Place, a street running from Washington Square to Broadway, flanked on one corner by a university and on another by a church. Later the Jameses moved into a house at Fourteenth Street and Sixth Avenue. But the family never spent much time at home, and wherever it went tranquillity rarely reigned. James's uncertainties, his many unsolved dilemmas, may have their origin at least in part in his possessing, as a child, no fixed place of abode – in being, as he said later, one of a group of 'hotel children'. Besides the future novelist there was William, born in 1842; two younger brothers, Garth Wilkinson (Wilky) and Robertson, born in 1845 and 1846, respectively; and a sister, Alice, born in 1848. The parents, Henry and Mary James, seemed to be happily married. The father was a Swedenborgian philosopher, a friend of Emerson and Thoreau and Thackeray, all of whom were seen by the young Jameses in Washington Place. Henry James Senior was unorthodox by any standards, unpredictable, perhaps a bit unstable. It was largely his belief that being in the same school for long could stifle learning and imagination that led him to turn his offspring into hotel children. He seemed to believe in a state of permanent domestic revolution to foster independence. By constantly uprooting his children, he could prevent them from becoming conformists, from falling under the influence of any particular teacher or institution or discipline, and indulge his own taste for change. In New York his children went from tutor to tutor, from school to school. But there was one cohesive force in their lives, according to Henry James Junior. Mary James, he wrote after her death, 'was our life, she was the house, she was the keystone of the arch. She held us all together.' James thought of his mother as being stronger than his father, an important fact in his life.

The moving about began early. At first there were trips to and from Albany, home of the children's grandparents and various aunts, uncles, and cousins. There were two visits to Europe when James was quite young, and extended stays in England, France, and Switzerland. In 1855 the Jameses went to Europe, where they lived for the next five years – in London, in Paris, in Geneva, in Boulogne, in Bonn. The father's experiments produced brilliant but eccentric children. Both William and Henry suffered from ill-health, real or imagined, throughout their lives. William endured three nervous breakdowns. Alice never recovered from her nervous ailments, and became a chronic invalid. The two younger brothers went off to the Civil War and were physically broken by it. All the James children sustained physical or emotional handicaps more spectacularly acute than most children find themselves subject to; in some ways none of them ever fully recovered from growing up a James. Perhaps this is what William meant when he said that his brother Henry could locate his identity only as 'a native of the James family'. Henry James's life was to become, among other things, a long search to understand the ambiguities of his youth.

The many illnesses of the James children were undoubtedly the retrospective response to the nightmare of their formative years, the lack of a centre in their lives. They became adept at the politics of invalidism to get what they wanted. Illness was a means of acquiring attention, sympathy, and support amidst the chaos of family life; they all became competitive experts at being ill.

Because of his haphazard education, James was largely self-taught; his own reading and observation would be his most vital form of 'experience'. As a child he was passive, often silent, and bookishly lethargic. His boyhood friend (and the recipient of almost all of his earliest letters) Thomas Sergeant Perry refers to the young James's 'slow speech, his halting choice of words'. James emerged as a formidable talker only after his fame as a writer brought him a certain degree of assurance. Part of his early tentativeness must have been due to the ambiguity of the role-model he was supposed to emulate. Leon Edel refers to James's parents in these terms: 'a father strong, robust, manly, yet weak and feminine, soft and yielding . . . and a mother, strong, firm, but irrational and contradictory'. Ralph Touchett, musing in *The Portrait of A Lady* (1880–81) about his parents, remembers his father as being 'the more motherly; his mother, on the other hand, was paternal, and even . . . gubernatorial.' If there was uncertainty and emotional confusion in the young Henry James, this sort of ambiguity may have been one cause of it.

Asked by the other boys at one of his many schools what his father 'did', James brought the question home. How should he answer it?

The elder Henry James's reply did not help the son to grasp the father's identity: 'Say I'm a philosopher, say I'm a seeker for truth, say I'm a lover of my kind, say I'm an author of books . . . or best of all, just say I'm a student.'

From his writings we can guess what James as a boy made of the marriage so closely under his observation. The men in his fiction often derive strength and sustenance from the women they marry; the women sometimes withhold that sustenance, thus depriving the men of strength, even of life. Men need women to survive – thus their lives are often in the control of women. (This was later reconfirmed for James when his father survived his mother by only six months.) The unequal relation between the sexes was to become one of his ubiquitous mature themes: not necessarily the weakness of men and the strength of women on every occasion, but rather the idea that in *any* human relationship there is a strong and a weak partner, that *no* relationship is wholly equal, that one member of it is *always* dependent on the other. Sometimes, though not often, it is the women who need the men in order to go on living. But the significant fact is that *nowhere* in James's fiction is there any relationship between the sexes that is wholly satisfactory, or wholly satisfactory for long. His is a tragic view of humanity. He used to call this aspect of his vision, somewhat euphemistically, 'the imagination of disaster'. In his fiction people use others, live off them, drain the life-blood out of them; no adults anywhere in James's many books live in complete equality or comfortable harmony. It is one of the most striking things about his work.

By extension, then, anyone who is so unfortunate as to love another human being may ultimately have to renounce his or her own individuality. To love is to give up oneself, to make oneself vulnerable – no more and no less. This 'vampire' theme – one human being taking the strength from another in an unequal relationship – is found in a great many of James's tales, from early to late. One of his first stories, 'De Grey: A Romance', written when he was twenty-five and published when he was twenty-six, expresses fear of sexual passion as a form of weakness, of vulnerability. Here, marriage equals fatality. In the next decade, 'Longstaff's Marriage' (1878) suggests that marriage can destroy a man unless the woman is removed or, as it were, de-fanged. In *The Sacred Fount* (1901) a young man appears to be drained of his youthfulness by an older woman who in turn grows

younger in the process, while at the same time another man is seen to
be acquiring wit and intelligence from a brilliant female companion
who, as a result (apparently), seems to grow dull, almost witless. This
list could be made much longer. For James, love can be a deterrent
rather than a spur to life; it may become a threat to existence itself.
To be led to the marriage bed is, in a sense, to be sacrificed. Or so the
young James thought, perhaps, as he watched his strong mother keep
his erratic father more or less on track. This may be one reason why
he never married. When, in 1878, William did marry, Henry James
wrote to him from London: 'I believe almost as much in matrimony
for most other people as I believe in it little for myself – which is
saying a good deal.'

There were many sources of uncertainty for James in these early
years, as we have seen: the constant travelling, having no fixed abode
and no school, the impossibility of making friends or retaining them
for long, the eccentricity of his parents. Perhaps because he was left so
much on his own, James sometimes had the feeling of being
orphaned. His younger brother Robertson is on record as having
thought, as a child, that he was a foundling. And being a second son
with a brilliant older brother could not have done Henry James's
fragile adolescent ego much good. *Roderick Hudson* (1875), which
James began to write in 1874 and was fond of calling, in later years,
his first novel – it wasn't, as we shall see – among other things
recounts a story about a father who disinherits his son; the
protagonist is a second son who feels, in his unhappiness, 'that he
should bear a little spoiling' from his father now and then. Valentin in
The American (1877) is a second son, as is Morgan Moreen in 'The
Pupil' (1891). In *The Wings of the Dove* (1902) Kate Croy lives in 'a
state of abasement as the second born'. Being a second son both
deflated James's ego and sharpened his competitive claws. It is at any
rate another significant fact about him; and throughout his early
years he found it discouraging and depressing to see his brother
William always just a few paces ahead of him. It was as if, he tells us
in *A Small Boy and Others* (1913) – which, significantly, takes four
hundred pages to describe his first fourteen years – William 'had
gained such an advantage of me in his sixteen months' experience of
the world before mine began that I never for all the time of childhood
and youth in the least caught up with him and overtook him. He was
always round the corner and out of sight.' When, in his twenties,

Henry James began to publish reviews and stories in some of the leading American periodicals of the day, William decided that he too wished to write for publication.

The two famous brothers suffered from bad backs and constipation throughout various periods of their lives, and even developed a sort of rivalry about their ailments. Henry James Senior, William, and Henry Junior had bad backs, which William called 'a family peculiarity'; but when Henry Junior complained of his back in 1869, William dismissed the complaint as 'dorsal insanity'. William took his brother's constipation more seriously – perhaps because, as a student of psychology, he knew that chronic constipation has something to do with the control, involuntary or not, one extends over oneself and with the desire to retain one's possessions. Constipation presents a classic case of what a good Freudian would describe as discipline versus desire: the discipline of keeping control over one's bodily functions versus the desire, literally, to let go, to relax. Throughout his twenties Henry James suffered tortures from constipation. Significantly, it was only when he found his vocation and his permanent residence, after years of uncertainty, that this particular complaint disappeared. The bad back, however, plagued him into old age.

What is most important to understand about James's youth, perhaps, is that it kept him living, from day to day and due to a number of different causes, under great strain. Today we would probably say *stress* rather than strain. Henry James Senior seemed to feel that he could introduce his children to transcendent experience only by making existence for them almost impossible. In this he succeeded; and in later years as well as earlier, all of his children, to one degree or another as we know, found life treacherously difficult to live. Henry Junior's ego seems to have undergone a sort of protective arrest. He tells us in *A Small Boy and Others* that he was frequently resentful and envious of others, and that he felt himself to be 'other' – strange, different – from his fellows. He was, of course, to turn this feeling of detachment to literary use.

James's passiveness – his envy of the robustness of other males, his habit of observing rather than actively taking part – dates from his earliest years. Ultimately he would decide that he was unfit for, disabled from participating in, active experience, and see his role as that of a recorder of the activities and experiences of others. The turning of hardship, real or imagined, into advantage was a James family habit, perhaps because there was no other alternative. We know that James identified himself with his mother – it was said that he looked very much like her – rather than his father. Slowly the abject, inarticulate second son transformed himself into the passive receptacle of experience. No wonder so many of his mature tales turn out to hinge upon the possible passions of observed others; no wonder the question of somebody else's innocence or experience is always at issue.

Experience, for James, came to be seen as something cerebral rather than physical, passive rather than active. In his famous essay 'The Art of Fiction' (1884) he was to call experience 'an immense sensibility', emphasizing its mental rather than its physical components. It was something you acquired through reflection rather than action, through observation of others rather than through knowledge obtained yourself. The usual narrative angle in James's mature fiction consists of the author's account of somebody else's impression of others; this is the 'point of view' he made famous, and its origin lies at least in part in the fact that from an early age he saw and felt and learned through indirection, through observation of others. Seeing things through others' eyes, life becomes something observed indirectly, at several removes from oneself. For the spectator, experience was concentrated, squeezed into images rather than photographs. Thus James's literary impressionism, explained and defended clearly enough in one of his most brilliant stories, 'The Real Thing' (1893). Cultivating his powers of observation and the process by which what he observed was turned in his work into images of the real. James eventually became, to borrow a phrase from 'The Art of Fiction', one of those 'people on whom nothing is lost'. In an autobiographical volume he describes himself (in the third person) as going 'without many things, ever so many – as all persons do in whom contemplation takes so much the place of action; but . . . he was really . . . much to profit by it.' James's passivity was by time and degree refined into a mode of artistic vision.

When he was eleven one of those moments of what he would later call 'apprehension' vividly occurred. It may help to document James's passivity, his tendency to turn observation into image – as well as his susceptibility to largely male stimuli. Several years older than Henry James, Gus Barker was one of his Albany cousins. One day the future novelist burst into a room to find William sketching Gus, who had discarded the uniform of the military school he was attending and was posing naked. Gus Barker, James wrote later, was someone he had always liked: 'Ingenuous and responsive, of a social disposition, a candour of gaiety, that matched his physical activity.' Seen thus unclothed, cousin Gus, James would recall, was 'the most beautifully made athletic little person', appealing and engaging in every way. 'Perched on a pedestal and divested of every garment', Gus Barker remained for the gaping James the very image of innocence, youth, strength, beauty, and action; and that image became even more sacred and powerful when, at the age of twenty-one, Gus's life was snuffed out by a sniper's bullet during the Civil War. James kept William's sketch of the boy athlete; it was all that remained of him. The healthy cousin, full of life and glowing with power, reinforced James's sense, at an early age, of his own hopeless weakness, the inevitability of his own inaction. His later memoir of Gus Barker makes this clear.

Around the same time – the age of eleven – James heard the celebrated preaching of Mrs Cora V. Hatch in an Astor Place basement. She was to resurface in several of his tales, most notably as a type of female orator familiar to readers of *The Bostonians* (1886). During this period in New York he went from tutor to tutor and from school to school before being propelled, in Europe, from country to country. Henry James Senior, as we know, feared pedantry and rigidity, dogma and moral judgement; he felt he must keep his family on the move lest anything in particular sink too deeply into it. As Henry James Junior wrote many years later, he felt himself almost forced to pay attention to everything – to be one of those people on whom nothing is lost – and through this process to try to wring order and sense out of the chaos of his young life. The absence of any conventional formal education forced James to translate, or 'convert', as he put it later, everything that happened to him into his own terms of understanding, to render them to himself in the light of his own comprehension. In other words, he was forced from an early age, if he wished to make sense of the things around him – and he did – to organize, to design, to apprehend the world in some orderly way of his own devising. Most middle-class children in the nineteenth century had their worlds carefully explained to them. But no one put things in order for Henry James; he was forced to do it for himself. In this way, perhaps, he began to develop the sharp observer's eye for detail, the sensual awareness without which no one can be an artist. James's conclusion, years later, was that 'no education avails for the intelligence that doesn't stir in it some subjective passion and almost anything that does so act is largely educative.' His intelligence was stirred not so much by the challenges of schoolmasters as their absence from his life and his own 'subjective passion' to make sense of the uncertainties around him.

From 1855 to 1860 – James's twelfth to seventeenth years, following his non-education in New York – the family was in Europe (except for the last half of 1858, spent in Newport). During this sojourn abroad it is likely that he began to develop a sense of style – or, more exactly, an awareness that different styles existed, styles not just different from America's, but different, in the European context, from one another. This developing sense alerted him to many possible artistic choices, made later. It was Paris, he was always to say, that first awoke him to the 'greatness' of Europe; this is not surprising, and it may help to explain why *The Ambassadors* (1903), in which the Parisian setting is crucial to everything that happens, is arguably his greatest novel. After 1860 James was not to see Europe again until 1869, by which time, at the age of twenty-six, many of his choices – including the most important one, to be a writer – had been made. The adolescent years abroad supplied data, impressions, and experiences without which that choice might not have been made. He had thought for a while that, like his brother William, he wanted to paint. Europe told him that he was not good enough. But it also made possible his interest in and studies of comparative art. French painting and the beginnings of Impressionism especially fascinated him. His studies taught him that at least he might become a knowledgeable critic of the work of others. The little read but copious art criticism of his later years is sophisticated and incisive. Differences in painting styles were also to alert him to the fact that a story could be told in a number of ways; the famous literary prefaces of his last years bulge with analogies between the novelist's art and the painter's.

On 8 July 1855 the family landed at Liverpool, and two days later James saw London, other than as an infant, for the first time. Soon the family found itself in the Paris of the Second Empire. On they went to Switzerland. Past and present, old and new, Europe and America – the comparisons would constantly have been in James's mind, and it is no wonder that he spent the next half-century attempting to work out their relationships to one another. American critics who have condemned him for not writing more about American life have not understood the plain facts of his boyhood: during his most impressionable years American life was known to him only dimly.

The Jameses went to Geneva, then back to Paris, then back to London, where they spent the winter of 1855–6, among other things taking long walks and going regularly to the theatre. By the summer of 1856 they were back in Paris again, where Henry James had another series of tutors, attended the theatre, and took long walks with William. One of his tutors was vaguely mixed up with anarchists; the young James heard from him stories of spies and 'subversives' which later had a role to play in one of his greatest but most undervalued novels, *The Princess Casamassima* (1886). More to the point, he learned to read French, and, voracious novel reader that he was, even at thirteen and fourteen, he began to read French fiction. From this period (1856–7) dates the beginning of the extraordinary fluency in French James was to preserve throughout the rest of his life. It was during their second year in Paris in 1857 that Henry James Senior described in a letter his second son as a 'devourer of libraries,' and reported that the boy had already begun to write 'novels and dramas'. Like his great disciple Edith Wharton, the habit of scribbling began early with him. He was fond of 'reading' rather than 'study', his father noted. But what sort of extended 'study' did he expect the fourteen-year-old boy to pursue as the family raced from place to place?

They spent the summer of 1857 in Boulogne, where Henry James nearly died of typhus fever, and then returned to Paris. It was during the winter of 1857–8 that whispers of Henry Senior's financial difficulties began to reach the family. They moved to less elegant lodgings, and a return to America was spoken of – though not, as yet, undertaken. When he came to write 'The Pupil', which among other things describes an itinerant and financially embarrassed American family in Europe, James undoubtedly remembered this winter in Paris. In the story it just happens to be a second son who suffers most acutely from the irresponsibility of his parents. As Mr Edel has observed, the plight of young Morgan in this tale recaptures the anguish of an adolescent for whom the world has no anchors, and who thus remains afloat among uneasy values and unrelieved anxieties. Inevitably, perhaps, Morgan develops an emotional dependency on his tutor, the only man around who offers loyalty, devotion, and stability. Probably Henry James in Paris was seeking, consciously or not, this sort of support. At any rate, he was not getting it from anyone in his family or, for that matter, anyone outside it.

The family finally returned to America and spent the rest of 1858 in Newport. James was now fifteen. President Buchanan was struggling unsuccessfully with the slavery question; Lincoln and Douglas, running for the Senate in Illinois, were about to debate the issue in public. A great and bloody civil war was about to overtake them all; but not yet. In Newport, James took a final fling at becoming a painter, and then gave up for good. His studies influenced his conception of the novel, as we have seen, and added a host of studio terms to his critical vocabulary. John La Farge, with whom he studied painting in Newport, gave him Balzac to read, and Merimée, and Gautier. The devourer of libraries swallowed them all.

In the next year the Jameses were off again, this time to Switzerland and Germany. From the novelist's autobiographical volumes one can tell that the adolescent boy continued to be disturbed by the constant upheavals, the restlessness, the apparent purposelessness of his parents. No wonder he felt 'disconnected', as he wrote later, from America. No wonder he was shy. His father admitted to a friend that his sons had been 'all along perfectly starved on their social side'. The intellect grew, but the heart, perhaps, could not keep up the same pace. Emotionally, Henry James continued to suffer from arrested development.

After one day in Le Havre, about as long as Caroline Spencer stops there in James's story 'Four Meetings' (1877), they all went back to Geneva, where the future novelist, sixteen now, was dispatched to a preparatory school for engineers and architects. Predictably, this was not a success; James later wrote of this period of his life that it was 'darkness, waste, and anguish . . . it was hard and bitter fruit all and turned to ashes in my mouth.' His poor mathematical skills made him feel inferior to the other students – yet another inferiority to worry about. James wondered if he was being punished by his parents for reading too many novels. Later he described himself in the Geneva school as a 'lost lamb, audibly bleating.' For the first time he felt homesick for America, especially for Newport and for the one great friend of his boyhood who lived there, Thomas Sergeant Perry. His letters from Geneva to Perry in Newport (1859–60), written just before the James family returned there more or less for good, beg for news. Read today, they appear to have been written by a precocious, and also a lonely and unhappy seventeen-year-old (James turned seventeen in April 1860). But who is happy at seventeen?

Toward the end of his time in Geneva, Henry James gave up any pretence of academic study and went back to devouring libraries. The new *Cornhill Magazine*, edited by Thackeray, introduced him, as it introduced much of the rest of the world, to Trollope, via *Framley Parsonage*. James continued to read French literature, including Racine; one of his Swiss tutors described for him Rachel's playing of Phèdre, a description he still remembered vividly when he wrote *The Tragic Muse* (1890). In July 1860 the family left Geneva and went to Bonn. James was too unhappy at Geneva to use it much in his fiction, but readers of 'Daisy Miller' (1878) may recall that Winterbourne, the protagonist, went to college there, 'on trial'; the city itself is described briefly as 'the little capital of Calvinism'.

William liked Germany and the Germans, but Henry could never stand them. He found them 'joyless', and later went out of his way to satirise the German character in 'A Bundle of Letters' (1879) and 'Pandora' (1884). The family had not been long in Bonn before the elder Jameses decided not to go to Frankfurt for the winter, which had been the plan, but instead to return to Newport in September. Again there were financial difficulties; and in any case Henry James Senior had decided that William, who still wished to paint, should study with William Morris Hunt in Newport. Henry James Junior was jubilant. 'I think that if we are to live in America it is about time we boys should take up our abode there,' he wrote to Perry. 'The more I see of this estrangement of American youngsters from the land of their birth, the less I believe in it.' For 'American youngsters', read Henry James. His own later expatriation, he came to feel, was a logical result of what he calls here his 'estrangement' from America. When he finally took up a permanent abode, it was not in 'the land of [his] birth'. Between July and September 1860 James longed desperately for America, which meant for him a respite from rootlessness. He now dispatched to Perry an astonishing series of what can only be called love letters (sublimated and indirect, to be sure); he wrote to his one friend as the living embodiment of the country he thought he missed.

For the next year and a half, until the spring of 1862, the family lived in Newport. During this period James was again sent desultorily to tutors, studied a little painting, read novels (mostly Balzac's), and discovered Browning, whose work was to hold a lifelong fascination for him. (The influence of Browning's dramatic method on James's is a potentially rich, and so far unexplored, field.) He renewed his friendship with Perry. And in January 1861 he was introduced to his first cousin, Minny Temple, a daughter of his father's widowed sister. Minny was considered by her Newport circle of friends and relations a rare free spirit, and generally admired. James enjoyed her company. Despite some speculation to the contrary, he was never in love with her, as the letters he wrote after her death vividly demonstrate. She died in 1870, at twenty-four, of a lingering consumption; and James, who rarely at that time of his life let pass an opportunity to feel, fired off across the Atlantic (he was then back in England) a series of documents which celebrate her life and memory and betray virtually every feeling it is possible to have about another person *except* love: we shall examine these letters in their place. Minny Temple was to become one of his great literary subjects: the doom of gratuitous impulse, the beautiful lost thing never able to achieve its promise, what Tennessee Williams was fond of calling 'the charm of the defeated'. Minny in memory was to join James's other beautiful lost young cousin, Gus Barker; together they gave him a theme, one he was to mine again and again throughout his career: the beautiful losers of life, the doom and death of the living – while those who have ceased to 'live' in every way except for the accident of continued existence go on merely surviving. There is something sado-masochistic in all of this. To dream of and exult in the damaging and ultimately the extinction of beauty and talent by the ugly or the commonplace surely is a sign of psychological or emotional instability or disturbance at some level. It suggests among other things that, through fantasy, the dreamer is 'getting even' with those he sees as more appealing or talented than himself. No wonder Henry James is a Freudian's delight.

He was to complain that though, now he was seventeen, his parents had not divined in him any aptitude for authorship; he had received from them no encouragement to pursue a literary life. While he doesn't say so directly, he seems to have resented the family's more obvious interest in William's short-lived career as a painter. Nonetheless, this was a period of relative stability for the future novelist; the family actually stayed in one place. Much later, in *The American Scene* (1907), he would speak of the years between 1860 and 1862 in Newport as a 'time of settled possession'.

On James's eighteenth birthday, 15 April 1861, President Lincoln issued his first call for volunteers (exactly four years later, to the day, he was shot). The Civil War had begun on 12 April in the harbour at Charleston, when Southern guns fired on Fort Sumter. Tangible evidence of struggle and choice abruptly confronted James: his generation was to face epic years of passion, division, upheaval, and change. At first he did what his friends were doing: he made bandages and rolled bullets, and watched the raw recruits hurry by – a scene transfigured by the very personal interest in life and death that now began to confront him. Two of his cousins, Gus Barker and William Temple, Minny's brother (who was also to die in the conflict), enlisted. Eventually, after some discussion with the family, the two younger James brothers, Wilky and Robertson, were allowed to join up. Until 1863, when Lincoln instituted America's first draft, young men of James's age had several choices. They could enlist, if they were medically fit; they could answer the military question by sending a substitute in their place, if one could be found; or they could buy, for $300, an exemption from service. Thus arose a cry in the North of 'a rich man's war and a poor man's fight', Lincoln's initial unpopularity, the anti-draft riots in New York in which a great many were killed or injured, and the early successes of the Confederacy.

In retrospect, it would seem to be no accident after all that it was now, in the spring of 1861, that James, faced with these momentous choices of life and death, of roles to be played out, allegedly suffered what he was later to call 'an obscure hurt' – an event which has spawned more speculation about him than any other event in his life. What exactly was this 'obscure hurt' – which, according to the novelist, disqualified him not only from participation in the Civil War but also, forever, from the normal physical exertions of life – including sexual exertions – and rendered him a sort of invalid, a permanent spectator of life, passive and celibate?

The stress on the young James, already acute as a result of factors we have examined, now grew almost insupportable. There was the challenge of war: should he take an active or a passive part? Should he put on a uniform, or roll bandages at home? Was he, indeed, like other men of his age – like William Temple and Gus Barker, like his

26

two unintellectual, physically healthy younger brothers, like all of the others marching off to the battlefields? Was he, indeed, a man? His friendship with Minny Temple was spiritual, but no more. As an aspiring, untried, untested writer and critic, he had so far done nothing to justify in anyone's eyes a decision to lead a sedentary life: he was, after all, just eighteen. The younger brother of a man of apparently brilliant promise, the son of a philosopher, it was assumed that of course he would 'do' something. But what would he do? Equally important: where would he do it? The geographical instability of his early years had posed an interesting question: of what country was he a citizen? Was he an American, like William Temple and Gus Barker? Should he fight for a country from which, as he said, he felt 'estranged'? Could he fight? If he failed to fight, would he be thought a shirker, a coward? Was he a coward?

The passional death of Henry James – if one can call it that – which now took place was in some way connected to these questions, especially those of gender, of sex. Probably they came into focus for him as a result of discoveries he made about himself, stimulated by the outbreak of war and the personal issues it inevitably raised. Was he like other men, or not? We can draw upon the evidence of later years, especially that from some of his recently published letters, to show, at the very least, sexual ambivalence, and more probably something like repressed homosexuality. Does it matter? Only insofar as it may help us to form part of the picture of these earlier years: that of a man hesitating between identities, cultures, occupations, and sexual roles, as well as having to make very practical decisions affecting his immediate fate and his future place in the life of his day. James may well have been asexual rather than homosexual: that is, just as he was 'above mere ideas', as T. S. Eliot put it, so he may have been above mere sex – if sex can ever be mere. Perhaps he was genuinely androgynous, everything and nothing, as many geniuses seem to have been. His insights into the minds of others were profound because his own mind, paraphrasing Eliot, was unfettered by anything so limiting as a particular sexual, or geographical, or cultural point of view.

This climactic moment in James's life was what today we might call a crisis of identity. It fixed forever certain preoccupations that were, in one way or another, to creep into everything he wrote: the question of innocence versus knowledge – how much it is good to know, especially about oneself; the perils as well as the virtues of unfettered vision; the moral advantages of renunciation, especially if you do not really wish to acquire what you seem to be renouncing. We come back to the beauty of loss. It is easier to recommend renunciation. It is easier to renounce what others want, if you have no loyalties and want nothing.

The lack of balance, the unsatisfactory nature of human relationships in James's work, articulate his ambivalent perception of his own place in the world and his relation to others. Is it so surprising, as this all-embracing ambivalence persisted, that such a man would develop a bad back, or that he might suffer for years from, of all things, constipation? The stress arising out of choices to be made and his inability to make them, realizations about himself that had the effect of traumatizing him even more deeply – these things, taken together, may well account for and add up to the 'obscure hurt' of James's eighteenth year. It need not have been a physical injury at all, as so many have speculated – a sacroiliac strain from pushing and pulling a fire-engine during a local fire, an impalement upon a fence, the other ingenious and sometimes derisive reasons we have been given by James's biographers and critics for his withdrawal into passivity. On evidence the obscure hurt is just as likely to have been mental, emotional and spiritual, as physical. In the Jamesian system of things, we should recall, 'experience' refers to spiritual rather than physical development.

So it was a crisis of identity that beset Henry James in 1861, a crisis that brought with it new knowledge of, or at the very least new questions about, himself. The call for troops and the stirring of the young men of his age around him to action made him look into his own heart and mind; and what he found there, or failed to find, wounded him deeply. The fact that James's obscure hurt apparently occurred at the moment the Civil War began cannot be coincidental. He was trying to define himself; it was a painful, complicated, searing, jarring experience. 'In his talk he tried word after word to express the precise shade he required,' E. F. Benson has written of James. 'He avoided ... any definite and final statement.' This is both crucial to an understanding of James the person and the writer, and symbolic of one of the ways in which his work reflected the imprecisions of his life. The search for the right word, the avoidance of any 'definite and final statement', helps account for the 'difficulty' of much that James wrote, but for its wonderful richness as well. The endless ambivalence of his personality provides the constant moral dilemmas of his literary personages.

What James said later of this time in his life, if critics would only read it, supports the argument that what happened to him in 1861 was a psychic rather than a physical event, a sort of epiphany. He tells us in the second volume of his autobiography, *Notes of A Son and Brother* (1914), that during this spring (1861) 'the breaking out of the War' and 'a passage of personal history the most entirely personal . . . bristling with embarrassments' coincided. He says here that a 'queer fusion or confusion [was] established in my consciousness . . . by the firing on Fort Sumter, Mr Lincoln's first call for volunteers' and a 'mishap' of his own, and that these things in conjunction 'were to draw themselves out incalculably and intolerably'. What could be more 'entirely personal' than self-examination? This caused the 'confusion . . . in [his] consciousness'. President Lincoln's call for troops, which James characterizes here as a 'great public convulsion', overtook him 'at the same dark hour' as this 'passage of personal history', and caused in him a great private 'convulsion' as well. He does not say that one provoked the other, that public events generated private events, but such a conclusion is compatible with everything else we know about him at this time.

He goes on in *Notes of A Son and Brother* to say that the crucial period – that is, the passage of personal history – lasted only 'twenty odious minutes'. This is more than enough time, at a moment of both national and personal crisis, coinciding with a demand for action and decision, to make, under duress, discoveries about oneself of the most incandescent variety. It does not take weeks or days or even hours to see, when you are forced finally and inescapably to come to the point, that you are unfit to fight, that you are not like your friends, that you are in fact disqualified from many of the traditional obligations of your sex. 'What might still happen to everyone about me, to the country at large,' James wrote of this time, obliged him to examine himself intimately, and subjected him to what in his old age he called 'a single vast visitation'; this 'vast visitation' brought on 'a huge comprehensive ache . . . which one could scarce have told whether it came most from one's own poor organism . . . which has suffered particular wrong . . . [or] from the enclosing social body.'

So much for the fire-engine and the fence. The 'vast visitation' which provoked in James 'a huge comprehensive ache' must have been emotional rather than physical, psychic rather than metallic. One is not 'visited' by a fire-engine or a fence. But one can be visited by thoughts, one can be visited by a sudden and unforeseen obligation to render up one's spiritual accounts. The novelist goes on to say at the end of this autobiographical reminiscence that the 'visitation' established 'a relation to everything occurring round me not only for the next four years' – that is, for the duration of the Civil War, which ended in April 1865 and in which he did *not* participate –

> but for long afterward . . . . [It] was at once extraordinarily intimate and quite awkwardly irrelevant. I must have felt in some befooled way in presence of a crisis – the smoke of Charleston Bay [where Fort Sumter was situated] still so acrid in the air – at which the likely young should be up and doing or . . . lend a hand much wanted; the willing youths, all round, were mostly starting to their feet.

But James looked within, and did not stand up. Finding himself, as he puts it in *Notes of A Son and Brother*, 'at a dire disadvantage of position', he examined, at this time of national emergency, not the contemporary political and military scene, but rather his own soul; and in doing so he caused himself, as he remarks here, 'a horrid even if an obscure hurt'. He concludes: 'What was interesting from the first was my not doubting in the least its duration.' He knew instantly that his wound would have lasting, even permanent, effects precisely because it was psychic rather than physical. The latter could heal; the former could not. He could not have said what he did about a physical 'hurt'. But a self-discovery, 'at once extraordinarily intimate and quite awkwardly irrelevant', fits the scenario.

Now it is also true that James injured himself while helping to fight a fire in Newport, and that he complained forever afterward of a back injury. But 'to have trumped up a lameness at such a juncture could be made to pass in no light for graceful,' as he freely admitted later. He did not 'trump up a lameness' – a bad back – to avoid fighting in the Civil War. His incapacity for action, his passiveness, was indigenous, as the rest of his life was to prove. Rather than shirking or cowering or hiding, he discovered in himself, intelligent as he was, symptoms which justified his decision not to fight. His passiveness, his withdrawal from the normal male activities of life (fighting and sex, for example), began here, with this epiphany; it was a result and a manifestation of the psychic wound he discovered in himself in April 1861, a very real wound indeed, though not visibly bleeding. For in that month and in that moment, he came face to face with himself in a way many of his fictional characters fail to do, or manage to do only when it is too late to help or save them. Henry James looked within and saw the beast in the closet. Three years later he began to grow a beard which effectively hid most of his face from the world for the next thirty-five years.

Some of the words James uses in these autobiographical passages have clouded the question of his failure to fight in the Civil War. They have also encouraged some critics to think, somewhat mischievously perhaps, that what happened during the twenty odious minutes was an event very physical indeed which could explain James's lifelong celibacy: some form of castration. But James was healthy enough in July 1861 to go mountain-climbing in New Hampshire with Perry; in later life he rode on horseback, fenced, lifted weights, walked prodigiously, travelled everywhere, pursued a vigorous social life, and of course worked hard, constantly, and productively. Only in an emotional sense can he be said to have been in any way an invalid. More to the point: it is a matter of record that the Newport fire during which James apparently injured himself occurred on the night of 28 October 1861, six months after the Civil War began (and three months, incidentally, after the Union forces suffered their notable disaster at the first battle of Bull Run). This is important. As long as the dates are not confused we should be able to see James's 'obscure hurt' as what in fact it was; an excruciating mental convulsion – 'a huge and comprehensive ache' – rather than a physical mishap. It was self-discovery, not impalement on a fence. James may well have hurt his back fighting the Newport fire in October 1861, and his later complaints about his bad back no doubt were genuine. Pains are painful no matter how induced. But there was nothing wrong with James's back in April 1861, when Lincoln called for troops, and the future novelist, discovering who and what he was, knew he could not answer. The obscure hurt is obscure indeed, made even more so by the roundabout, orotund way in which James tells the story; his account in *Notes of A Son and Brother* is, perhaps, deliberately obfuscatory. But it is not an impenetrable matter if, as often with

James, we can steel ourselves to gather clues and read between the lines. The wound which kept him out of the Civil War was no trumped-up lameness, to use James's own words – a ruse he considered beneath him; it was a lifelong fact.

From this time forward Henry James thought of himself as a semi-invalid; and having established his difference from others on a physical basis, he was free – indeed, by what we might call the rule of conversion, he was obligated – to try to compensate for his passivity in an appropriate way, which ultimately led to a return to life through art. If he could not live life himself, he could at least create it for others and write about the ways in which they lived it. He began his career as a writer by sending essays to the *North American Review* (the first of these appeared in October 1864) and stories to the *Continental Monthly* ('A Tragedy of Error' was published in February 1864) and the *Atlantic Monthly*.

It was in March 1865 that 'The Story of A Year' appeared in the *Atlantic*. Written early in 1864, when James was twenty, it became in later years his first 'acknowledged' tale. Set against the background of the Civil War – indeed, his fiction was the only contribution James was able to make to the war, which ended a month after it was published – 'The Story of A Year' is about the illusion of love. As in so much of his later fiction there are young people here who think they may love one another but are unsure of themselves and of each other and thus reluctant to assert or commit themselves. When they find themselves able to do so, one of them pays for this rashness, this presumption, with his life. Emotions, feelings – above all, love – can kill, the story tells us. Though very early, it is already vintage James. In 'The Story of A Year' the narrator does *not* go to war, and thus can relate to us a harrowing tale of love and death. His passiveness enables him to become a storyteller. He consistently sees things through the eyes of his leading woman, as James the novelist was so often to do – a woman who, we are told, 'like most weak persons . . . was glad to step out of the current of life' whenever it begins 'to quicken into action', and who harbours recurring fantasies of self-mutilation. The hero of the story is wounded on the Rappahannock River in Virginia, where James's charismatic young cousin Gus Barker had been cut down by a sniper's bullet in 1863. The wounded soldier in the story is brought back to his mother's door, very much as James's brother Wilky was returned to the

James family after being badly wounded; the description, judging from family accounts of Wilky's traumatic return, is an exact one. Among other things, what happened to Wilky confirmed James in his conviction, as he wrote of it later, that his role in life was appropriately reduced to 'seeing, sharing, envying, applauding, pitying, all from the far-off'.

'A Tragedy of Error', written after 'The Story of A Year' but published earlier, is a melodramatic tale set in France and notable chiefly for its theme: a weak husband (with an injured leg) married to a strong woman who does not scruple to destroy him in pursuit of selfish goals. (Freudian writers on James have been fond of commenting on the fact that Henry James Senior was an amputee with one good leg who appears to have been weaker than his wife.) Again, the early James is recognizably the later James. These first two tales, like many that were to follow, introduce James's usual narrative method of assuming another guise in order to relate the action. Telling stories was, on several levels, a way of escape for Henry James. It is not he himself, he makes clear, who is telling us what happens: it is someone else, of whose impressions he is simply giving an account. The point of view in the first tales is the same – used more complexly, to be sure – as that in James's great last novel, *The Golden Bowl* (1904).

Having as he did some sense of permanent physical inadequacy (rather than injury), James found himself, in 1861, a prey to anxiety that he might be considered a malingerer ('to have trumped up a lameness at such a juncture could be made to pass in no light for graceful'). Would others conclude that he was deficient in the masculinity being displayed so conspicuously on the battlefields of the Civil War by others of his generation? This worry is reflected, one way or another, in most of his early stories. After 'The Story of A Year' and 'A Tragedy of Error' in the 1860s came 'A Landscape Painter' (1866), 'A Day of Days' (1866), 'My Friend Bingham' (1867), 'Poor Richard' (1867), 'The Story of A Masterpiece' (1868), 'A Most Extraordinary Case' (1868), 'De Grey: A Romance' (1868), 'The Romance of Certain Old Clothes' (1868), 'Osborne's Revenge' (1868), 'A Problem' (1868), 'A Light Man' (1869), and 'Gabrielle de Bergerac' (1869). All of them have autobiographical overtones.

The hero of 'A Landscape Painter', who disguises himself as a poor artist in the hope of eluding women looking for husbands, is told to 'be a man'. In 'A Day of Days' the hero recoils from the attentions of a woman in love with him. The narrator of 'My Friend Bingham' notes in the protagonist, who is relatively young and healthy but not very masculine, 'the ravages . . . of a solemn act of renunciation. Bingham had forsworn marriage.' Taxed with this by his friend, Bingham replies: 'I feel a foreboding that I shall live and die alone . . . my marriage is improbable.' In 'Poor Richard' two brothers go off to the Civil War while a third, with whom the author seems to identify, suffers from a deep sense of inadequacy and stays at home. He comes down with typhus, as James had done at Boulogne in 1857. Richard ultimately becomes 'poor' through the death of passion in the course of an aborted romance, snuffed out by his obligation to fight in the war.

'The Story of A Masterpiece' strikes many notes heard later in James's work. There is an interest in painting and in how paintings get painted, and familiarity with Paris and the world of artists, a number of whom, including many dilettantes, make appearances. There are references to Browning, and especially to 'Andrea del Sarto', which is never quoted but whose famous credo – 'give us no more of body than shows soul' – seems to inform the tale. The story also demonstrates James's interest in Impressionism; and it suggests that art can be truer, more 'real', than life itself, and that imagination is more powerful than knowledge. Primarily, however, 'The Story of A Masterpiece' is the first of James's many tales about art and the artist, about how art is achieved – a subject he addressed often during his long writing career. Artists, James says here, 'claim their property wherever they find it'. Of Baxter, the painter in the story, James makes an interesting observation: 'Deep . . . in the unfathomed recesses of his . . . sensitive nature, his genius had held communion with his heart and had transferred to canvas the burden of its disenchantment and its resignation.' Very recently James too had 'held communion with his heart', and his response to what he found there was to turn to art and arrange his life to suit its requirements, transferring to 'canvas' the burden of his own disenchantment and resignation.

'A Most Extraordinary Case' is about a veteran of the Civil War who, though apparently healthy, loses the will to live, and dies of some unnamed and unnameable disease, obviously psychosomatic. Wounded by the war in invisible ways, he dies, in fact, of an obscure hurt. In both 'De Grey: A Romance' and 'The Romance of Certain

Old Clothes', as in 'The Story of A Year', James's narrator speaks from the point of view of a young lady. 'De Grey' is notable for the fear it expresses of sexual passion. It is also the first of James's many ghostly tales; and in it the 'vampire' theme appears undisguised. De Grey's young fiancée 'remorselessly drained the life from his being. As she bloomed and prospered, he drooped and languished. While she was living for him, he was dying of her.' The vision of woman as the destroyer is typical especially of the younger James; later on he saw emotional vampirism working in the other direction too. In the meantime, here, he writes of a hero who dies 'of' woman. 'The Romance of Certain Old Clothes' is another ghostly tale, this time of the rivalry of two sisters for the same man. One of the sisters is named Viola, and it has been said by some critics that she resembles the heroine of *Twelfth Night*, who spends much of the play dressed as a man. Howard M. Feinstein, William James's biographer and himself a psychiatrist, has declared that 'The Romance of Certain Old Clothes' is typical of much of Henry James's fiction in that in it we encounter a female consciousness masquerading in the body of a man. In 'Osborne's Revenge' the woman/vampire is seen by the man once again as his destroyer: 'she drained honest men's hearts to the last drop and bloomed white upon the monstrous diet.' The story suggests, however, that men may sometimes be deluded in their perceptions of women. Indeed, like *The Turn of the Screw* (1898) many years later, 'Osborne's Revenge' describes man's ultimate failure to comprehend the second sex. In the course of the story a woman bewilders not one but two men, causing the death of one of them. In 'A Problem' marriage results in pathos and tragedy. And 'A Light Man', Dr Feinstein claims, is 'transparently homosexual' and almost pornographic in the sado-masochistic byplay and blushing affection between the men in it. Whatever else it might be, 'A Light Man' reverses the gender of Browning's poem 'A Light Woman', quoted in the story's epigraph. One of the story's chief characters is a weak, idiosyncratic, effeminate man, brilliantly and sympathetically sketched, who seems to combine in his personality traits both masculine and feminine. James retained an unusually distinct fondness for 'A Light Man' in his later years.

Thus thirteen of the fourteen tales James published in the 1860s, in his early to middle twenties. Considering his tender age, some of them are astonishingly well done. He continued to write reviews as well, many of them for *The Nation*. Often he would complain that native authors were ignorant of their European forebears and contemporaries, and *The Nation* soon came to be known as 'the weekly Day of Judgement'. James's assessment of Dickens, his contemporary in the 1860s, has (some might say) stood the test of time: 'it is one of the chief conditions of his genius not to see below the surface of things.' James also reviewed novels by Trollope and Miss Braddon, and gave a drubbing to Whitman's *Drum Taps*. He was later to change his mind about Whitman; in old age he could declaim Whitman by heart. But now, in 1865, he declared that in Whitman's poetry one found 'imitations of ideas' rather than the things themselves. Art, James declares in the most striking passage of this essay, 'requires, above all things, a suppression of oneself, a subordination of oneself to an idea'. (This was to become Conrad's credo as well.) The early reviews and the early fiction eventually reached an interesting intersection of sorts in James's life when, in the late Sixties and early Seventies, he began to write stories and, finally, novels, in which the hero's pursuit of his manhood became associated with and inseparable from his discovery – in James's case, a rediscovery – of Europe.

But this was some years off. In September 1862, nineteen now and still uncertain what profession he might follow, Henry James went to Cambridge and registered at the Harvard Law School. Beyond providing important background for *The Bostonians* and *The Europeans* (1878), this experience contributed little to James's career. He considered Boston hostile to art and creativity, and was never to change his mind. One of the city's most familiar voices, that of James Russell Lowell, had recently declared, in the style of Dickens's Mr Podsnap, 'Let no man write a line that he would not have his daughter read.' Nurtured on European fiction, James complained that American editors liked to reduce if they could the things they published to the intellectual level of adolescent maidens.

Curiously enough, it is a matter of record that while in Cambridge James made no attempt to study law, continuing instead to devote his energies to reading and to writing stories and reviews. One of the virtues of his Cambridge sojourn was to get him, temporarily at least, out of his parents' house, and to give him, for the first time, a sense of his own independent existence, which he seems to have savoured. He stayed at Harvard only a year. By the time his first critical piece appeared in 1864 he had decided that literature in some form, either as a writer of it or as a critic of it, would be his profession. He spent the last half of this year in Northampton, Massachusetts – a residence put to use in the opening pages of *Roderick Hudson* – writing reviews, polishing his first efforts in fiction, and drinking the local waters, said to be beneficial to his condition. For he had begun, as the Civil War drew to a close and his literary labours began in earnest, to suffer from the constipation that was to plague him for the next decade. He was now twenty-one.

While in Northampton, James was never without a novel to read. 'It cannot be said that this desire [to read novels] is one of the elementary cravings of mankind. We take to it as to our mother's milk,' he wrote to Perry. The analogy might interest a Freudian. 'My *work* is my salvation,' he declared. By the time of 'The Middle Years' (1893), one of his most famous stories, the *cri de coeur* of the (highly autobiographical) protagonist/novelist may be longer and more eloquent, but it is not substantially revised: 'We work in the dark – we do what we can – we give what we have. Our doubt is our passion and our passion is our task. The rest is the madness of art.'

James spent the summer of 1865, the first since the end of the war, in the White Mountains of New Hampshire, in close proximity to his cousin Minny Temple. He was twenty-two, she was twenty. He came to 'adore' her – but more as a literary subject than as a woman, it turned out. Like the good Victorian which in some ways he resembled, James both feared and worshipped women; physical love was out of the question. Instead, as his letters testify, he formed a series of friendships with spinsters, safe women who could never inject a sexual threat into the comfortable, gossipy relationships thus established.

In New Hampshire one day the Temples entertained two Civil War veterans still in uniform. One of them was Oliver Wendell Holmes, Jr., the future Supreme Court justice. Two years older than Henry James, Holmes was a friend of William, who was now enrolled at the Harvard Medical School. The novelist later described this encounter vividly; as it turned out, Holmes was to remain a lifelong friend. The two men in uniform were full of stories, and told them to the attentive Temples. Yet again James felt on an unequal footing among his fellows: he was the civilian stay-at-home, looking on from the outer edges as both men flirted with Minny. The 'very smell' of war service seemed to surround James's 'supersensitive nostril', and to have the effect of hedging the two veterans round with 'an emotion the most masculine' – a circle from which the future novelist felt debarred. In a more tangible way this time, he tells us in *Notes of A Son and Brother*, he felt his masculinity being directly questioned. In the immediate aftermath of the war, with the Northern states awash with heroes in uniform, he must frequently have had this disturbing experience. Holmes himself, in a Memorial Day address in 1884, commented that, 'as life is action and passion, it is required of a man that he should share the passion and action of his time at peril of being judged not to have lived.' And he added: 'The generation that carried on the war has been set aside by its experience. Through our great good fortune, in our youth our hearts were touched with fire. It was given to us to learn at the outset that life is a profound and passionate thing.' The same could be said of America's Vietnam generation. But the point to be made here is this. The divergent courses followed by Holmes and James demonstrate that, in the crucible of their youth, different paths were open to their generation to follow toward profundity and passion, to use Holmes's terms. Those who came of age in the 1860s necessarily found themselves under close scrutiny. James shared 'the passion and actions of this time' in an unusual but no less affecting way, having determined to 'live' through observation rather than through action. Observation *was* his passion and his action, and ultimately the source of his profundity as well.

James spent part of the year 1866 in Swampscott, Massachusetts, this time nursing his bad back. He continued to produce stories and reviews (his notice of George Eliot's *Felix Holt* appeared in *The Nation*). As a result of his writing he was now earning several hundred dollars a month, enough for him to live independently of his parents; in the post-war North, he could rent lodgings for a few dollars a month and eat a steak for a few cents. The elder Jameses had moved from Newport to Cambridge to be near their eldest boys; neither son as yet showed any inclination to leave the nest permanently. It is an oddity that when Henry James, at the age of twenty-five, was offered the editorship of the *North American Review* in 1868, he was still living at home with his parents. Using ill health as an excuse, he turned the job down in order to be able to concentrate on the writing of fiction. James was twenty-six before he first ventured abroad on his own – fourteen months in Europe in 1869–70 – and thirty-two before he moved out of his parents' house for good and settled, initially, in Paris in 1875.

William, nearing the end of his medical studies at Harvard in the later 1860s, was never an admirer of his brother's work, surely at least in part an unconscious residue of the unspoken competition that always existed between the brilliant older boys. In the first of many such comments ungenerously dispatched to his younger brother over a lifetime, William complained of the 'want of heartiness' and the 'want of blood' in Henry James's early stories. William said he found them 'thin'. As he always would be, Henry was upset by his brother's criticism, but gave it no particular attention; he simply went on with his work. It is interesting to note that Henry James never stinted his praise for the writings of William, always more insecure about his work than his younger brother, who knew very well what he was about. Surely the novelist's nature was a finer and more benevolent one than the philosopher's.

'It is a question . . . whether a man gets the *bulk* of his society [from] man . . . and not rather [from] books,' the devourer of libraries wrote to his friend Perry in 1867. And he added, presaging the decision he was soon to make to go abroad, that the society he found in Cambridge 'was provincial, common and inelegant'. Indeed, he was finding fault with most things American these days: perhaps all those blue uniforms around him were a contributing factor. 'American literature is at a dreadful pass,' James wrote to Perry. 'Nothing decent' is to be found in it. On the other hand – 'When a man has seen Paris somewhat attentively, he has seen (I suppose) the biggest achievement of civilization in a certain direction and he will always carry with him a certain little *reflet* of its splendour.' James was setting the stage for his famous decision to leave America – and the women he could not love, the brother who would not love him, the parents he could not live with forever, the society he detested, the literature he could not read, the culture from which he could take no sustenance, the circle of men from which he felt excluded. His ultimate self-exile, the most important act of his life, was the act of an outsider, a loner; Henry James was a man who by his very nature felt compelled to retire from what he called the 'common scene'. He could not simply become a native writer. 'It's a complex fate being an American,' he wrote to Perry, 'and one of the responsibilities it entails is fighting against a superstitious valuation of Europe.' On the other hand Europeans, especially the English, had 'manners and a language', and he could not find these things in the gilt-edged glitter of post-Civil War America. What de Tocqueville had observed three decades earlier applied to James as he saw himself and his life now: 'Nothing conceivable is so . . . anti-poetic as the life of a man in the United States.' James thought he might like to make on his own that 'valuation of Europe' he felt Americans needed to have.

So that when, in September 1867, he wrote his famous letter to Perry on the subject of comparative cultures, we need not be surprised either to find him poised to leave the land of his birth, or by the reasons he gives for doing so. It is a long letter, James obviously gave a great deal of thought to it, and at the time Perry was the only human being he could speak and write to without reservation.

'There is nothing new . . . in the universe of American letters,' James begins, a familiar opening. He goes on to say that 'deep in the timorous recesses of my being is a vague desire to do for our dear old English letters' what Sainte-Beuve and others did for theirs. James now felt 'English letters' rather than American to be his. To accomplish what he wished to do he must return to England: 'It is by this constant exchange and comparison, by the wear and tear of living and talking and observing that works of art shape themselves into completeness.' And he adds: 'I think that to be an American is an excellent preparation for culture.' He means that, unlike Europeans, Americans 'can deal freely with forms of civilization not our own. . . . To have no national stamp has hitherto been a defect and a drawback.' But he intends to make a virtue of having 'no national stamp', of being a cultural *tabula rasa*, and to do so by developing, deliberately cultivating, what he calls here his 'moral consciousness'. He hopes that 'something original and beautiful [may] disengage itself from [the] ceaseless fermentation and turmoil' he finds going on within himself. And so, just as he had given up – or, to use one of his favourite words, renounced – almost every other aspect of the identity with which he had come into the world, Henry James, at the age of twenty-four, was resolving to give up his tenuous nationality in order to turn himself into an English man of letters. He had to be nothing before he could be something; like many of his characters, he had to renounce in order to gain.

Most of James's early tales, as we know, have an American setting; and the action of his first novel, *Watch and Ward* (written 1870; published 1871) would take place largely in Boston. When, eventually, James was able to see Europe with adult eyes, his venue would move across the Atlantic. Later still he would refer to his American birth as a 'terrible burden' which no European writer had ever had to face. Americans, James told Perry, were more or less required to deal, 'if only by implication, with Europe; whereas no European is obliged to deal in the least with America. No one dreams of calling him less complete for not doing so ... The painter of manners who neglects America is not thereby incomplete.' Flaubert needn't pay any attention to America; but could Hawthorne have written his novels without reference to Europe? The American writer who neglected Europe was 'incomplete', and this is what James meant when he talked about the 'terrible burden' of being an American who also wished to be a novelist of manners. And so he would expatriate himself: seen in this light, the decision now seems inevitable. He needed to learn, to soak up Europe. And so George Moore could make his celebrated remark some years later that whereas Henry James went abroad and read Turgenev, William Dean Howells stayed at home and read Henry James. James gave his successors in the field a theme: comparative manners. It did not exist as a subject for American writers until he made it one. Before James there had been, among his fellow Americans writing of Europe, only Irving and Cooper and Hawthorne, whose point of view remained unambiguously American. After James came Howells and Twain and Edith Wharton and Sinclair Lewis and Scott Fitzgerald and *their* disciples, and so the international theme entered American letters forever.

By 1868 James was panting for Europe. He needed it. 'Paris ... haunts my imagination,' he told Perry. He required, he said, a '*donnée*', a seed, ideas for stories: 'There are none here ... in literature or in art.' He wrote for the magazines, saved his money, bided his time, and planned to leave. Merging his literary with his other self, he had by now decided that he must abandon, for a time at least, the native scene of so many humiliations and losses, and try living abroad. On 17 February 1869, two months shy of his twenty-sixth birthday, he left America, hoping to complicate his life, to add to its artifices and rituals — the exact opposite of what most men of his age usually find themselves seeking. But then James was not like other men of his age, and we have seen why he might wish to exile himself from the 'common scene' of his past life. He was, for the first time, altogether on his own.

He went initially to London – 'this murky metropolis' which, now that he could see the city with a man's eyes instead of a boy's, 'sits on you, broods on you, stamps on you', he told his sister Alice. Writing to his mother, he declared: 'The truth is that the face of things here throws a sensitive American back on himself – back on his prejudices and national passions, and benumbs for a while the faculty of appreciation and the sense of justice.' Still very much an American, he was nonetheless doing what he had come to Europe to do: he was comparing cultures. 'I should like to settle down for a year and expose my body to the English climate and my mind to English institutions,' he added. He noted in himself a sort of literary vampirism, the desire to 'hang on to a place till it has yielded me its drop of life-blood . . . I feel that it is in my power to "do" any place . . . as thoroughly as it can be done.' But his chronic constipation was preventing him from doing much of anything. He tried the first of many 'cures': hydrotherapy at Dr Gully's famous establishment in Great Malvern. From there he went to Oxford, which he adored. In the college gardens, he wrote, he wished to lie in the grass 'in the happy belief the world is all an English garden and time a fine old English afternoon . . . The whole place gives a deeper sense of English life than anything yet,' he wrote to William. He added some sentiments the significance of which the embryo philosopher and psychologist could hardly have misconstrued: 'As I walked along the river I saw hundreds of the mighty lads of England, clad in white flannel and blue, immense, fairhaired, magnificent in their youth . . . and rejoicing in their godlike strength.' One is inevitably reminded of the famous photograph taken of James in old age in a punt at Cambridge, gaping upward at the blond, muscular, dashing undergraduate with the pole in his hands named Rupert Brooke; the very last thing the novelist wrote was a moving preface to a volume of Brooke's posthumous poetry, *1914 and Other Poems* (1915). All his life James worshipped masculinity – though Rupert Brooke might be considered a more dubious object of such worship than, half a century earlier, Gus Barker had been – largely because he felt excluded from its magic circle. We tend, perversely, to worship what we are not.

At any rate, his fascination with the beautiful losers his fiction would immortalize was already well-developed; Brooke was simply the last, as Gus Barker and Minny Temple were the first, in a long procession of a type James described willingly enough in his letter to William from Oxford in 1869. The assaults of these and other emotions, more cultural than sexual, were to spill over into 'A Passionate Pilgrim' (1871), the first of his stories James chose to revive many years later when arranging the contents of the New York Edition of his works. Among other things the tale demonstrates how deeply his first adult impressions of England had struck through his sensibilities. This almost instant Anglophilia would last and strengthen during his intervening flirtations with Italy and France in the 1870s. Indeed, read carefully, 'A Passionate Pilgrim' seems to announce that its author was well on the way to becoming an Englishman; 'haven't I been all my life long sick for England?' exclaims an English character in this story, for many years an exile from his native land. While critical of English snobbery, 'A Passionate Pilgrim' speaks of the country in transcendent, almost mythopoeic terms: 'There is a rare emotion, familiar to every intelligent traveller, in which the mind with a great passionate throb, asserts a magical synthesis of its impressions. You feel England.' The American narrator of the story speaks for the author when he declares: 'The latent preparedness of the American mind for even the most delectable features of English life is a fact which I never fairly probed to its depths. The roots of it are so deeply buried in the virgin soil of our primary culture . . . It makes an American's enjoyment of England an emotion more fatal and sacred than his enjoyment, say, of Italy or Spain.'

Back in London, James was introduced to George Eliot, and in May 1869 dispatched to his father the much-quoted description of her at fifty: 'she is magnificently ugly – deliciously hideous . . . Now in this vast ugliness resides a most powerful beauty . . . so that you end . . . in falling in love with her. Yes behold me literally in love with this great horse-faced blue-stocking.' Well, not literally. There lay, James declared, 'great feminine dignity and character in those massively plain features'. George Eliot and her work fascinated him; he was to get to know her better in the 1870s. The fascination lingered; he would write more essays on her – nine – than on any other subject (Balzac comes second). Only his monograph on Hawthorne contains more words about another author than his essays on George Eliot.

The question of a residence remained; James found his constipation unabated. Searching for relief from his complaint, he spent the summer of 1869 at various establishments in Switzerland, where he also did a good deal of walking and mountain-climbing. There is no mention in his letters now of a bad back – only of his continuous constipation. Otherwise, he was obviously healthy. He took the long trek, for example, from Geneva to Vevey, and renewed his acquaintance with the Castle of Chillon, to which Daisy Miller was to make an excursion a decade later. He also did some work, writing during this summer two more tales, 'Gabrielle de Bergerac' and 'At Isella' (1871). The first, set in France before the Revolution, is the only historical romance he ever produced; it seems to have cured whatever momentary impulse he might have had to leave, in fiction, his own time. 'At Isella' suggests that Italy rather than England, France, or Switzerland is the true land of passion and thus an appropriate venue for the would-be artist. By September 1869 James had reached Venice.

The ultimate sacredness of Venice for him will be clear to anyone who has read *The Wings of the Dove*, or even 'The Aspern Papers' (1888). 'It takes a great deal to make a successful American, but to make a happy Venetian takes only a handful of quick sensibility,' James was later to declare. He stayed, on this occasion, just two weeks, but his first impressions of the place can be seen, like those of England in 'A Passionate Pilgrim', as prophetic. 'I personally prefer Oxford' to Venice, he wrote to William. 'It told me deeper and richer things than any I have learned here . . . I feel I shall never look at Italy . . . but from without; whereas it seemed to me . . . in England . . . that I was breathing the air of home.' He would try living in Italy a few years later, and discover that it didn't, after all, work for him: it wasn't the right place, as he suspected. But now he haunted the Venetian galleries. He was impressed by Tintoretto, especially his 'Cain and Abel'. In *Roderick Hudson* this is the subject the young American sculptor wishes to carve.

James spent the next month – October 1869 – in Florence; like Gissing two decades later, he preferred it to Venice. From Florence he dispatched to his mother another much-quoted letter. Though he was in Italy, he remained chiefly concerned with the comparison between Americans and the English, especially those abroad. What are they like outside of their native lands? James says: 'the Englishmen I have met . . . bury in unfathomable depths the Americans I have met. A set of people less framed to provoke national self-complacency than the latter it would be hard to imagine. There is but one word to use in regard to them – vulgar; vulgar; vulgar.' Gissing would apply the same epithet to the English tourists he found in Italy and Greece; perhaps none of us likes to see our countrymen in close proximity when we have taken so much trouble (and expense) to leave them, we thought, so many miles behind us. James, at any rate, was finding his great subject: Americans abroad, the international theme. *The American*, *The Portrait of A Lady*, *The Ambassadors*, *The Golden Bowl* – all of these, and much else James was to write, may be glimpsed in this reflected light. About Americans abroad he adds here, in his letter to Mary James: 'Their ignorance – their stingy, grudging, defiant attitude towards everything European – their perpetual reference of all things to some American standard or precedent which exists only in their own unscrupulous wind-bags – and then our unhappy poverty of voice and of physiognomy – these things glare at you hideously.' Americans were still, for him, both 'theirs' and 'ours'; soon they would be only 'theirs'. The contemporary American, James told his mother, was 'the modern man with *culture* quite left out. It's the absolute and incredible lack of *culture* that strikes you.' These are James's italics; again here we can see his great literary subject forming. The English, on the other hand, 'have been smoothed and polished by mutual social attrition. They have manners and a language. We lack both, but particularly the latter.' The English looked especially good to James in Italy. 'In the midst of these false and beautiful Italians they glow with the light of the great fact, that after all they love a bath-tub and they hate a lie.'

This letter is signed 'Thy lone and loving exile'. That James was feeling increasingly estranged from his native land is clear enough from what he writes here. The same word is used again a few days later in a letter to his father in the course of which he refers to 'the cheerlessness of solitude and the bitterness of exile'. But there were compensations, in this false dawn of exile, of a very specific kind. 'I've been vastly struck . . . with the beauty of the Italian race, especially the men,' James tells his father. 'Never in my life . . . have I seen so many young men of princely aspect.' He says nothing of the women. To William, as so often, he wrote of his various ailments, including the one they competitively shared: 'my back . . . is so chronically affected by my constipated state that there are times when I can hardly drag myself about.'

By the end of October James was tired of Florence; he went off to Rome. While there, he methodically studied the work of Michelangelo. He considered Michelangelo the greatest of all of the Italian artists – a 'real man of action of art' is James's interesting phrase. Passiveness or inversion in life need not preclude high 'action' in art. He glimpsed Pius IX in his gilded coach drawn by four black horses, a vision which was to figure in *Roderick Hudson*. And he visited the graves of Shelley and Keats in the Protestant Cemetery; here he would set the last scene of 'Daisy Miller'. James says of himself that in Rome he 'went reeling and moaning thro' the streets, in a fever of enjoyment'. One of the things he was learning in Italy, he told Alice, was to 'value a good portrait'; and often throughout his long career, as we have seen, he would remark on the similarities of the novelist's craft to that of the portrait painter. A fair number of his tales, both short and long, are about painters, whom James sometimes uses as stand-ins for the more generalized idea in his fiction of 'the artist'.

His continuing constipation, of which he writes in copious detail to almost all of his correspondents during this period, decided him to return to England. He started northwards in January 1870, stopping in Genoa and Paris, reached London in February, and set off almost immediately to get more of Dr Gully's hydrotherapy treatments. His letters betray moodiness. 'This *beastly* London,' he writes to his mother upon his arrival there, 'its darkness and grim and grime and filth and misery are . . . overwhelming.' 'I find I like England still,' he tells William a few weeks later. 'I shall get my fill of old England yet.' He informs his brother that he means to start writing a novel 'one of these days' as good as *The House of the Seven Gables*. He has been reading Browning's *The Ring and the Book*, recently published. He remarks on the frumpishness of Englishwomen, comparing them unfavourably with American women in terms of 'beauty and grace and elegance and alertness . . . cleverness and self assistance.' As always, he was interested more in differences than in similarities. He had been in Europe for six months now. 'My memory . . . is a storehouse of treasure,' he wrote to his father.

On 8 March 1870 Minny Temple died of consumption. James, at Great Malvern, received the tidings there on the 26th. He was to make a great deal of this death. The theme of a life unachieved spoke to many things in his own spirit. Here was another epoch-making moment in the private history of beautiful losers, and James was to cherish it for years. He was nearing his twenty-seventh birthday; the author of fourteen tales, he was poised to write his first novel. The death of Minny Temple, as some critics have noted, helped to crystallize for him a lifelong, though disembodied, subject: the premature death, physical or emotional, of someone who desperately wants to live. What sort of life would Minny have had? James found himself brooding over this question. More specifically: what might her collision with Europe have been like had she ever achieved one? How would such 'a plant of pure American growth' have prospered in foreign soil? Years later, in *The Wings of the Dove*, he was still writing about her, and about this subject. But we know all that. The issue now, in the spring of 1870, was this: how did Minny Temple's death seem to speak to Henry James? And what was his response?

On the day he received the sad news, James wrote to his mother that he 'must wait . . . to comprehend it,' but in the meantime he was 'almost *enjoying* [his italics] the exquisite pain' of his recollections of Minny. We have noted an element of sado-masochism in the beautiful losers theme – the beautiful person destroyed, annihilated by ugliness. 'The thought of . . . rest and immortal absence' for Minny gave James, he told his mother, 'absolute balm'. That his dead young cousin was already becoming a literary subject in James's imagination is clear from what he says next. 'I feel immensely curious for all the small facts and details of her last week. Write me any gossip that comes to your head . . . Try and remember anything she may have said and done.' His mother would have been the member of the family most likely to have such treasures stored up, and so it was to her that James wrote on the day of Minny's death. He goes on in this letter to describe Minny as 'the very heroine of our common scene'. We can almost feel him hugging to himself his new subject: 'Twenty years hence what a pure elegant vision she will be . . . What a pregnant reference in future years. . . . I feel absolutely *vulgarly* [James's italics] eager for any fact whatever' his mother could add to the story. He muses 'on the dramatic fitness . . . of her early death'. Fit for whom? He becomes more specific as the great theme seems to spread out before him: 'I couldn't help thinking this afternoon how strange it is for me to be pondering her death in the midst of this vast indifferent England which she fancied she would have liked.' But would she have liked it? How would she have 'done' in Europe? We can see being born in this letter Daisy Miller, Isabel Archer, Milly Theale, Bessie Alden of 'An International Episode' (1878), and a dozen others. In a sense, James was now appropriating the vampire theme for his own use, and turning it around. The death of this woman, an inspiring and sustaining death for him, was to carry the novelist well beyond the next few years of composition. Drinking the blood of Minny Temple was to become a lifelong addiction for Henry James. Her death gave him life as a writer.

James comments on the event, a few days later, to William. Minny's demise, he says, now seems 'the most natural – the happiest, fact ... in her whole career ... to the eye of feeling there is something immensely moving in the sudden and complete extinction of a vitality so exquisite and so apparently infinite as Minny's.' It was always the 'extinction' of vitality that was to move James, not its fulfilment or its triumph. Largely, perhaps for autobiographical reasons, his 'eye of feeling' was caught by those who, due to various causes, did *not* live a complete and satisfying life. For Henry James there was something fascinating, 'something immensely moving', in this failure, this defeat. Seeing himself as one of those who, for private reasons, could not live a life considered 'normal' by others, he never left off being fascinated by the destruction of the normal; and after Minny Temple's death he never stopped thinking and writing about this destruction. James's feelings of inadequacy had been building up for a very long time indeed – since the call for troops in April 1861, and before that during the unsettling family life of his earliest years. Now he began to create a series of characters who, unlike himself as he had come to see himself, were both 'normal' and innocent, and who found themselves put out of the way – destroyed, defeated, demeaned – or in some other way distinctly disposed of. So James took his revenge upon those who hadn't looked sufficiently deeply inside themselves, as he had (the innocent), and those who wished to love the other sex, and to marry (the 'normal').

In the letter Henry wrote to William, he makes no attempt to be coy about the connection between Minny and himself. 'It seems as if she *represented* [his italics] in my life several of the elements or phases of a life at large.' Among these he names '*Youth*, with which owing to my invalidism, I always felt in rather indirect relation.' Minny Temple's death released a great many things in Henry James.

His relation to Minny in life could never have been stronger than it was at the time of her death. He goes on to make it clear to William what the true nature of that relation was. 'Everyone was supposed . . . to be more or less in love with her: others may answer for themselves; I never was.' But now that she is dead and has become for him a subject – he doesn't say this, but it is clear from what he writes – she has in effect 'served her purpose' for him. This he *does* say. He seems to see her, moreover, 'inviting me onward by all the bright intensity of her example' – not to die, but to interpret and assimilate her death for himself. He too may be, though living, unfulfilled, a sort of chronic invalid, excluded from 'life,' but what he can still do is make use of what he has left to give, part of which is the story she exemplifies of the doom of promise. This story he can tell. James perceives himself, in the wake of his cousin's death, as 'slowly crawling from weakness and inaction and suffering into strength and health and hope: she sinking out of brightness and youth into decline and death.' Here is the vampire theme writ large. Minny is the beautiful loser whose life's blood he, the ugly survivor, will drink to sustain himself in literature, and thus in life. No wonder he understood so well how and why human beings use one another up to gain unequal advantages. 'I can't put away the thought that just as I am beginning life, she has ended it,' he tells William. Her loss was his gain, and he knew it. It was as if Minny had sacrificed herself so that he could live. The vision James had of what Minny Temple did for him is expressed, among all the tales, most specifically perhaps in 'Longstaff's Marriage', in which the man's health seems to require the woman's death.

In this long letter to William of March 1870 we can see Henry James feeling his cousin's death not as a lover but rather as an artist who has suddenly stumbled into marvellous material and knows how to value it. 'The more I think of her,' he tells William, 'the more perfectly satisfied I am to have her translated from this changing realm of fact to the steady realm of thought' – by which he means imagination, his own. Now that she is out of life, he will make her immortal. The emphasis is on what Minny's death may do for *him*. 'There,' in his thought, 'she may bloom into a beauty more radiant,' James declares, and we can see him resolving that this should be so. The letter to William goes on: 'What once was life is always life, in one form or another . . . I feel as if in effect and influence Minny had lost very little by her change of state.' And so it was to be, for him if not for her; she remained 'alive' in his fiction, a living presence there. He seems, a few weeks after her death, already to know this would happen. 'She lives,' he writes to William, 'as a steady unfaltering luminary in the mind . . . Among all my thoughts and conceptions I am sure I shall never have one of greater sereneness and purity: her image will preside in my intellect.' Truth beats fiction as the true stuff of art every time. James's work was almost always, in one way or another, to begin with the truth, and to take off from there. Thus his well-known habit on social occasions in later years of listening to the beginnings of anecdotes of the personal histories of others and absenting himself before the full story could be told. All he wanted was the seed; he would feed the plant himself and grow what he liked. The death of Minny Temple was one of the earliest and most important of his '*données*'; he would finish her story in innumerable ways, over and over again. And in fact he notes with some satisfaction at this point in his letter that thinking of Minny has already inspired him to produce twelve pages for William to read.

'It's the *living* ones that die; the writing ones that survive.' It appeared to James that to write one first had to die to life; one could not both 'live' and write. In Proustian terms, you could only write about the people you had detached yourself from; you could not write about people at the same time you were seeing them. In Jamesian terms, only the 'dead' could write about the living. That is how he saw it, now, in the spring of 1870, as he viewed from every possible angle the spectacle of Minny's fate and the ways in which he could make use of it. He must have been relieved as well. Now no one who might have thought that he loved her could expect him to do anything about it – to become 'more active and masculine,' as James phrases it in his letter to William. Minny's death gave him not only a subject, but also an excuse not to marry. And it gave him a permanent means of subterfuge, for he could hide forever in his literary response to this death. Part of James's exalted state just after this event can surely be traced to his realization of his good luck, which in turn produced in his letter home a barely concealed sense of emotional release. He was off the hook now, and without really losing her. Indeed, he would have her now, he tells William, 'forever talking to me'. In exchange, he would 'keep [her] future' in his work. 'Don't fancy that your task is done,' he admonishes the dead girl. Should we be surprised that a novelist of James's stature returned so often to the ghost story? For him, the tissue dividing the living from the dead was very thin indeed.

To his friend Grace Norton, James wrote a few days later that Minny's was a 'death which has cut short the sweetness of . . . youth.' He continued to hug his theme. 'Her life,' he tells Miss Norton, 'was a strenuous, almost passionate *question*,' and one which he intended to answer.

Thus the story, or at least the first part of it, of Henry James and Minny Temple. Consciously or unconsciously, in her he cultivated a brief and limited heterosexual intimacy, an intimacy guaranteed in one way or another to fail in order to set itself free. Whether he knew it or not, this is what he must have wanted to happen; that is, the failure of this friendship was, at some level of his being, his true desire. Psychiatry tells us that episodes such as this not infrequently form part of the adolescent history of future homosexuals. Proust's disappointed love, at the age of fifteen, for Marie de Bernardaky, the Gilberte of *A l'ombre des jeunes filles en fleurs*, is another case in point. As C. P. Snow has written, 'In your deepest relations, there is only one test of what you profoundly want: it consists of what happens to you.'

By May 1870 James had returned to America, and to Cambridge. Almost immediately he began to write *Watch and Ward*. While doing so, as he told Miss Norton, 'I am constantly beset by the vision of my return to Europe.' Indeed, he would soon go back to Europe for good, and he seemed to sense this. He stood, in the summer of 1870, somewhere between the two continents and all they meant to him. Out of this emotional crucible and this past personal history, Henry James's first novel emerged.

Its major preoccupations reflect what we know about James's youth, and in a number of ways too they anticipate much of what we know he was soon to write. Like so many Jamesian heroines, Nora in *Watch and Ward* is a 'free' young woman faced with crushing choices: already the 'Minny theme' is paramount, though James's cousin had been dead for only a few months. Typically too, Roger, the leading man, is weak, prone to illness, and always in doubt about his strength and even his manhood; he is a shrinking and stricken hero. An invalid, throughout much of the book he lies in bed and fusses. His helplessness is associated with sincerities and scruples which are supposed to make him morally superior to others, but the young novelist doesn't quite bring this off. As he had done in his earliest stories, and as he would do in many of his subsequent tales, James creates in *Watch and Ward* a hero who is the exact opposite of the hero of traditional romance. The Jamesian hero tends often to be a loyal sufferer, a dying invalid, passive and unassertive, capable of being manipulated by others, especially women. Roger Lawrence, in *Watch and Ward*, adds another dimension to this portrait by apparently being half in love with his handsome, dashing cousin Hubert. Even the virile Hubert, however, often sounds like the Henry James of the letters. 'There are men born to imagine things, others born to do them,' he says. 'Evidently I am not one of the doers. But I imagine things, I assure you!'

Having been refused in marriage, Roger vows everlasting celibacy, a version of the disappointed youthful heterosexual love theme. But Roger ultimately breaks his vow to make what appears to some readers of *Watch and Ward* an incestuous marriage with the girl he has raised as his adopted daughter (incapable of being a real father, he can be only a surrogate one), whom he has treated throughout as a child. It is *Henry Esmond* in reverse, and then some. As Nora flourishes and grows, Roger sickens and fades, in good Jamesian vampire fashion. James's first novel, like so many to follow, bulges with sublimation and repression, and sketches the unequal relation of the sexes. In this it is a faithful portrait of its young author's state of mind. James writes candidly in *Watch and Ward* that 'we love as we must, not as we should.'

Here is the first sentence of James's first novel: 'Roger Lawrence had come to town for the express purpose of doing a certain act, but as the hour for action approached he felt his ardour rapidly ebbing.' The weakness and indecisiveness of the man shrinking from action are what is emphasized. Decisions, as we know, were always difficult things for Henry James; he was aware, as he wrote the novel, that he was facing, that he was on the brink of having to make, several more of crucial importance, including that of where – and therefore, how – to live. The hero of his first novel, not surprisingly, has trouble deciding *everything*. The description of Roger Lawrence goes on: 'He should fail, he was sure, but he must fail again before he could rest.' Fail, then rest; thus James's first protagonist at full length. The picture widens. We learn that Roger's 'desire to get the better of his diffidence had given him a certain formalism of manner which many persons found extremely amusing.' The young Henry James, fussy and formal, sometimes amused people by a premature gravity interpreted as pompous. But, significantly, Roger is 'an undervalued man, and . . . in the long run he would come out even with the best.' So James believed, quietly, about himself, and so it proved to be. Undervalued as a youth, he took his revenge – principally, it may be, against his older brother – by becoming famous, more famous than William, and much earlier. We learn further that Roger had made a feeble attempt to marry, dreaming of 'gentle bondage', but has been utterly unsuccessful with women before Nora came along. And no wonder. 'How can I ever have . . . that charm of infallibility, that romance of omniscience, that a woman demands of her lover?' If James thought anything like this – that women look for infallibility and omniscience in their lovers, or that these are attributes men have to have in order to interest them – it could be another reason why he steered clear of them. No woman was going to devour him! A little 'gentle bondage' was one thing; to be swallowed whole was something quite different.

At the end of *Watch and Ward*, Nora reads in Roger's eyes 'the whole record of his suffering. It is a strange truth that this seemed the most beautiful thing she had ever looked upon; the sight of it was delicious.' The beauty of suffering is one of the novel's ubiquitous themes, and it is significant that Nora takes pleasure in Roger's. Here at the start of James's career as a novelist we can discern that strain of sado-masochism which in one way or another, sublimated or not, runs through everything he wrote. What other novelist of James's stature describes the sight of someone's suffering as 'delicious'?

Nora's story anticipates much of what was to come. Like many another Jamesian heroine, she loses her spiritual innocence as the novel unfolds; the process is accelerated by a trip to Europe with an older woman who becomes her confidante, a Jamesian pattern that was to become well-worn. The novelist refers to Nora as wrapped in a 'blessed bandage of innocence'. She goes to Europe: 'Nothing can ever be the same after a winter in Rome.' She is the first of a string of heroines who find this out: one thinks of Daisy Miller and Isabel Archer. What is it, exactly, that happens to Nora in Europe? 'It was as if she had bloomed into ripeness in the sunshine of a great contentment; as if, fed by the sources of aesthetic delight, her nature had risen calmly to its allotted level.' In acquiring culture she loses her innocence. It is the corruption of her acquired knowledge, no doubt, that impels her to find suffering 'delicious'; she could not have felt anything like this before going abroad. Exposure to Europe is in itself a death of innocence; here one thinks not only of Daisy and Isabel, but also of Christopher Newman, Milly Theale, Lambert Strether, Maggie Verver – one could go on and on. Only a child can stay innocent forever. Interestingly, James in his work often associates loss of spiritual innocence with Europe. It may well be that the 'education' he received there, which consisted chiefly of exposure to a series of alien cultures, helped him to see what was in his heart, to acquire that self-knowledge that in him was equivalent to a death of innocence.

Nora is taken to Europe by the experienced Mrs Keith, who plays Madame Merle to Nora's Isabel: 'Nora . . . had too much to learn, and Mrs Keith too much to unlearn.' Nora comes back from Europe capable of understanding Roger's true feelings and his true intentions: he wishes to possess her for life, not just for the years of her minority; and he wishes this to happen as a result of her agency, since he is not capable of acting for himself. He wishes to be taken possession of, to become the victim of 'gentle bondage', of a covert rape. She now sees this. 'The whole face of things was hideously altered; a sudden horror had sprung up in her innocent past, and it seemed to fling forward a shadow which made the future a blank darkness.' In Nora's understanding of the past lies the end of innocence. Like so many of her fictional successors, she ends up renouncing the romance and adventure, the experience and experimentation she craved. Her wings will be clipped by her marriage to Roger, to whom she is not physically attracted. When she finally reaches the point of feeling 'capable of erecting a monument of self sacrifice' her story ends, for James has got Nora and Roger where he wants them. Their marriage, the story of which is not told, is bound to be a disaster. For Roger it will be the end of celibate freedom; for Nora it will be the end of 'experience'. Marriage is the perfect Jamesian disaster – logical, expected, and absolutely fatal.

It was of course a mistake he never made himself. He knew himself too well – had known himself ever since Lincoln called for troops in April 1861 and James, on his eighteenth birthday, began to work out who he was and what his fate must be. Like the hero of his first novel, he was bound to love as he must, not as he should.

Thomas Hardy in 1856, aged sixteen (*Trustees of the Thomas Hardy Memorial Collection in the Dorset County Museum, Dorchester, Dorset*)

CHAPTER TWO

Hardy Rising

'Poetry, you know — well, of course, there'd be
nothing like it if it was all true, if the poets
really believed what they say. But as often as not
you'll find that there's no one so mean and
calculating as those fellows.'
Odette in *Du côté de chez Swann*

His nature was really like a sheet of paper that
has been folded so often in every direction that it
is impossible to straighten it out.
Proust, *Sodome et Gomorrhe II*

One must die to life in order to be utterly a
creator . . . Nobody but a beginner imagines that
he who creates must feel.
Mann, 'Tonio Kröger'

Thomas Hardy had enough peasant cunning to outwit several
generations of would-be biographers. The 'life' he wrote of himself in
old age, to which his second wife was made to sign her name, leaves
out everything he did not want known. It can only be described as a
deliberate deception; even the corrections he made on the final
typescript are in a 'disguised' hand. The letters he did not destroy
either are full of lies, or, like most of Trollope's, perfunctory communications about business matters. True, his family and earliest
friends were poorly educated country people not accustomed to

writing or receiving letters. But this does not explain all. For Hardy, secrecy was a passion, concealment an art, and distortion a rule. He was always abnormally sensitive about any reference to his private life. Despite the fact that as a writer he took great risks and issued many challenges, as a private man he was always self-defensive and misleading. His habitual reserve makes him one of the most elusive of biographical subjects, despite all the biographies.

Why? What did he wish to hide? The answers are rooted in his origins, his early obscurity and failures, and especially in his exaggerated class-consciousness. The blatant mendacity of some of his most apparently 'intimate' communications originated in the circumstances of his upbringing and in his emotional development during the first thirty years of his life. His fiction, especially the early fiction, betrays an obsession with matters of class. His attempt to write his own biography, to pass it off as the work of someone else, and to suppress the facts about himself, especially those concerning his early life – these things had as their goal wholesale obfuscation of the truth about his family and his origins. It is no accident that much of Hardy's earliest fiction focuses upon social distinctions and how they can paralyze and destroy the hopes of individuals not to the manor born. While the same social animus can also be found in the later work, it is supplemented there by other kinds of social commentary and more wide-ranging observation of the effects of the English class system on marriage, on education, on man's condition itself. But the earliest work is much more stark and specific, written as it was by a young man who feared, as George Gissing would do later, that the circumstances of his birth might become an indestructible, immovable barrier to success in his chosen profession, to acceptance by his intellectual peers, and above all to that most cherished of Victorian aspirations, Respectability.

Hardy was born on 2 June 1840, in an area in which social distinctions were patent, wide, and in a sense built into the landscape. The railway, which was beginning to transform both life and countryside in many parts of England in the 1840s, had not yet reached Dorset. Dorchester, its small county seat, contained areas in which the rural poor lived as many as 1,100 to five acres and in which the typical cottage could be composed of a single room as small as eight square feet and stand as close as four feet from its nearest neighbour. Most Dorset cottages lacked a privy; sewage would be disposed of in the nearest mill pond, also used for washing and cooking. The cottage at Higher Bockhampton where Thomas Hardy was born was situated a few miles both from Dorchester and the picturesque manors of the local gentry: it was neither a hovel nor a house, exactly, which helped guarantee Hardy's longstanding interest in its, and his, precise social status. The Bockhampton cottage was relatively comfortable, but from an early age Hardy was impressed by the social extremes even in this small but still beautiful corner of rural Dorset.

He was prone in later years to claim kinship with various notable Hardys over several centuries of English history. The fact is, however, that both of his parents came from humble local families in obscure corners of the countryside. Hardy's father, a builder, spoke dialect to his workmen. His mother had been a domestic servant. Several of his female cousins were ladies' maids. It was generally thought that the family had come down in the world.

One of Hardy's earliest forms of juvenile recreation, significantly, was to wrap himself in a tablecloth and imitate the local vicar – the first of many Hardyesque disguises which might be characterised as embodying fantasies of gentility. In later years, when his name was widely known and he had achieved the respectable status he had always sought, he could neither forget his origins nor bring himself to reveal them. 'The less people know of a writer's antecedents (till he is dead) the better,' he told a friend in 1881. Here, perhaps, lies part of the explanation for the very real discrepancy between his public boldness as an author and his defensive reticence as an individual. Even after he was dead Hardy in effect was still trying to manipulate the record of his life from the grave, having perpetrated on his English audience that highly expurgated and selective biography of himself and burnt most of the personal papers on which it was based. Many of the letters were destroyed, as well as excerpts from diaries and notebooks used to prepare the 'biography' signed by his second wife. Hardy also left instructions to burn any of his private papers that might have been overlooked, especially those relating to his early life.

One of the important facts about Hardy – one which he never acknowledged and yet which must have haunted him in an age when Respectability seemed so important, and the circumstances of one's birth constituted a crucial route to it – was that he was conceived out of wedlock. He was born less than six months after his father married his mother. The extent to which Hardy went to bury this fact about himself, and his success in doing so, may be measured by the general ignorance of it today even among his most devoted students. That any form of illegitimacy was an unambiguous stigma for the Victorians may be glimpsed in Wilkie Collins's brilliant novel *No Name* (1862), published twenty-two years after Hardy's birth, as well as by the most cursory examination of nineteenth-century British law.

Not surprisingly, then, the 'life' Hardy wrote of himself tends to raise the status of his family significantly, and omits his humblest connections. The rule for omission or inclusion in *The Life of Thomas Hardy* (1928–30), by Florence Emily Hardy, seems to have been based on social class. Hardy's memoir of himself leaves out all the ordinary labourers, cobblers, bricklayers, carpenters, farm servants, house servants, cooks, butlers, and journeyman joiners among his relations, as Robert Gittings, who has written the only dependable biography of Hardy among dozens, points out. Hardy did not want even the existence of his lower-class relatives known. The few 'relations' he does mention in the *Life* are of a comparatively high social status, and were not close connections. His whole life may be seen as a fight against the Victorian social stratification of which he saw himself, as a young man, the victim. No wonder then that his slamming of the door on the real facts of his own past became obsessive, and remained so up to the moment of his death in 1928.

In Hardy's books the peasants are often idealized; in his life he avoided them – just as Dickens avoided the poor he romanticised – and sought the company of the educated middle classes. Yet certain early habits remained. He always spoke with a broad Dorset accent, and retained his country manners: Gissing noted in his diary that during luncheon at Max Gate in the 1890s Hardy threw a knife at an insect on the wall. He never wore a watch, saying he could tell the time by the sun. His novels and his poetry are deeply rooted in the place, the age, and the milieu into which he was born; his fiction, taken together, constitutes among other things a history of nineteenth-century Dorset. It is this memory of a buried life which gives so much power to the best works of Hardy's maturity, especially his poetry.

Though Hardy all of his life seems to have been obsessed by what he called the decline and fall of a family – a crucial theme of *Tess of the d'Urbervilles* (1891) – in fact this obsession was largely a self-induced delusion. The Hardys had no place to fall from. The writer's father rose from extremely humble beginnings to earn a considerable income as a mason. His mother was a servant and the daughter of a servant; her family had been brought up as paupers on parish relief – in fact, she seems to have been the recipient of a small Poor Law dole throughout her life. Hardy's father married her because she was pregnant; he would have had few other compelling reasons to do so.

And so it was into this family, and not into that described in the *Life*, that the illegitimate Thomas Hardy was born. The mother's labour was difficult, and almost killed her. When it finally appeared, the child was thought by the surgeon to be dead, and thrown aside into a basket. It was left to the midwife to discover life in the fragile infant. The theme of class differences, one might say, began with Hardy's emergence from the womb.

In the *Life*, Hardy serenely describes his birth in a 'seven-roomed rambling house'. The low social standing of the family of course goes unmentioned; instead he declares the Hardys to have been on 'substantial footing'. And in the opening sentences of the volume he manages to work in references to various military officers character-ised as close relations, a fabrication pure and simple. There follows a long and largely irrelevant account of 'the Hardys of the south-west, derived from the Jersey le Hardys who had sailed across to Dorset for centuries.' A seed of *Tess of the d'Urbervilles* may be found in Hardy's statement early in the *Life* that he (writing in the third person) 'often thought he would like to restore the "le" to his name, and call himself Thomas le Hardy.' He goes on to talk about so-called ancestors who fought in the Wars of the Roses, and claims, falsely, to be related to the famous Captain Hardy of Trafalgar, in whose arms on the *Victory* Lord Nelson died. One of the few genuine military connections he mentions is a dashing uncle in the Lancers who may have been the model for Sergeant Troy in *Far from the Madding Crowd* (1874). Hardy's mother's family is declared to be 'Anglo-Saxon', and the author of the *Life* goes on to conjure out of nowhere some well-heeled maternal antecedents. His great-grandmother, he says nonchalantly, was fond of *Paradise Lost* and *The Pilgrim's Progress* and the *Spectator* and Richardson and Fielding. Probably she could not read at all. Hardy's maternal grandmother had been left by her husband on the day after their wedding, yet another seed of

Tess. His mother is said to be a great reader, a woman at her ease 'in London, Weymouth, and other towns'; in fact she could barely read or write, and for years Hardy had to compose her letters for her. His father is described as 'a manager of and contractor for all [building] trades' who looked like the famous Captain Hardy and was considered by women irresistible. The latter may be true. Everyone in the family was interested in music, according to Hardy. It is a fact that the Dorset Hardys became well-known country fiddlers, and his paternal grandfather played the violoncello in a church whose vaults contained, Hardy is quick to point out, 'many members of the Grey and Pitt families'.

Thus the extraordinary opening of Hardy's biography of himself. He manages to work all of these subterfuges into its first half-dozen pages, as if the most important fact about himself, which he wished his readers to know immediately, was that he came from a gentle rather than a humble background. Both in its placement in the volume and in its wholesale mendacity this is revealing. From the first, and on to the end of his life, when the memoir was written, Hardy had a quarrel with 'society', and wished to delude it. Writing his biography in old age, that quarrel seemed to him no less acute, no less relevant, than it had seemed to him as a young man.

Stories abound from Hardy's early years of embryonic sexual attractions reaching across class barriers. What he could not have seemed especially alluring to him during his years of striving; in later years he was attracted to women, regardless of class, everywhere he found them – on omnibuses, glimpsed across the street or in a shop window, anywhere else. He was always interested in the women who were not his wives – a large part of the population.

Hardy's lifelong susceptibility to women seems to have begun with his first teacher, a local lady of good family named Mrs Martin. Hers was a Church of England school in nearby Stinsford; Hardy started attending it in 1848, when he was eight. Indeed, he was the first pupil through its doors, an early measure of his passion for learning. In 1850 he was sent by his mother, who had no difficulty discerning her son's obsessive attachment to Mrs Martin, to a Nonconformist school in Dorchester. But Hardy remembered Mrs Martin, who first awakened his sexuality, all his life; in his story 'The Withered Arm' (1888) the aphrodisiac effect of her dress rustling close to him is described in detail. Her husband ran an estate farm and lost money on it after employing a Scottish bailiff, in outline a foreshadowing of the Henchard-Farfrae relationship in *The Mayor of Casterbridge* (1886). This novel also recounts the visit of Prince Albert to Dorchester in 1849; Hardy never forgot that as a boy he had once found himself just a few feet from a prince.

He must have noted the dissimilarities between the Martins' household, in which he could come and go as he pleased, and his own; it was a revealing first-hand experience of the differences between classes. The Martins were prosperous, at least before the Scottish bailiff came upon the scene. Hardy's inflation in the *Life* of his father's social position was perhaps an attempt, after the fact, to bridge a class gap that had been unbridgeable for him as a child and an adolescent. His father at this time was only marginally better off than when he had married Hardy's mother; and, as Hardy well knew, his father's brother was an ordinary labourer. The life the Martins led was a universe away from that of the Hardy family, and young Thomas Hardy never forgot it. This story, however, is not touched upon in the *Life*. Nor does Hardy mention that his mother's brothers were, all of them, bricklayers, and heavy drinkers; one of them got his name in the newspapers for battering his wife. Hardy's cousins, the Sparks girls, started life as seamstresses and later became ladies' maids who might well have been employed by someone like Mrs Martin. None of this finds its way into the *Life* either. One of his uncles, like Jude in *Jude the Obscure* (1894–5), had a 'great mass of unruly black hair'; though only a carpenter, he taught himself Latin, and died in circumstances similar to Jude's. The point is that, unlike the Martins, the Hardys were real labouring families, not the middle-class people the author of the *Life* dreams up as his relations in his 'biography'. It is a matter of record that a local boy Hardy knew died of starvation, and that he saw for himself people, some of them related to him, living on top of one another like dogs at close quarters in mud-floored and leaky cottages. Again, none of these coarse social realities is mentioned in the *Life*.

Had Hardy told the whole truth it would in fact have made a moving story. He could have been perceived as what he was: a man who surmounted tremendous social obstacles to become one of England's greatest poets and novelists. Certainly Dickens exaggerated the horrors of his youth in order to be seen, as he wished to be seen and was seen, as having by sheer force of will and talent burst out of nowhere to become a Great Man. This is a different kind of snobbery, the reverse of Hardy's. But Hardy did not want his story told. Like Meredith and Gissing, he wished to be thought of as someone for whom mingling with the middle classes was as natural as breathing, as someone who quite naturally belonged where he was – when in fact nothing could be farther from the truth. There are all kinds of snobbery. To the end of his days, as the *Life* testifies, Hardy remained sensitive and secretive and misleading about his origins. Never was he able to overcome either his class consciousness or his obsession with his place, wherever it might be, in the social hierarchy. One way or another this fact is reflected in every novel he wrote, and in many of the poems as well.

Hardy's paternal grandmother was a collector of folklore and legends, and she was fond of narrating them to her precocious, inquisitive grandson. His mother loved local legends, and also passed many of them on to the young Hardy. His father, a great walker, often took the boy along on his rambles, and Hardy quickly developed an interest in and sensitivity to physical nature – though to the end of his days he couldn't name half the plants growing in his own backyard, as Gissing, an expert botanist, noted in his diary after a visit to Max Gate. Hardy was taken by his father for walks on the wild heath that came up to the back door of the cottage at Higher Bockhampton. They would often stop, at the top of the heath, at a place called Rainbarrows. The father would take out his telescope and survey the valley beneath – as Tess, sans telescope, would do years later. Here too, of course, are some of the seeds of *The Return of the Native* (1878; it is at Rainbarrows that Eustacia is building her bonfire when we first meet her), arguably Hardy's greatest novel, and of 'Wessex Heights' (1896), one of his most famous poems. The observation of nature encouraged by his father, along with the fund of local legends learned in childhood from his grandmother and his mother, together filled Hardy's mind from his earliest years, as Mr Gittings points out, with both landscape and human foibles, that special blend of emotion, place, and action that was to coalesce so brilliantly in his imaginative works. As a boy, as in many of the works of his mature years, distance for Hardy between the natural and the human worlds was blurred. We may not be surprised to learn that snakes and bats were sometimes discovered in his boyhood home, while heath-cropping ponies and deer often looked at him through its windows. All his life he loved animals; and while in later years it was only with great difficulty that he could be persuaded to join any society, he was always interested in, and supported, groups and committees dedicated to the protection of animals.

The Hardys and their neighbours frequently found around them relics of Stone Age and Roman and other inhabitants of earlier eras, for the Hardy country remained virgin, untouched, throughout the nineteenth century. Such relics in turn evoked in the young Hardy memories of accounts he had heard or read of rougher and more brutal periods in Dorset's history, themes we find him pursuing as a writer. As a schoolboy in Dorchester he saw stage-coaches rush through town at a time – the 1850s – when much of the rest of England was accessible by travel on the railways.

Early on, Hardy developed a passion for reading; what he was not given at school or was unable to find in Dorchester's circulating library and bookshops, he picked up on his own. Among other things, as a boy he read Dryden's *Virgil*, which he was to quote copiously in his earliest novels; Johnson's *Rasselas, Paul and Virginia*, the romances of Dumas *père* (in translation), Shakespeare's tragedies, and various histories of the Napoleonic wars, which particularly fascinated him – a fascination that was to last many years and bear fruit in *The Trumpet-Major* (1880) and *The Dynasts* (1904–8). He asked to be taught Latin; this was 'extra', but his parents agreed to additional tutoring, and at twelve he started on Eutropius and Caesar. At thirteen he won the Latin prize at his school.

The studious young Hardy was often seen by his neighbours reading a book or a magazine as he walked the three miles between Bockhampton and Dorchester. Hardy says of himself that he could 'read almost before he could walk'. He also mentions his sensitivity to music, which was certainly genuine, and notes that the first gift he remembers receiving from his father was a small accordion, presented to him at the age of four. While still quite young he could play the violin, as he informs readers of the *Life*. He then goes on to tell the story of how he wrapped himself up in a tablecloth and read the Morning Prayer standing on a chair, impersonating the local vicar. All of these things are related – the reading, the music, the mimicry of the vicar, for they paint the picture of a middle-class boy for whom access to culture constituted no special problem. In fact he had to fight to learn; and his reticence about the struggle, not the results, is one of the most unattractive things about what is in fact a very attractive story. From his earliest years Hardy aspired to live in a genteel world; and yet in the *Life*, which suggests by omission that such a world was always within his grasp when in fact it wasn't, he refers ingenuously to a 'lack of social ambition' in himself as a young man. He does admit in the *Life* that he would use any means he could find to get himself near Mrs Martin long after his mother had removed him from her school. Mrs Martin was attractive, cultured, and well-to-do, and Hardy, who of course never admits this, found the combination enticing and irresistible, whatever he may say in the *Life* about 'lack of social ambition'. He went on dreaming of her for years, though she was thirty years older than he, and later, when he was living in London, he tried yet again to rekindle their friendship.

In 1853 Hardy was thirteen and had reached the time when the education of many boys ceased. But he was allowed by his parents to follow his Latin master to a new school the man was opening, and here the future writer studied mathematics, German, and French, in addition to Latin. Around this time Hardy won a prize of five shillings at a local raffle, in those days conducted by the throwing of dice, a form of gambling that was to figure importantly in *The Return of the Native*. He used the money to buy a volume on sports and pastimes called *The Boys' Own Book*, the reading of which he never forgot; it is the source, for example, of Sergeant Troy's method of treading water, and of Farmer Shiner's technique for catching bullfinches in *Under the Greenwood Tree* (1872).

At school Hardy made virtually no friends of his own sex, though in the *Life* he complains, typically, that he was so popular with his schoolmates that 'their friendship . . . became burdensome,' and that he had to struggle to be able to walk home unaccompanied. The fact is that he was a solitary boy by choice and knew practically none of his schoolmates.

When he was fourteen he saw a pretty girl ride by on a horse one day, and fell instantly in love with her: such was his susceptibility from an early age to the briefest of encounters with members of the opposite sex. This was the first of many short-lived obsessions. When he saw the same girl go by some time later with another young man, his fantasies abruptly ended. The story of this very brief romance is retold in exact detail four decades later in *The Well-Beloved* (1892). Hardy next fell in love with a local girl, a gamekeeper's pretty daughter named Elizabeth Bishop, the subject of his poem, 'To Lizbie Browne' (1899). Then there was a girl called Rachel Hurst, whose 'rich colour and vanity, and frailty, and artificial dimple-making' Hardy noted carefully, and incorporated years later into Arabella in *Jude the Obscure*. He was always in love with somebody. In the Sunday School of his parish he met a 'pink and plump damsel' (unnamed) who was to sit for the portrait of the dairymaid Marian in *Tess of the d'Urbervilles*; Hardy comments, ingenuously and inaccurately, that this was 'one of the few portraits from life in his works'. There was a girl from Windsor he was taken with, but saw only once. And there was a farmer's attractive daughter named Louisa, to whom he was too shy to say anything other than 'good evening' when they passed on a path. A few months before his death Hardy still remembered this stinging moment in his youth and wrote a poem about it, 'Louisa in the Lane' (1928). He spent years gazing at Louisa in church, but that 'good evening', uttered when he was fifteen, was all he ever said to her. When she died in 1913 he composed several poems about her, and as a very old man he sought out her grave. In 1895, when Hardy was fifty-four, he met, and was very much taken with, Agnes Lane Fox, afterwards Agnes Fox-Pitt. When she died in 1926 he wrote a moving elegy, 'Concerning Agnes', published in *Winter Words* (1928). A number of Hardy's poems have their origin in the deaths of women he had met briefly, or only glimpsed once or twice; both of his wives were to find irksome his habit of never forgetting a pretty woman. But this susceptibility surely helped Hardy to become the creator of some of the most memorable women in English fiction as well as the author of some of the greatest love poems in the language. The death of his first wife in 1912 provoked him – he was by then in his seventies – to write some of his most tender and eloquent verses.

As an adolescent, Hardy could be characterized as both emotionally susceptible and physically aloof. In the *Life* he admits to a 'lateness of development in virility, while mentally precocious'. He adds, in a memorable passage, 'he was a child till he was sixteen, a youth till he was five-and-twenty, and a young man till he was nearly fifty.' Delayed physical development and sexual curiosity are often partners, and this may help to explain the persistence of Hardy's voyeuristic nature well into old age. One sees it in his work as well as in his life. Interestingly, as he himself admitted, he always hated to be touched by anyone; and yet he not only noticed pretty women go by, he seemed unable to forget them. He was always mooning around about some long-lost but not-quite-forgotten girl – a source at the same time of poetic impulse and, later on, of domestic embroilments. No wonder he drove both his wives into periodic bouts of rage, impatience, jealousy, resentment, and despair. At various times as a youth and a young man he seems to have been in love with three of his four Sparks cousins, Rebecca, Martha, and Tryphena, who were separated in age by twenty-one years. Undoubtedly this particular susceptibility of Hardy's led to the story of Pierston in *The Well-Beloved*, who falls in love with three generations of women, all of whom resemble each other physically, in the same family. Of Pierston's obsession with women, Hardy writes: 'In the streets he would observe a face . . . and follow the owner like a detective; in omnibus, in cab, in steamboat, through crowds, into shops, churches, theatres, public-houses, and slums . . . he . . . was tossed like a cork hither and thither upon the nest of every fancy.' Like Pierston, Hardy often seems to have been in love with the idea of love as much as with any particular woman. Nowhere in the *Life* does he mention Rebecca or Martha, who went into domestic service. Tryphena, with whom he was more taken than with any of the others, and who became a schoolteacher, rates a few bland references.

A month after his sixteenth birthday Hardy started work as an architect's apprentice at the Dorchester offices of John Hicks, who specialized in church restorations. 'Restoration' was at this time in full gear in Dorset and many neighbouring counties. 'Much beautiful ancient Gothic, as well as Jacobean and Georgian work, he was passively instrumental in destroying or in altering beyond identification,' Hardy writes in the *Life*, 'a matter for his deep regret in later years.' *The Mayor of Casterbridge*, however, contains a brief defence of Victorian Gothic restoration of Palladian churches. Hardy rarely admired eighteenth-century architecture, seeing it largely as the result of a jumble and confusion of other styles. John Hicks, who also employed Hardy's father to do some of his building work, had noticed the younger Hardy's academic talents, asked him as a test to help with a survey, and then offered to hire him. So Hardy got his first job, and went to work. He contined to read omnivorously, often getting up at four or five in the morning and reading until eight, when office hours began at Hicks's. He read the *Aeneid*, Horace, and Ovid;

and, having taught himself some Greek, embarked on the *Iliad*, the Greek Testament, the *Agamemnon*, and the *Oedipus*, working on the Greek texts mostly at night. No one pushed him; he wished to be an educated man, seeing learning as the key to and the path towards the 'respectability' he coveted. He also began to write for the *Dorset Chronicle* accounts of the church restorations carried out by Hicks and his assistants. These articles, Hardy's first publications, continued to appear between 1856 and 1862 – that is, between Hardy's sixteenth and twenty-second years. They show he could write prose competently, and that he knew one architectural style from another, but they show little else. Hardy's journalism led to the acquaintance of the well-known Dorset poet William Barnes, who may be said to have been the young writer's first literary mentor. The friendship began when Hardy consulted Barnes about some grammatical questions, and lasted until the latter's death. Barnes's poetry tends to provide minute evocations of natural landscapes, and undoubtedly Hardy learned something about poetic composition and subject matter by careful reading of his friend's verse.

One morning, instead of going directly to the office, Hardy got himself a good view of a public hanging in front of the Dorchester goal. The criminal was a woman who had killed her husband in a fit of jealous rage. The impression made on Hardy by the hanging lasted into old age; typically, in his eighties he still remembered 'what a fine figure she showed against the sky as she hung in the misty rain, and how the tight black silk gown set off her shape as she wheeled round and back.' The execution witnessed that morning provided, many years later, the dénouement for *Tess of the d'Urbervilles*. Two years later, watching through a telescope while on the heath, Hardy saw a man hanged at Dorchester goal for a particularly offensive crime, the murder of a helpless and deformed young woman. This became the inspiration for a memorable incident in his first published novel, *Desperate Remedies* (1871), in which the heroine's architect father is seen from a distance by his daughter to drop to his death from a scaffold around a church tower.

Hardy's grandmother, at whose knee he had heard so many fascinating tales, died in 1857. Her death inspired, half a century later, his poem 'One We Knew' (1902). The death of a woman was always a powerful inspiration for Hardy. In fact deaths, whether natural or otherwise, female or male, were always to stimulate him, both as a poet and a novelist; as a writer he rarely 'wasted' the death of someone he knew. If Hardy's readers often find him macabre, this early fascination of the emotionally passive youth with death and violence may provide one clue to the working of the mature mind.

Hardy continued to work for Hicks and to learn from Barnes. His sceptical nature was stimulated to further doubts about religion when he read *The Origin of Species* in 1859 and *Essays and Reviews* in 1860; the latter provided a textual and critical interpretation of the Bible, arguing that it should be read and analyzed like any other book. Many of Hardy's later poems were the result of the religious doubts and controversies of the 1860s, the decade in which Victorian England began to lose its faith. Meanwhile Hardy continued to study Greek, now getting help from a local Scottish Baptist clergyman named Perkins, who sat for the portrait of the Baptist minister in *A Laodicean* (1880–81). This, Hardy remarks in the *Life*, as he had previously remarked of the model for the dairymaid Marian in *Tess*, was 'among the few portraits of actual persons in Hardy's novels'.

Now, in 1861, he began writing poems, though many years were to pass before he could publish his verses. The earliest of these was 'Domicilium', finished in 1862, which describes Hardy's Higher Bockhampton home as set in the midst of a wild natural scene, and recalls conversations about earlier days with his late grandmother. He did get into print a fanciful piece, arising out of one of Hicks's restorations – an account, published in the *Dorset Chronicle*, of the disappearance of the local almshouse clock, written as if from the point of view of the departed clock's ghost.

In the spring of 1862, approaching his twenty-second birthday, Hardy toyed briefly with the idea of a university career, but decided instead to put his apprenticeship in Hicks's office to immediate pecuniary use and enter, if possible, the employment of a prosperous London architect, which he reasoned would also allow him to pursue his fledgling career as a writer. He was uncertain about his scholastic abilities and training: his education had been rather haphazard. There is no question, however, that his university fees would have been paid by his father, who was now a fairly prosperous employer of labourers. Hardy's rejection by Oxbridge on grounds of class, poverty, or insufficient training in the classical languages is pure myth, fostered by *Jude the Obscure*; in later years its author never bothered to correct the inaccurate assumptions readers drew from the novel. He certainly could have had, or at least tried to obtain, a university education; the fact is that he chose not to try, lacking self-confidence and wishing to earn some money instead.

So in April 1862 he went off to London armed with several letters of reference, the traditional Victorian poor boy with the world all before him and his fortune to make. After some initial rebuffs, he was briefly hired as a draughtsman by a kindly man named Norton, who had no need of one – as Owen Graye is hired as a superfluous draughtsman by the kindly Mr Gradfield in *Desperate Remedies*. Soon, however, Hardy landed just the job he wanted: it was in the office of Arthur Blomfield, a fashionable London architect engaged chiefly in the design and restoration of churches and rectories.

Hardy was to work for Blomfield until 1867. His five years in London were both exhilarating and disappointing. He went to music halls and met girls, not all of them respectable; he read a great deal at the British Museum; he attended the opera and the theatre regularly; he did some writing. But he was lonely, his health suffered while he was on his own in the metropolis, and he failed to advance very far either as an architect or as a writer – due, he always believed, to his social gracelessness and what was known about his background. Still, his London years were to provide him with material for some of his early novels, and ultimately to confirm his conviction that he was meant to live in Dorset, the country of his heart.

Life in London provided Hardy with ample observation of the social classes at close quarters, and led directly to the composition of his first – now lost, and never published – novel, called 'The Poor Man and the Lady', the tale of what happens (nothing good) when two people from different social classes fall in love. London made him think, if possible, even more intensely about class divisions. As he listened to the accents of Eton in his West End office describing various pleasures of the night before, 80,000 prostitutes were roaming the streets outside. Hardy was impressed by the poverty he saw in London – much more spectacular than anything he had seen in Dorset – and by the distance, both physical and metaphysical, between those who wanted for nothing and those who had nothing. He noted the monogrammed carriages in Hyde Park passing within feet of hopeless men and women sleeping on the ground in a bundle of rags – a scene he was able to reproduce vividly in *A Pair of Blue Eyes* (1872–3). Like Gissing a few years later, he saw with fascination that the difference between everything and nothing could be measured on a London street by a matter of inches.

Hardy spent many evenings at the opera. There can be little doubt that the study of opera, even more than the study of architecture, helped shape the plots of his novels, most of which could be described as 'operatic' in structure, though critics have rarely noted this. The exaggerated nature of his plots – the gratuitous tragedies, the bizarre coincidences, the ultimate revenge of fate upon the erring and the unerring alike – render them more than merely 'theatrical' or 'architectonic', epithets often applied to them; they are, these plots, quite consciously 'operatic' in this sense, and it is surprising that Hardy's tales have not been turned more methodically into operas. He attended the opera two or three nights a week; like Edith Wharton in New York in the 1870s, he heard Nilsson (among others) sing. Like Gissing in the 1880s, Hardy's insatiable appetite for learning led him again and again to the British Museum reading room. And like Dickens, he made the mistake of seeing once too often a first 'love' of his youth. He called on Mrs Martin, and found her, now in her fifties, 'altered'. The visit was not repeated.

The evidence is murky, but Hardy probably had an affair with his cousin Martha Sparks, born between Rebecca and Tryphena. Martha was now a lady's maid in a Paddington house. The two of them were thrown together more by the accident of sharing the same distant home town than anything else, and the affair, if that is what it was, neither lasted very long nor seemed to transform Hardy in any significant way.

Late in 1862 he won the silver medal of the Royal Institute of British Architects for his essay 'On the Application of Coloured Bricks and Terra Cotta to Modern Architecture'. In the spring of the next year he won the prize offered by the Royal Exchange for plans submitted for the Embankment, built in the late 1860s. In the latter instance Hardy was awarded £3, which he spent on a set of translations of the Greek dramatists. But the £10 which should have accompanied the R.I.B.A. prize was withheld; the winning essay was rated by the judges unworthy of the cash award. Hardy never mentioned this, but it must have helped to convince him that social barriers would impede his entry into influential 'sets' and prevent him from having a lucrative architectural practice. Certainly he could not have been denied the prize money if he had come from the 'right' background – family, public school, and university – and he knew this. He redoubled his efforts in literary self-improvement; and it was probably toward the end of this year, 1863, or at the beginning of the next, that he decided to try to make his way as a writer, perhaps as a journalist or a critic. He was then twenty-three. Like Henry James in 1861, he had reached a sort of spiritual crossroads. Architecture or literature? He wrote to a friend around this time that he was beginning to consider 'the pen as one of my weapons' in what he called the *'struggle for life'*.

He began to study literature like a doctoral candidate preparing for exams. In one of his earliest extant letters he recommends to his sister that she read Thackeray, obviously his favourite novelist; this is something else almost always overlooked in studies of Hardy. In his letter to Mary Hardy he calls Thackeray 'the greatest novelist of the day' because he alone considered the writing of fiction 'of the highest kind as a perfect and truthful representation of actual life – which is no doubt the proper view to take.' Thackeray's novels, Hardy concludes, 'stand so high as works of Art . . . from their very truthfulness'. Though he would often be accused of not telling it in his own tales, Hardy was obviously impressed by Thackeray's rating of 'truth' as the highest of the novelistic virtues; Thackeray himself had made no bones about wanting to convey in his fiction what he called the 'sentiment of reality'. Undoubtedly Hardy also became interested in the way Thackeray used memory in his novels; memory has an important role to play in many of his stories, most notably *The Trumpet-Major*. In turn, Hardy's use of memory attracted the notice of Proust; Hardy was one of the few English novelists Proust admired (George Eliot was another). It is interesting to note that in his letter to his sister, Hardy does not recommend Dickens, Trollope, or George Eliot – they were the three major novelists of the day, Thackeray having just died – though he does remark laconically in a later letter to Mary that *Barchester Towers* 'is considered the best' of Trollope's books.

Hardy writes in the *Life* that by 1865 – after three years in Blomfield's office – he was beginning to find 'architectural drawing', in which he had little to say about matters of design, 'monotonous and mechanical'. Having, he remarks, 'little inclination' (translation: improper credentials) to become a fashionable architect, 'Hardy's tastes reverted to . . . literary pursuits . . . and by 1865 he had begun to write verses, and by 1866 to send his productions to magazines. These were rejected by editors.' In those early days Hardy took one rejection as a total rejection, and never submitted a poem more than once; he was less fastidious about his fiction, as we shall see. He kept these spurned early verses, and the high quality of what he was writing by 1865–6 may be gauged by the fact that in later years he was able, as he says in the *Life*, 'by the mere change of a few words or the rewriting of a line or two to make them quite worthy of publication'. Two other factors are relevant here. Until he was an old man, the frugal Hardy never threw anything away; indeed, he would frequently cannibalize his own past work in constructing something apparently fresh. And – by the time most of these early verses were resubmitted, he had become a famous novelist. But that he was, by the age of twenty-five, already beginning to embark on the career which would land him on almost everyone's list of the dozen or so greatest English poets is astonishing when one considers his origins, his lack of advantages, the absence of any sustained formal education, and the necessity from the time he was an adolescent to earn his daily bread. Yet there can be no doubt that the earliest of his many great poems – and surely it can be agreed that Hardy in poetry, like Trollope in prose, produced, in the mass, as much first-rate literature as any other English writer – date from around the year 1865.

His desire to turn the Book of Ecclesiastes into Spenserian stanzas was, fortunately, short-lived. The only actual publication he achieved in 1865 was an essay called 'How I Built Myself a House', which appeared in *Chambers's Journal* – it earned Hardy £3.15s – and which possesses a lightness and charm he was not always able to recapture in the prose he subsequently produced. That lightheartedness was not necessarily his dominant mood may be seen in a diary note for 1865: 'The world does not despise us; it only neglects us.' This anticipates the more usual tone of the later Hardy; his temperamental pessimism preceded the famous novels by many years. His feeling that he was an outsider 'neglected' by Providence may well have contributed to his periodic gloominess as a young man, an attitude of mind that was to become habitual and instinctive in later years.

Throughout the rest of 1865 and on into 1866 Hardy, while still attending Blomfield's, turned his mind chiefly to poetry, reading Keats and Shelley carefully, and buying various rhyming dictionaries.

His copy of Shelley is heavily marked; and *Desperate Remedies*, his first published novel, is packed with quotations and stolen passages from Shelley, who never for a moment ceased to be Hardy's favourite poet. A renewed burst of enthusiasm for Shelley in the 1890s left its mark as well on *The Well-Beloved* and *Jude the Obscure*; the most casual perusal of the former shows it to be utterly soaked in Shelley. In his reading of *Prometheus Unbound* in the 1860s, Hardy paid special attention to passages of natural description and the effect of the interplay of natural forces, frequently a theme in his own poems and stories. (In later years he was certain, but unable to prove, that he had once slept in the same room as Shelley.) He also read carefully Meredith's *Modern Love* (1862), a sonnet-sequence about an unhappy marriage; *Modern Love* clearly influenced the sonnets Hardy wrote during the late 1860s. Later, in *A Laodicean*, he delineates himself as a poet in his mid-twenties in his young architect-hero's addiction to writing poetry: 'For two whole years he did nothing but write verse in every conceivable metre, and on every conceivable subject, from . . . sonnets on the singing of his tea-kettle to epic fragments on the Fall of Empires.' What Hardy was doing in these years, in a word, was learning the language *as a poet*.

He continued to read – Spenser, Milton, Herbert, Thomson, Crabbe, Coleridge, Scott, and others; he seems to have remained largely uninterested in Wordsworth. His poems of this period tend to emphasize the hopelessness of unrequited love – for example, '1967' (1867) – a theme he was to mine again and again. Swinburne's *Atalanta in Calydon* (1865) and *Poems and Ballads* (1866) became instant favourites. Hardy would often walk to his office in the morning through the crowded streets reading the poems of his new hero, 'to my imminent risk of being knocked down'. To his credit, Hardy always in later years stuck up for the controversial Swinburne, unhesitatingly recommending his appointment as Poet Laureate when Tennyson died (Alfred Austin was chosen instead).

In 'The Ruined Maid' and 'The Bride-Night Fire', both written in 1866, Hardy manages to take a humorous view of love and marriage, but these poems also give notice that his treatment of sexual matters will be candid. 'Hap' and 'Discouragement', both also 1866, are more sombre, containing references to suffering, doom, pain, and a 'vengeful god', very much in the manner of the later Hardy. 'Annabel' (1865) and 'The Musing Maiden' (1867), less successful products of this period, are about the devastation and agony of unrequited love. 'Neutral Tones' (1867), the best of these early efforts, concerns a failed affair, possibly a censored account of Hardy's abortive romance with Martha Sparks. Other poems of these years include 'In Vision I Roamed' (1866), which portrays man as a speck in the universe; 'A Confession to a Friend in Trouble' (1866), about the pain and grief of 'bitter knowledge'; 'Her Dilemma' (1866), in which a young lover, about to die, characterises 'humanity' as 'mocked'; 'She, to Him' (1866), four sonnets suggesting that love is no match for time, another favourite theme of the older Hardy; 'Her Reproach' (1867), which tells us that nothing lasts; and 'Heiress and Architect' (1867), which prefigures 'The Poor Man and the Lady' both in its title and in its argument that all human plans are foiled by death. Hardy, it is clear, was not in a hilarious mood during his last years in London.

He was in regular attendance at Drury Lane during the mid-Sixties whenever Shakespeare was produced. The architect-hero of *Desperate Remedies* is said to 'know Shakespeare to the very dregs of the footnotes'; Hardy would bring to each performance a text of the play and follow it as he watched the action. It has often been said that Hardy learned a lot from Shakespeare, especially from his use of rustic and choral characters. Certainly he studied Shakespeare carefully during these London years. His assiduous attendance at the theatre and a fleeting desire to write plays in blank verse landed him, after laying siege to several theatre-managers, a walk-on part in *The Forty Thieves* at Covent Garden. Thus began and ended Hardy's career as an actor, though he remained stage-struck well into old age. He seems briefly to have fallen in love with the granddaughter of Mrs Siddons, a young actress praised by the press in her debut as Rosalind in *As You Like It* – primarily for her figure. Hardy went to see her perform again and again; 'To an Impersonator of Rosalind' (1867), another poem about unrequited love, was written to her, but never sent. Again we find Hardy watching an attractive woman from afar but afraid to speak to her, even through the post. Half a century later, while in his seventies, he fell briefly in love with the teenaged actress chosen to play Tess in the first stage version of the novel.

At this important time in his development and growing maturity as a writer, Hardy was becoming increasingly unhappy in London. On his twenty-fifth birthday we find him writing a note to this effect: 'Not very cheerful. Feel as if I had lived a long time and done very little . . . Wondered what woman, if any, I should be thinking about in five years' time.' He was depressed by his failure to place any poem of his in any journal – and by a shadowy and ultimately painful affair with a girl whose initials were H.A. and about whom we are unlikely to know any more. Poems of 1866 such as 'At A Bridal', 'Postponement', and 'Revulsion' hint at bitter and disillusioning emotional situations under the glazed eye of an indifferent universe. Indeed, the last of these poems suggests, in the gloomy tones Hardy was to use so often, that all love is so ineluctably doomed to disappointment that it may be better not to love at all. Certainly by 1866 he was desperately unhappy, heading for a breakdown, and contemplating radical changes in his life. He toyed with the idea of going to Cambridge, but decided, as he wrote to Mary, that the three or four years it would take him to get a degree was a prospect that 'seems absurd to live on now with such a remote object in view'. He would also have found it impossible to take seriously the theological study demanded of all undergraduates in those days, as he acknowledges readily enough in the *Life*. He did work at French at King's College, London, in the evenings for several months. He haunted the National Gallery, spending part of his lunch-hour there day after day, studying in his methodical way the canvases of a different painter on each visit. And he went to hear some of Dickens's readings. But these vicarious cultural exercises did not satisfy him. And he found life in London unhealthy; he was not eating properly or getting enough fresh air. He contemplated changes but for the moment did nothing, going to work as usual every day at Blomfield's. His architectural career, however, was not blossoming, and he was bored. 'He constitutionally shrank from the business of social advancement,' Hardy writes of these years, 'caring for life as an emotion rather than for life as a science of climbing.' More likely, as we have seen, he was inept at putting himself forward – as an architect, a poet, or a lover.

Almost in desperation, it would seem, Hardy turned to the writing of fiction. He rated the novel as a *genre* inferior to poetry, an attitude maintained all his life; his decision to write a novel seems to have been made with the sole object of making as much money as he could as quickly as possible. Indeed, for the rest of his career as a novelist Hardy looked upon fiction chiefly as a way of acquiring the means to enable him to go on with his poetry without starving to death. He could not place his poems; perhaps he could sell a novel. Three decades later Somerset Maugham would start work on a novel because he was unable to get his plays produced – deciding (rightly) that fiction might provide a convenient short-cut to gain the attention of theatre managers. In any case, at the end of 1866 and the beginning of 1867 Hardy turned his attention to fiction as a way of escape from his chronic penuriousness and his apparent failure as a poet. 'Editors . . . [do] not know good poetry from bad,' he remarks bitterly in the *Life*. Yet he also describes himself there, with his usual ingenuousness, as 'not so keenly anxious to get into print as many young men are'.

At any rate, it was in a savage but hopeful mood that 'The Poor Man and the Lady' was begun. Hardy wrote it between August 1867 and June 1868, by which time he had left London for Bockhampton in an attempt to regain his health and peace of mind. He went back to work in Hicks's Dorchester office, took long walks in his favourite countryside, and let his mother feed him up. 'The Poor Man and the Lady' was never published, and the manuscript was later destroyed by its disillusioned author. But we can piece together a good deal about it; and in 1878 Hardy published a chunk of it in revised form as a long short story in the *New Quarterly Magazine* under the title 'An Indiscretion in the Life of An Heiress'. He also drew on 'The Poor Man and the Lady' when he wrote the Rotten Row scene in the fourteenth chapter of *A Pair of Blue Eyes*, as well as the scene at the Tranter's house on Christmas Eve in *Under the Greenwood Tree*. At the end of Hardy's career as a novelist he put into Jude's mouth a public narrative of his life which resembles Will Strong's autobiographical speech to the working men in 'The Poor Man and the Lady'. So for years he continued to cannibalize the rejected tale; like many authors, he was loath to let anything he wrote go entirely to waste.

Hardy called 'The Poor Man and the Lady' a 'striking socialist novel'. It was told in the first person by an obviously autobiographical figure called Strong (instead of Hardy), the son of a Dorset labourer. Strong shows academic promise, and his education is encouraged by the local squire and his lady, based on the Martins. He becomes an architect's draughtsman, falls in love with the squire's daughter, and is sent away. In London he works in the office of a leading architect and wins a prize which is later withdrawn. All of this, of course, comes directly from Hardy's life.

Strong adopts radical politics, even making a socialist speech in Trafalgar Square. In the first of many plagiarisms over a long career,

Hardy used the 'Address to working-men' by Felix Holt as the basis for the speech; that portion of George Eliot's novel was published in the January 1868 number of *Blackwood's*. After Strong's speech, the squire's daughter breaks with him. At a concert, with the girl in the last row of the expensive seats and Strong in the first row of the cheap ones, they re-establish contact. She invites him to call on her. He does, but she is out at the time – the first of many unfortunate accidents Hardy grew so fond of using in his fiction. Strong is asked not to call again. The squire's family returns to Dorset. Strong continues his studies in London, going temporarily blind from continued study at night of small print and Greek characters (a decade later, in *The Return of the Native*, the hero goes temporarily blind as a result of compulsive reading and study). Hearing that the squire's daughter is to be married in Dorset, Strong rushes back to the country, and on the night before the wedding they meet in a church. She confesses her love for him, then falls ill and dies. Strong designs her tombstone, free of charge.

Judging from the reports of publishers' readers and the account Hardy gave of it years later, 'The Poor Man and the Lady' was not so much a 'socialist novel' as a story about class-consciousness, articulated primarily through crude satire of the ruling classes. In this respect it captured Hardy's mood in the 1860s and expressed one of his lifelong grievances. It was, as a matter of fact, the logical outcome of nearly everything that preceded it in the young author's life. Obsessed by matters of class and status, Hardy in his first work of fiction could speak of almost nothing else. His chief targets in the tale were London society, middle-class values, religious cant, and the general run of what he thought of as the political and domestic morals of his day. It should not be surprising that the hallmark throughout was, quite simply, class hostility.

On 25 July 1868 Hardy sent the completed manuscript to Alexander Macmillan along with a letter in which he made plain his desire to attack, in the story, the manners of the prosperous classes, insisting that the novelty of his tale lay in its point of view, which was that of an 'outsider' – a role which the author saw himself as occupying in real life. Macmillan replied on 10 August, criticising the 'utter heartlessness' of Hardy's depiction of the upper middle classes and informing him that he, Hardy, knew next to nothing about them. In his zeal to condemn, said Macmillan, Hardy was guilty of thoughtless generalisation and groundless hostility. 'Nothing,' Macmillan wrote, 'could justify such a wholesale blackening of a class but large & intimate knowledge of it,' which the author lacked. He compared 'The Poor Man and the Lady', interestingly enough, to the work of Hardy's hero Thackeray – who, Macmillan said, often makes the well-to-do seem foolish in his novels, but also gives them 'many redeeming traits & characters, besides he did it all in a light chaffing way that gave no offence ... He meant fair, you *mean mischief*.' Macmillan also commented on 'a certain rawness and absurdity that is very displeasing, and makes it read like some clever lad's dream,' which is exactly what it was. Macmillan concluded: 'It is inconceivable that any considerable number of human beings ... should be so bad without going to utter wreck within a week.' It was the first time that Hardy's fiction nettled a reader, and by no means the last.

However, Macmillan and his literary adviser, John Morley, were able to spot intermittent passages of promise in 'The Poor Man and the Lady'. They praised the rural scenes and the strength and freshness of some of the writing. But they went on to suggest that Hardy 'study form and composition, in such writers as Balzac and Thackeray', who seemed to them to be Hardy's 'natural masters'. Macmillan and Morley complained of poor or non-existent plotting, but ended on a note of encouragement. He was addressing the letter, Macmillan said, to 'a writer who seems to me, at least potentially, of considerable mark, of power and purpose. If this is your first book I think you ought to go on.' He advised Hardy to stick to rural life, and to write only of what he knew at firsthand – good advice indeed, of which Hardy was soon to take advantage in *Under the Greenwood Tree*.

He saw this response, optimistically, as not quite an absolute refusal to publish, and asked for more information. Did Macmillan and his reader mean, in saying that he needed to 'study form and composition', that he was deficient in English composition, or in 'the building up of a story'? They meant the latter, of course. In December 1868 Hardy went to London to see Macmillan, who said that he could not publish the novel. But he encouraged Hardy to go on writing, and gave him a letter of introduction to Frederick Chapman of Chapman and Hall. Chapman took over 'The Poor Man and the Lady' and sent it to his reader, who was George Meredith. Meredith complained that the story was not interesting and that some of the 'episodic scenes are fatally injured'. Chapman told Hardy, however, that the firm might publish the novel if Hardy made some revisions and agreed to put up £20 against the publisher's possible loss. This would have been about £450 in today's terms, and Hardy, quite understandably, hesitated.

On his next trip to London he saw Carlyle in Chapman and Hall's front bookshop, and in the firm's back room the young author was lectured copiously by Meredith in person. Recently turned forty, Meredith waved the manuscript of 'The Poor Man and the Lady' in the air and declaimed on the necessity of learning how to devise plots. He told Hardy to write a new novel with less social purpose and more attention to construction. He advised him not to publish 'The Poor Man and the Lady', which he thought might cripple the younger man's fledgling career as a novelist. It was again good advice, given this time by the author of a sonnet-sequence – *Modern Love* – that had influenced some of Hardy's early poetry, and of a novel – *The Ordeal of Richard Feverel* – everyone had heard of. The seriousness with which Hardy took to heart Meredith's advice about construction may be seen in his next tale, the sensational *Desperate Remedies*, an unashamed and skilful Gothic story reminiscent of Mrs Radcliffe at her best and of a popular writer of the day, Wilkie Collins.

Early in 1869, however, Hardy was informed by Chapman of the firm's decision not to publish 'The Poor Man and the Lady' without a guarantee against loss much greater than the £20 Macmillan had asked for: they suspected it would be savagely attacked, and might injure their reputation. The (unknown) amount asked for was beyond Hardy's means, and he decided to withdraw. Before giving up entirely, however, he obstinately tried one more house, Tinsley's. Tinsley also asked for a large guarantee against loss, and it was at this point that Hardy decided to put 'The Poor Man and the Lady' on the shelf. Probably he never forgot how bitterly dashed his high hopes for the tale had been. Still, he was encouraged by the fact that he had been taken seriously by such eminent men as Macmillan, Morley, Meredith, and Chapman, and resolved to try his hand at another work of fiction. Meanwhile bits of 'The Poor Man and the Lady' kept turning up in his stories for years afterwards.

Hardy's most spectacular cannibalization of this first novel resulted in the novella called 'An Indiscretion in the Life of An Heiress'. There can be no doubt that 'An Indiscretion' came directly out of the earlier tale. The architect Strong is turned into Mayne the schoolmaster, but resembles his author no less; the second Mrs Hardy remarked, in fact, that Mayne was certainly based on Hardy himself. The novella's setting, Tollamore, resembles the Tolmare valley and farm in Dorset. Indeed, the country settings are largely in and around Stinsford, and the church in which the climactic scene takes place is Stinsford church. Stinsford is called Mellstock, and Weymouth, Budmouth – names Hardy was to retain in later novels. There are additional connections to Hardy's other fiction. When Mayne leaves Dorset for London to seek his fortune, as Hardy had done in 1862, the heroine tells him: 'If you cannot in the least succeed, I shall never think the less of you. The truly great stand on no middle ledge; they are either famous or unknown.' Cytherea says to Springrove, in similar circumstances in *Desperate Remedies*: 'And if you should fail – utterly fail . . . don't be perturbed. The truly great stand on no middle ledge; they are either famous or unknown.' In Geraldine's death scene in 'An Indiscretion', Hardy writes: 'Everything was so still that her weak act of trying to live seemed a silent wrestling with all the powers of the universe.' When Miss Aldclyffe lies dying in *Desperate Remedies*, Hardy writes: 'In the room everything was still, and . . . the lady's weak act of trying to live seemed a silent wrestling with all the powers of the universe.' A passage quoted in the text of *Desperate Remedies*, taken from Dryden's translation of the *Aeneid*, is also used as the epigraph to a chapter in 'An Indiscretion'.

More importantly, the resemblances between Hardy and his hero are as striking here as they were in 'The Poor Man and the Lady'. Terry Coleman, who edited in 1976 the first publication of 'An Indiscretion in the Life of An Heiress' since its initial appearance a century earlier, reminds us that Mayne, like Hardy, lives in a cottage built by his grandfather. Both have the habit of reading as they walk, and both read *Childe Harold* as young men. Mayne knows the areas of London frequented by Hardy during his stay there. Like Hardy, Mayne finds London inimical to his bodily strength and yearns for fresh air, exercise, and home-cooked food. Mayne is a schoolmaster who wishes to become a writer. In 1865 Hardy, as an assistant architect, attended the laying of a foundation stone at New Windsor by the Crown Princess of Germany. Blomfield gave her the ceremonial trowel, she managed to get her glove smeared with mortar, and handed the trowel back to him, saying 'Take it, take it.'

In 'An Indiscretion' the same thing happens to the heiress on a similar occasion, and she utters identical words. Broadford, the old farmer who is obsessed by the fear that he will have to leave the cottage he has lived in all his life, and who then dies, is an early version of John South in *The Woodlanders* (1886–7). The steam-thresher from which Mayne saves Geraldine reappears years later in *Tess of the d'Urbervilles*. Angel Clare's declaration on his wedding night that the woman he thought he was marrying is not Tess is prefigured in Geraldine's letter to Mayne in which she says she is no longer the girl he loved. They meet, after a lengthy separation, at a concert; the heroine is sitting in the last row of the expensive seats, the hero in the first row of the cheap seats. All of this is familiar territory.

With his acute class-consciousness and his array of social insecurities and yearnings, Mayne resembles Hardy in his twenties so exactly that some passages of 'An Indiscretion in the Life of An Heiress' read like pure autobiography. Here is Mayne meditating on his love for the wealthy Geraldine Allenville: 'He entered on rational considerations of what a vast gulf lay between the lady and himself, what a troublesome world it was to live in where such divisions could exist, and how painful was the evil when a man of his unequal history was possessed of a keen susceptibility.' And: 'That the habits of men should be so subversive of the law of nature as to indicate that he was not worthy to marry a woman whose own instincts said he was worthy, was a great anomaly.' Anyone familiar with Hardy's origins and his attitude toward their social liabilities should be able to recognize such a passage as coming from his pen – or George Gissing's, since they sound identical when discussing in their fiction such subjects as these. Mayne's susceptibility to feminine beauty is unconsciously emphasized on almost every page of 'An Indiscretion'. His encounters with women 'above' him always provoke in him, as in many of Gissing's heroes, 'a sharp struggle of sweet and bitter'; yet Mayne also declares, in Hardyesque tones, that men's 'love is strong while it lasts, but it soon withers at sight of a new face.'

All in all, 'An Indiscretion' provides an ample gloss on Hardy's sensitivity to his 'declassed' status, which is also Mayne's: that of an educated, sensitive man – no mere peasant, like his forebears – who nonetheless is prevented by the accident of lack of means from associating with his natural intellectual equals. It is the same conflict we find in Gissing's novels, and for similar reasons. Mayne assumes that people say whatever they like to him because he is 'only' a schoolmaster. He in his turn carefully monitors his own speech to avoid grammatical irregularities. Gissing behaved the same way in 'society', for the same reasons; so, apparently, did the young Hardy.

Like Hardy, Mayne leaves home to learn a trade, works hard, and dreams of writing 'a work of really sterling merit, which appeared anonymously'; *Desperate Remedies* appeared anonymously, as did *Far from the Madding Crowd* when it was serialized in the *Cornhill* in 1874. The latter became an instant popular success and made Hardy famous once it became known that the tale was not, as many had surmised, by George Eliot. 'The perpetual strain, the lack of that quiet to which he had been accustomed in early life, the absence of all personal interest in things around him, told upon [Mayne's] health of body and of mind,' as it told upon Hardy's in London. Significantly, thinking so much of Geraldine and her class and so little about 'the peasantry about him – his mother's ancestry . . . forgetting his old acquaintance[s], neighbours, and his grandfather's familiar friends, with their rough and honest ways,' causes Mayne to feel guilty.

Geraldine Allenville and Mayne meet in 'Wessex'; Hardy uses the same name in *Far from the Madding Crowd*, which appeared four years before 'An Indiscretion in the Life of An Heiress'. We shall never know if he used 'Wessex' in 'The Poor Man and the Lady'; what can safely be said is that the name by which Hardy chose to call that area of Dorset he wrote about in novel after novel, indeed the name by which his novels are known today, originated in the story of Strong/Mayne.

When, in 'An Indiscretion in the Life of An Heiress', Mayne finally makes up his mind to kiss Geraldine, 'The madness of the action was apparent to him almost before it was completed . . . he had committed a crime.' Hardy in his early fiction, like Gissing in his, exaggerates class differences and their impact upon human life because he felt them so keenly. What was he, after all, but the son of a stone-mason and a domestic servant, a man who aspired to a professional career and had yet, now nearly thirty, to attain one? His insecurities invade every page of 'An Indiscretion'. Mayne's grandfather succinctly articulates Hardy's social paranoia. 'However honourable your love may be' for Geraldine, the old man tells Mayne, 'you'll never get credit for your honour. Nothing you can do will ever root out the notion of people that where the man is poor and the woman is high-born he's a scamp.' Attracted to Mayne, Geraldine sees herself, Hardy puts it, as being 'on the verge of committing the most horrible social sin – that of loving beneath her, and owning that she so loved.' The overly sensitive Hardy exaggerates all of these feelings. Exogamous marriages, though of course they often went against the social grain, were taking place all the time in the latter decades of the nineteenth century: Geraldine could have found much worse 'social sins' to commit.

In a chapter headed by an epigraph from Thackeray's *Book of Snobs* (1855), Geraldine asks how many hours a particular trip might take. Mayne gives her an answer, and immediately they discover that he has been measuring the time in terms of walking and she in terms of driving. 'It was that horrid thought of their differing habits and of those contrasting positions which could not be reconciled' surfacing again, remarks the relentless author. Poor Mayne, Hardy feels compelled to add, 'had never . . . made use of a carriage in his life.' If they do marry, society's verdict, Mayne assumes, will be that he was 'one of the mere scum of the earth' who was 'an artful fellow to win [Geraldine's] affections.'

The pessimism grown of social paranoia and personal insecurity, so endemic to so much of Hardy's better-known work, may be seen in many guises in 'An Indiscretion in the Life of An Heiress'. Mayne's idea of 'ransacking the future for a germ of hope,' being 'a man not yet blinded to the limits of the possible,' identifies him as a character who could have stepped out of the pages of any of Hardy's books. Like a number of Hardy's heroes, the masochistic Mayne basks in his pain; at a concert he finds 'a certain half-pleasant misery in sitting behind [Geraldine] . . . as a possibly despised lover.' Among British novelists only Gissing is capable of writing such a sentence as that. At the end of 'An Indiscretion', the lovers must meet two conditions imposed by the author before their story completes its course. They must 'rigorously [exclude] all thoughts of the future'; and they must be separated by a death. As Geraldine lies dying, Mayne's existence is perceived by him to be 'apparently forgotten by the whole world'. Thus ends 'An Indiscretion in the Life of An Heiress' – a remnant of Hardy's first foray into fiction, yet utterly characteristic, due to his early life, his thought, and his character, of much that he would produce in subsequent years.

'The Poor Man and the Lady' having been rejected by Tinsley, Hardy went back to Dorset, where he started a poem on the Battle of the Nile, never completed – another indication of his interest in the Napoleonic wars. It is likely that in this year, 1869, he visited his cousin Tryphena Sparks, the last of the Sparks girls he was destined to fall in love with. Various biographers' speculations about a possible affair between them – culminating, in some of the more colourful versions, with the birth of an illegitimate child – must be wildly exaggerated. Tryphena was now a schoolteacher, whose conduct was necessarily open to wide scrutiny. While visiting Tryphena, Hardy heard something of her friends the Spillers. Robert Spiller worked as bailiff for an enterprising young widow named Catherine Hawkins, who owned and ran a large farm. The unusual story of the farm managed by an attractive woman stuck in his memory, and a few years later, in *Far from the Madding Crowd*, Bathsheba Everdene is said to employ the same number of men and boys Mrs Hawkins employed on her 525-acre farm at Waddon House.

As Hicks's assistant once again, Hardy was visiting interesting houses and churches of the district. One of these, Turnworth House, became the model for both Knapwater House in *Desperate Remedies* and Hintock House in *The Woodlanders*. In 1869 Hicks died, and Hardy suddenly found himself having to look for work elsewhere. Almost immediately he was invited by G. R. Crickmay, a prosperous Weymouth architect, to assist his firm with some unfinished church restoration. The work was expected to keep Hardy in Weymouth during the summer, but no longer. And so in June he took lodgings in Weymouth, which was to figure so largely in *Desperate Remedies*, and to a lesser extent in *The Trumpet-Major*.

Hardy enjoyed the summer in Weymouth, and memorialized it, among other places, in the poem 'At a Seaside Town in 1869', which appeared a half-century later in *Moments of Vision* (1917). He swam in the sea every morning, rowed a boat on the bay every evening, listened to the military bands on the seafront, and felt better than he had in years. He was also, unknowingly at first, gathering material for the setting of his first published novel. Being Hardy, he continued to struggle through passages of personal despair. The poem 'At Waking' (1869) describes life as 'appalling', hopeless, and 'blank'. In mid-September he re-engaged himself to Crickmay, who had more work in hand and was pleased to take him on in addition to a new young assistant who had joined the firm; the circumstances resemble those in *Desperate Remedies* when Springrove goes to work in

Weymouth. Hardy reckoned that his fairly light work for Crickmay would leave him time to try some more fiction-writing. He was determined now to follow Meredith's advice and contrive a more carefully plotted tale of incident. In late summer or early autumn of 1869 he began to write *Desperate Remedies*. From this period we also have the poem 'The Dawn after the Dance' (1869), which narrates the chilling, cheerless sentiments of a man during the morning after a dance, and ends with the thought 'That the vows of man and maid are frail as filmy gossamer.' Hardy always believed, as he said once, that 'love lives on propinquity and dies on contact' – that it is the most fickle, unpredictable, and short-lived of human emotions. Again in this he resembles Gissing, who was fond of referring to love as the 'hallucination' which precedes the 'chill' of physical contact. Hardy's poems of 1869, perhaps owing in part to his (surely) unconsummated passion for Tryphena Sparks, not to mention his failures as a writer, emphasize the hopelessness and frailty of human happiness.

Hardy's labour for Crickmay came to an end along with the year. Early in 1870 he returned to Dorchester, working at speed on his new book. By the beginning of March he had finished a first draft of *Desperate Remedies*, the last few chapters of which he was to rewrite before its publication by Tinsley in 1871. And so this heavily plotted and deliberately sensational story, touching among other things upon murder, abduction, impersonation, illegitimacy, adultery, and lesbianism, became Thomas Hardy's first published novel.

It was submitted initially to Macmillan, and refused in April 1870. Morley told Macmillan that 'the story is ruined by the disgusting and absurd outrage which is the key to its mystery – The violation of a young lady at an evening party, and the subsequent birth of a child, is too abominable to be tolerated.' Macmillan himself thought the book 'far too sensational'. In May, a month before his thirtieth birthday, Hardy received an offer from Tinsley to publish *Desperate Remedies* if the author would make some revisions and pay £75 towards the cost of publication. Hardy agreed to these terms, though he had only £123 to his name at the time (his savings from Crickmay's), and Tinsley contracted for an edition of 500 copies. Hardy did not try Chapman and Hall this time; perhaps he feared Meredith's opinion. In any case the revised version of *Desperate Remedies*, with some of the sexuality toned down, the 'violation' excised and the ending rewritten, was delivered to Tinsley in December 1870, and published anonymously in three volumes in March 1871. 'Never will I forget the thrill that ran through me from head to foot,' Hardy wrote many years later, 'when I held my first copy of *Desperate Remedies* in my hand.' The reviews were mixed but by no means flattering, the book was remaindered three months after it appeared, and Hardy lost his £75.

But it has always been one of Hardy's most underrated novels, and remains to this day spellbinding reading. He once described himself, deprecatingly, as a good hand at a serial; *Desperate Remedies* was not published serially, but Hardy early on figured out how to leave his audience gasping for more, and it is too bad that he never wrote another 'thriller'. As *Desperate Remedies* demonstrates, he came naturally to the *genre*: his instinctive sense of the macabre and the bizarre, his ability to cook up chilling coincidences and crushing accidents, his feeling that men and women have little control over their destinies in a universe at best indifferent to them and at worst positively malign, guaranteed this.

It must be remembered that Hardy wrote *Desperate Remedies* at breakneck speed. Inevitably it is filled with descriptive and incidental details from actual experiences and events in his own life, as well as with characters and happenings culled from 'The Poor Man and the Lady' (Hardy employed the same calendar, that for 1864, in writing both tales). The power of landlords over tenants and the social barriers between lovers are themes in 'The Poor Man and the Lady' transferred directly to *Desperate Remedies*. The scene in the later story in which Cytherea and Edward clasp hands across a stream is an adaptation of the cheap seats/expensive seats scenes in 'The Poor Man' and 'An Indiscretion'. Cytherea's speech to Springrove about the truly great being 'either famous or unknown' is taken out of Geraldine's address to Mayne on the same subject, as we know. In each of these early tales Hardy quotes the same passage from Browning's 'The Statue and the Bust':

> The world and its ways have a certain worth,
> And to press a point where these oppose
> Were a simple policy.

The last hours of Miss Aldclyffe and those of Geraldine are described in almost identical terms.

Springrove has a good deal of Hardy in him, being an architect from a country family, a man of humble origins who loves books, knows

Shakespeare, and writes poetry. The setting is Weymouth, though in early editions of the novel it was called Creston before Hardy settled on Budmouth. There are scenes in *Desperate Remedies* in which the lovers row on Weymouth Bay, as Hardy did every evening during the summer of 1869, and the areas around the bay are described with almost photographic accuracy. The melodramatic incident of the heroine's father falling to his death off a building scaffold came out of Hardy's memory of the man he saw hanged. The fire caused by smouldering couchgrass which burns down an inn and several cottages is based on a similar fire on the property of a Mrs Wood near Puddletown, during which sparks were blown by the wind on to the roof of the barn, as in the novel. The failure of Farmer Springrove (who bears some resemblance to Farmer Broadford in 'An Indiscretion in the Life of An Heiress') to insure his property has its real life analogue in another Puddletown fire. One William Brown, whose premises had been insured for the past forty years and who had just recently discontinued his policy, lost about £500 worth of property to fire; the senior Springrove, who has recently let his insurance lapse, loses £600 in his fire. The Puddletown fires were widely reported in the Dorset newspapers of the day. Hardy got Owen Graye's lameness and its symptoms directly out of his heavily annotated copy of *Modern Domestic Medicine*, by Thomas J. Graham. *Desperate Remedies* is liberally sprinkled with quotations from some of Hardy's favourite authors – a great many from Shelley, and some from Virgil, Shakespeare, Dryden, Keats, Browning, among others – and, typically, with various unattributed plagiarisms from *The Merchant of Venice*, 'Il Penseroso', Collins's 'The Passions: An Ode for Music', 'Ode to a Nightingale', 'Ode to the West Wind', and *David Copperfield*, to mention just a few.

Desperate Remedies is a Gothic mystery with a murder precisely in the middle and a complicated plot reminiscent of one contrived by Wilkie Collins, then a bestseller. In fact the plot is impossible to describe; it is too complex. But it works. Unlike many sensation novels of the day – and they were all the rage with contemporary readers – *Desperate Remedies* is also filled with the quiet realism that surrounds the rather ordinary heroine, her lame brother, her architect lover, and his farmer father. These characters are close to Hardy's experience, and are convincing. He portrays himself not only in Springrove but also to some extent in Owen Graye, who is bright but shy, socially undeveloped, and intimidated by servants. Owen is asked to come into an architect's office where there is no vacancy, as Hardy himself had been when he got to London in 1862. Owen's first job is the rebuilding of a church not far from Weymouth, a recapitulation of Hardy's experiences at Turnworth. (With his usual desire to mislead, Hardy allowed an illustration of Kingston Maurward House to serve as a frontispiece to both the 1896 and 1912 editions of *Desperate Remedies*.)

Despite the fact that this first published novel of Hardy's does not always resemble the sort of fiction he was to produce later, it remains a fascinating distillation of the first thirty years of his life. The story begins with a young architect falling in love with a woman who apparently does not reciprocate his passion. He marries another woman and they produce two children, a boy and a girl; the former becomes a pupil in an architect's office. The architect father accidentally hangs himself on a building site. The children, Cytherea and Owen, wonder what will become of them. Their lives, says Hardy, have nothing special about them: they will turn out 'like those of other people similarly circumstanced', period. Providence in Hardy is always indifferent. His ultra-sensitivity about himself and his past history may be reflected in the novel's declaration that in human experience 'It is the exchange of ideas about us that we dread most; and the possession by a hundred acquaintances . . . of the knowledge of our skeleton's closet's whereabouts, is not so distressing to the nerves as a chat over it by a party of half-a-dozen.' Were people talking about him? Like Gissing, Hardy detested and feared the possibility that 'society' discussed him behind his back; it affected his social 'nerves'.

After his architectural apprenticeship has gone on for two years, Owen's 'knowledge of plans, elevations, sections, and specifications, was not greater . . . than might easily have been acquired in six months by a youth of average ability . . . amid a bustling London practice.' This describes Hardy in the 1860s, a disillusioned architect's assistant who saw no prospect of further advancement. Owen's characterisation of Springrove, the head draughtsman in Gradfield's Weymouth architectural practice, could apply as well to Hardy:

> though he is not a public school man he has read widely, and has a sharp appreciation of what's good in books and art . . . [he] is rather of a melancholy turn of mind . . . He is a thorough artist,

but a man of rather humble origin. . . . He's a thorough bookworm . . . knows Shakespeare to the very dregs of the footnotes. Indeed, he's a poet himself in a small way.

This is quite exact. At Gradfield's, the young men agree that falling in love is like trying to catch something in the dark, and that afterwards one often regrets snaring anything. Again, pure Hardy. Hearing about Springrove from her brother, Cytherea begins to fall in love with him long before she sees him, as Eustacia is determined to have Clym before he appears in *The Return of the Native*.

Owen's poor health obliges Cytherea to take work as a lady's maid, as did three of the Sparks sisters. Like Hardy, Springrove goes to London to try to make his fortune as an architect. The growing love between Cytherea and Springrove is described in *Desperate Remedies* in terms that were characteristic of Hardy's thought in the 1860s and were to grow more intrusive and strident in the later novels: 'perhaps . . . the only bliss in the course of love which can truly be called Eden-like is that which prevails immediately after doubt has ended and before reflection has set in . . . before the consideration of what love is, has given birth to the consideration of what difficulties it tends to create.' Before he leaves for London, Springrove tells Cytherea that he will not prosper there as an architect, since success in the arts has nothing to do with the skill of the artist: it depends instead upon 'earnestness in making acquaintances, and a love for using them'; 'the art of dining out' is more important than the mastery of a profession. Thus the London-weary Hardy speaks in his own disillusioned and bitter voice. A city makes one cynical, *Desperate Remedies* argues. Springrove also remarks to Cytherea that 'If anything on earth ruins a man for useful occupation, and for content with reasonable success in a profession or trade, it is the habit of writing verses on emotional subjects' – a transcription of Hardy's state of mind during the years 1865–7, his last in London, when he was writing poetry to try to comfort himself for professional disappointments. On the subject of survival, Cytherea makes a comment worthy of Hardy's later pessimists: 'we desire as a blessing what was given us as a curse, and even that is denied.'

The heroine, by birth and education fitted for better things than domestic service, is forced by necessity to 'declass' herself – a favourite Hardy theme – and becomes lady's maid to the eccentric

Miss Aldclyffe. Her house at Knapwater, its furnishings and its outbuildings, are described in the sort of knowing, technical, minute detail accessible, perhaps, only to an architect. In an astonishing scene Miss Aldclyffe gets into bed with Cytherea and attempts to make love to her. The lesbian theme was passed over by contemporary critics, but it seems patent to today's post-Freudian readers. Fifteen years before Henry James's *The Bostonians* (1886), which is often cited as the first novel in English to concern itself with lesbianism, Hardy places a lesbian at the centre of his novel; unlike James, he puts two women into bed with one another, and lets us see and hear them there. Significantly, Miss Aldclyffe's 'sensuous' instincts were toned down in later editions of the novel published during Hardy's lifetime.

Disillusioned with London, Springrove returns to his father's farm, as Hardy went back to his father's Dorset cottage in 1867. This gives Hardy the first of many opportunities he was to take to use rural characters in a choric capacity. Meanwhile, at Knapwater, Miss Aldclyffe hires the villainous Aeneas Manston, yet another architect, as her steward. Can there be another novel in any language with so many architects in it? The detailed description of Farmer Springrove's cider-making, like the sheep-shearing sequences in *Far from the Madding Crowd*, is pure Hardy; he had observed these things at first-hand, and in such episodes took Meredith's advice to write about what he knew.

When Owen comes to visit Cytherea at Knapwater, he walks from the station to the house in order to avoid the company of Miss Aldclyffe's servants, who would, he is certain, look 'down upon him as a hybrid monster in social phrase'. This is vivid wording, and it undoubtedly reflects Hardy's embarrassment about his own anomalous social position. Was he a servant or a master? To what class, exactly, did he belong? His birth provided one answer, his education, his training, and his professional attainments another. No doubt like Owen Graye he often felt, as a visitor in other people's houses, like 'a hybrid monster'. Hardy always had great sympathy for the 'declassed' of the world; he was one of them himself.

A series of harrowing and breathtaking coincidences moves the plot briskly along. Farmer Springrove has his rick-yard fire. The younger Springrove considers suicide, but decides instead to take a job as assistant to an architect. Describing Springrove's interview with Miss Aldclyffe after the fire, Hardy goes out of his way to point out that for such a woman to realise that 'a son of her tenant and inferior could have become an educated man, who had learnt to feel his individuality and that hence he had all a developed man's unorthodox opinion about the subordination of classes' (like the author himself) would take a great deal of imagination on her part. There is also some Hardyesque exasperation about the nature of women expressed near the end of *Desperate Remedies*. In one passage the narrator refers to woman's 'sheer inability to be simply just, her exercise of an illogical power entirely denied to men in general,' and her 'punctilious observance of the self-immolating doctrines in the Sermon on the Mount'. Hardy begins in *Desperate Remedies* the exploration of female logic which continues through most of his subsequent books.

Another foretaste of the later Hardy is the theme of mediated desire. Had Manston been encouraged by Cytherea to make advances to her, we are told, he 'would have become indifferent'. Instead, 'Her supreme indifference [to him] added fuel to Manston's ardour.' Readers of Hardy's novels will be familiar with his idea, present in all of the fiction but perhaps most noticeable in *Far from the Madding Crowd*, *The Return of the Native* and *Jude the Obscure*, that what we easily get we are prone to undervalue, while what we cannot have always seems more desirable. Manston doesn't get very far with Cytherea; his only weapon is conversation. Watching her play the piano, he remarks that she 'would soon acquire the touch of an organ'.

Miss Aldclyffe advises Cytherea to accept Manston (her illegitimate son) in language almost identical to Sir Thomas Bertram's in *Mansfield Park* when he advises Fanny Price to marry Henry Crawford: 'The chance which he offers you of settling in life is one that may possibly . . . not occur again. His position is good and secure, and the life of his wife would be a happy one.' The marriage theme is broadened by actions of the novel's choric characters. One of these is Mrs Higgins, the wife of a carpenter 'who from want of employment one winter had decided to marry.' The result is predictable: 'Afterwards they both took to drink, and sank into desperate circumstances.' Hardy comments acidly: 'The most wretched of men can, in the twinkling of an eye, find a wife ready to be more wretched still for the sake of his company.' One of the other rustics advises: 'Choose your wife as you choose your pig – a small

ear and a small tale [*sic*].' *Desperate Remedies* shows Hardy already a
confirmed sceptic on the question of the relation of the sexes.

Like a novel by Mrs Radcliffe or Wilkie Collins at their
considerable best, *Desperate Remedies* races toward its dénouement,
led by Hardy's characteristic idea that one's fate is always at variance
with one's deserts and expectations. Humanity, he tells us, 'followed
a solitary trail like the interwoven threads which form a banner, and
all were equally unconscious of the significant whole they collectively
showed forth.' Human beings' unconsciousness of the true nature of
things – and just as well too, according to Hardy's contemporary,
Conrad – is an idea Hardy was to develop more carefully later on.
'Believing in God is a mistake made by very few people,' he adds
succinctly at the end of *Desperate Remedies* – the sort of sentiment
which, after he became famous, tended to enrage unsympathetic
critics. The novel concludes in a welter of spectacular revelations and
deaths. Through Springrove, Hardy comments that 'there's no
difference . . . between sudden death and death of any other sort.
There's no such thing as a random snapping off of what was laid
down to last longer.' The capriciousness of fate, the invisibility of
poetic justice, the unfulfilment of human expectations – *Desperate
Remedies*, the first published novel, is as lucid in its depiction of these
themes as *Jude the Obscure*, the last. Manston's declaration that
'man's life [is] a wretchedly conceived scheme' echoes down the
book's final pages. Hardy manages to spare some of the characters
from disaster, an indulgence he came more and more to avoid as the
years went by and the essential bitterness of his nature expanded.

Hardy wrote *Desperate Remedies* at the age of thirty. While it may
resemble none of the other novels in terms of form, its pessimism is of
a piece with many of the poems of this period of his life and with the
more famous novelistic declarations of unfaith that were soon to
follow it, book by book.

Hardy's work was the product of an early history notable both for
its triumphs over superior odds and its bitterness attributable to the
apparently insurmountable barriers to his ambitions thrown up by
the accident of his origins. He never forgot, and he never forgave. The
youthful striving to rise, the turning to fiction as a desperate remedy
after his early failure as a poet, the great successes after great trials,
the later obfuscation of earlier truths – it is all there in embryo in his
first three decades. How well, one might wonder, did Hardy the

Shakespeare scholar know his *Othello*? Think of Iago, so ambitious, so malicious, so brilliant, so fond of pontificating on the nature of man while hiding his own. ''Tis in ourselves that we are thus and thus,' Iago declares. He reminds Othello that 'men should be what they seem.' But 'I am not what I am,' he admits when he is alone. After all, it is Iago's play: he makes everything happen. He is a great character, though not a great man. The second Mrs Hardy's verdict on her husband was that he was a great writer, but not a great man. And yet, when we consider what Hardy had to fight against, the odds he had to overcome, when we remember that stonemason's cottage in the middle of nowhere, out of which emerged one of England's greatest poets, we may perhaps be excused for forgiving Hardy the various plots and schemes by which he wished to befuddle and confuse posterity. That we continue to read him with great pleasure is the final verdict on his life, and the only one that counts.

George Gissing in June 1884, aged twenty-six (*Beinacke Rare Book and Manuscript Library, Yale University*)

CHAPTER THREE

Gissing Agonistes

It almost seems as though a writer's works, like the water in an artesian well, mount to a height which is in proportion to the depth to which suffering has penetrated his heart.

> Proust, *Le temps retrouvé*

I had already realised long ago that it is not the man with the liveliest mind, the most well-informed, the best supplied with friends and acquaintances, but the one who knows how to become a mirror and in this way can reflect his life, commonplace though it may be, who becomes a [novelist].

> Proust, *Le temps retrouvé*

'Why will these literary men make these unfortunate marriages? It's all very sad, very sad.'

> Maugham, *Cakes and Ale*

Manchester, 31 May 1876, dusk. The students of Owens College (now the University of Manchester) have been worried by the disappearance from their cloak-room of money, clothing, books. A police trap has been laid for the thief: some marked money – five shillings and twopence, to be exact – has been left in an obvious place. A detective hides in a contiguous room.

And now a handsome, tall, well-built and freckled but pale youth of eighteen, with thick brown hair and blue-grey eyes, walks among the lockers. He is the College's most distinguished scholar. Four years earlier he received the highest mark in the Manchester District when he sat for the Oxford Local Examination. Now he is a scholarship student who, during his career at Owens, has carried off the prizes for German, Greek, Latin, English, and poetry; during the previous year, at the age of seventeen, he passed the matriculation examination for the University of London.

The young man looks nervously around the room; sees the money; takes it. Out swoops the detective; makes the arrest; transports the young man to prison. The news circulates. Among those to hear it, the Principal of the College is particularly upset by the news; the thief was to have been his guest at dinner that evening. Later, at a special meeting of the College Senate, all of the young man's awards are revoked and he is summarily dismissed.

This is the central event of the young man's early years. It explains a good deal about his youth, and also a good deal of what was to come. In fact an understanding of the motive for the theft and of the overall significance of this moment is central to any examination of his life and art. For the thief, of course, was George Gissing.

In Wakefield in the West Riding of Yorkshire, a town once described as 'ingeniously designed for the torment of any man who cares for beauty or tradition', George Gissing was born. The date was 22 November 1857, and the place a room above his father's chemist's shop in an old three-storeyed brick building in the market centre.

Thomas Gissing, the future novelist's father, was an amateur botanist, would-be poet, sometime Liberal politician in local elections, and an avowed agnostic with an interest in education – a hard-working and intelligent man, the author of several volumes devoted (separately) to plants and poetry. 'Taciturn' but 'pleasant', according to George Gissing's childhood friend Henry Hick, Thomas Gissing was a great reader and advocate of culture. Early on he won the undiluted admiration of his intellectually precocious eldest son, an admiration which never diminished. Years later, long after the father's death, the novelist remarked that he owed everything to his father and that he regularly saw him in his dreams, but some obstacle always arose to prevent their coming together.

Thomas Gissing was fond of airing his hatred of snobbery and hypocrisy, but he prohibited his children from associating with the children of other tradesmen, and he chose his own friends from among the professional classes. This is important. Thomas Gissing was not, strictly speaking, a member of the prosperous middle class, though his aspirations undoubtedly tended in that direction, nor was he of the more humble working class. Today we would probably classify him as lower middle class and be done with it, but in the middle of the nineteenth century in England his position was ambiguous: he had the education and the intellectual pretensions of the comfortable *bourgeois* and the income, never very much, of an ordinary worker. George Gissing grew up in a household in which such distinctions were often discussed; early on he seems to have picked up from his father the exaggerated interest in class that was to characterize the rest of his life. To which class, exactly, did he belong? His lifelong fear and abhorrence of the working classes began with his father's social pretensions and aspirations. The novelist certainly was *not* born into the lower classes, as those who have read only his slum-life novels have assumed, but rather into that twilight zone between 'middle' and 'working' – almost a guarantee in itself that one's life will be devoted at least in part to sorting the problem out. Dickens grew up in very roughly the same circumstances, and this was one of many things that attracted Gissing in later years to the work of his great predecessor. In any case, the father apparently made class an obsession in the Gissing household, seeing himself as fitted by learning and inclination to live amongst the respectable middle classes yet plagued by his failure to escape altogether the financial circumstances of the ordinary working classes. It is in this way that the 'exile' motif – the man *déclassé*, 'exiled' from his natural or appropriate social class – came into the future novelist's life at an unusually early age. He always remembered his father with that admiring pity one feels for worthy men and women handicapped by their origin and overtaken by fate. George Gissing's obsession with class was inherited from his father along with the interest in physical nature and the passion for culture, especially literature. If his fiction is mostly about class, this is one reason why. V. S. Pritchett rightly calls him 'the most class-conscious of [English] novelists'.

Gissing's mother, Margaret Bedford, married Thomas Gissing in February 1857. The wedding took place in the parish church of

Grasmere, in the yard of which may be found the simple grave of Wordsworth. Margaret Gissing was immune to this potential influence and this contiguity; her interests were domestic and religious. She was less educated and more devout than her husband, and to the end of her days remained uninterested in ideas. She was the disciplinarian of the family; her eldest son never liked her very much. Years later he described her as a 'a stranger' to him and said that he could not remember ever having received a caress from her. It must have contributed to the feeling he had all of his life, articulated plainly in his novel *Born in Exile* (1892) and elsewhere, that he was unlovable to women. The only other early account of her on record comes from Gissing's friend Hick, who recalled that she once locked his cousin's sister up in a dark cupboard for being naughty and left her there for a very long time. When, as a grown man and a published novelist, Gissing revisited his Yorkshire home, which he did as rarely as possible, his mother, he complained in letter after letter to friends, took interest only in her house and her religion, and none at all in her son. Age did not mellow her.

Gissing had two brothers and two sisters, all younger than he. William, born in 1859, died young. Algernon, the other brother, failed both as a solicitor and a novelist, but managed always to get by. He was three years younger than George. Margaret and Ellen were, respectively, six and ten years younger than their eldest brother. Neither of the girls escaped the narrow Anglican puritanism of their unimaginative mother, though the novelist seems always to have felt the younger sister, Ellen, more in sympathy with him than the elder and more religious Margaret. All of the Gissing women, however, were outraged by *The Emancipated* (1890), a novel in which Gissing attacked head on their favourite theories of existence. Indeed, the novelist was not close to any member of his family, though he would correspond prodigiously with Algernon. 'I never in my life exchanged a serious confidence with any relative, – I mean, concerning the inner things of one's heart & mind,' Gissing noted in his Commonplace Book in 1889.

The Gissing children grew up wanting for little, though there were no luxuries. Gissing as a boy is described by all who knew him as thirsting for knowledge, tireless in his studies, and fascinated by almost every aspect of physical nature – a passion which he inherited from his botanist father, as we have seen, and which contributed to his lifelong penchant for sketching whatever interested him. Indeed, his interest and skill in sketching led him to sprinkle a sizeable number of artists among his literary characters – *The Emancipated*, *The Whirlpool* (1897), and *Will Warburton* (1905) come especially to mind – and to contribute his own illustrations to one of his most successful and popular volumes, *By the Ionian Sea* (1900), an account of his travels in Calabria. The young Gissing read everything he could get his hands on. As a schoolboy he is remembered chiefly for the ferocity of his devotion to his studies, his hunger for learning, and his high marks. Compulsiveness, signs of great natural intelligence, and tremendous intellectual curiosity are the hallmarks of Gissing's boyhood. He worked hard because he could not help it. Hick describes Gissing as a rather shy, ingenuous boy, popular with his schoolmates.

In December 1870 Thomas Gissing died of congestion of the lungs – oddly enough the same ailment was to kill his novelist son thirty-three years later to the day. The elder Gissing's illness may have been precipitated by some sudden financial calamity. This has never been clear, but if so it helps account for the large number of precipitate economic reversals found among his son's novels. The sudden loss of this guide philosopher, and friend was traumatic for the thirteen-year-old boy. Gone was his most intimate associate; left was a parent with whom he had nothing in common and who obviously could not understand him, along with brothers and sisters too immature to be intellectual companions. From this time onward the shadow of loneliness and unhappiness begins to loom over the young Gissing's life.

Mrs Gissing was left with five young children to raise and very little money with which to do it. Of course she herself had no occupation. The house and the chemist's shop were sold and the family moved to more modest lodgings in Wakefield. A fund in the town was raised by public subscription for the schooling of the Gissing boys. All three were sent away as boarders, further reducing Mrs Gissing's domestic expenses, to the Lindow Grove School at Alderley Edge in Cheshire, a decent place run by non-sectarian Quakers in which the teaching standards were relatively high. All three brothers did well there. George, who avoided games and devoted himself exclusively to academic pursuits, soon became head boy, amazing the teachers with his scholarly zeal. He worked as he ate; he read as he walked. He saw himself as the prospective head of a large family; he felt he must get on quickly to help support his mother and brothers and sisters. Undoubtedly his mother made it clear that this and no less was what she expected of him. Being poor, he knew he would need scholarships to continue his studies, and he drove himself accordingly. Indeed, from the time of his father's death, for one reason or another, he never stopped driving himself; on his deathbed the plot and characters of his unfinished novel *Veranilda* (1904) continued to whirl through his brain. His death at forty-six was due, officially, to pulmonary failure, but in fact he wore himself out.

At fifteen – if we take the fifteen-year-old Harvey Rolfe in *The Whirlpool* as a portrait of the novelist at that age, which is not unreasonable – Gissing was, or saw himself as, loutish, ungainly, scholarly, conceited, bashful, and tormented by his bashfulness. At sixteen, according to his sister Ellen, he was 'a tall boy with dark auburn hair, high white brow and eyes slightly short-sighted so that the lids had to be drawn together when looking at any distant object.' She said 'he showed a marked gentleness of manner' and was 'over-sensitive . . . to what others were feeling or thinking'; this was, she says, 'all through [his] life, a very strong characteristic'. She also remembers him at home on holiday using 'scathing words to denounce the boyish pursuits and love of adventurous literature' of his younger brothers. The uneasy relationship between the overbearing Godwin Peak and his unintellectual younger brother in *Born in Exile* is obviously drawn from Gissing's memories of his own youth.

Gissing did equally well in all of his subjects during his two years at Lindow Grove, carrying off so many of the school's prizes that he had to take them home in a cab. In May 1872 he passed the Oxford Local Examination, having characteristically worked himself into exhaustion in the process. His examination paper was ranked the best in the district, and on the basis of this performance he was offered a three-years tuition-free scholarship to Owens College, exactly what he was hoping for. He matriculated there in January 1873, apparently knowing where he was going, and why. Founded in the early 1850s, Owens offered something between a secondary and a university education; many of the young men who went there did so to prepare for Oxford, Cambridge, or London University, as Gissing did.

During his first two years at Owens he continued to board at Alderley Edge, but in his third year he moved into Manchester, a change that was to have far-reaching consequences. Sounding suspiciously like Dickens on the blacking-factory episode – Gissing carefully read Forster's *Life of Dickens* in 1874 – he declared later to his friend Morley Roberts: 'It was a cruel . . . thing that I, at the age of sixteen, should have been turned loose in a big city, compelled to live alone in lodgings, with nobody interested in me.' Turned loose he certainly was, but Gissing did most of the unfastening himself. For a boy of studious habits, with no experience of less intellectual temptations and an extremely sentimental cast of mind, the results of such sudden freedom were to be disastrous.

Roberts remembers Gissing at this time as a young man of exceptional promise who hated science and was fascinated by Hogarth's paintings, a great talker when in the mood but often reserved, capable of great hilarity on occasions. He describes the future novelist, now in his seventeenth year, as 'curiously bright, with a mobile face' and 'abundant masses of brown hair combed backwards over his head, grey-blue eyes, a very sympathetic mouth, and extraordinarily well-shaped chin . . . and a great capacity for talking and laughing.'

Gissing's academic career continued to prosper. He won prizes at Owens for English poetry, Greek, Latin, and German. He rested little, and avoided social engagements so that he might work. He replied to an invitation to a theatre-party as follows: 'I am afraid the uneasiness caused by neglect of duty would surpass in degree the pleasure afforded by the spectacle,' followed by his regrets. He regularly rose at 4 a.m. and worked until 10 p.m.; overwork quickly became his most settled habit. In June and October of 1874 he sat for the matriculation examinations of London University – he hoped for a scholarship – and to the surprise of nobody performed brilliantly in them, winning national prizes for English, Latin, and history. Owens gave him prizes for Greek, Latin, history, mathematics, and classics. It was clear that he had a distinguished university career ahead of him. During the autumn of 1875, his last at Owens, he began preparing himself to enter the University of London in the autumn of the following year. His teachers and schoolmates predicted that he would become a professor of classics at one of the universities. He was a fine literary scholar and an exceptional linguist.

During the first months of 1876 Gissing, now just turned eighteen, was living by himself in furnished rooms near the College. He had, of course, complete freedom of action, his mother and brothers and sisters being far away and his few friends at the College kept, much of the time, at arm's length. One day Gissing showed his friend Roberts a photograph. It was that of a young girl, about seventeen, who, Roberts observed, wore 'her hair down her back. She was not beautiful, but she had a certain prettiness ... and she was undoubtedly not a lady.' Her name was Marianne Helen ('Nell') Harrison; she was a prostitute Gissing had picked up in a pub. During the early stages of their affair the naive, romantic, sentimental, sex-starved Gissing had been an easy prey for Nell and her landlady-procuress. As he got more passionately involved, however, the relationship began to change, and he became Nell's lover instead of her client. Roberts advised him to give her up; Gissing warned him to watch what he said about his future wife. Roberts was horrified.

John George Black, another friend of Gissing's, slept with Nell too; a venereal disease was his reward. Gissing himself had a bout of gonorrhoea in February 1876, but not even this could cool his passion. He haunted the streets she haunted, and sometimes saw her with other men. He seems to have viewed her as a victim of society and to have set out to redeem her. Gladstone also had a mania for 'saving' prostitutes, though only those with striking figures.

Attempting to give Nell the means of a respectable livelihood off the streets, Gissing bought her a sewing-machine and suggested that she set up as a seamstress. Nell was not interested. But Gissing continued to see her as saveable. He gave her, eventually, all of his money, even selling his late father's treasured watch to acquire additional funds. For Nell Harrison, however, there was no such thing as enough money. She was a hopeless alcoholic, and had become a prostitute to feed her habit, a habit she never succeeded in overcoming; she was to die, at thirty, of exposure, alone and penniless – in doing so providing Gissing with one of his most passionate subjects in *The Nether World* (1889).

The available evidence suggests that Gissing completely misread her from the start, attributing to her special qualities she never had or could have had, such as the desire to improve herself, to learn, to become respectable, and so on. He had fatal sexual susceptibilities, and this was the first tragic illustration of them. At eighteen, in any case, he understood neither his own sexual needs nor those of the women he met. He projected onto Nell his own idealistic social values. She was immune to them. The more money he gave her, the more she spent on drink; the sewing-machine remained unused. Still he persisted in his mad desire to marry her, assuming apparently that marriage would provide a moral framework which would rehabilitate her. It is what educated men and women attracted to their social and cultural inferiors always assume and hope and suffer the consequences of. Gissing's friends, those in on the secret, begged him to give her up. He refused to listen. He seemed bent on self-destruction, throughout his life a persistent theme. He would, he announced, save her, save her at all costs. It should surprise no one to learn that *The Ordeal of Richard Feverel* was his favourite novel. During the spring of 1876 he took her on several trips; for the first time in his life he began to neglect his studies. He was completely infatuated. The scheme to save Nell cost him more and more. He had exhausted his scholarship funds. He began to take things from the locker-room of the College and to sell them. And so the trap was sprung and the culprit caught, and Gissing's world suddenly came crashing down on him.

And now at one blow all those years of careful academic preparation, of planning and work to overcome the financial circumstances of his background and to justify his father's faith in education and the town of Wakefield's faith in himself as a scholar, went down the drain. Caught, jailed, and dismissed from the College, Gissing's admission to the University of London was cancelled. Like any ordinary criminal, he had committed a crime and been arrested. Overnight he was transformed from a respectable college student to a common felon, a prostitute's fancy-man. The effects of this mighty and sudden transformation were to last all of Gissing's lifetime and to determine many of his most characteristic social attitudes. They were also to give shape to his art in a number of ways – among these the many sudden reversals of fortune to be found in his books. Above all, however, the affair with Nell Harrison and the stealing episode were always and inevitably connected in Gissing's mind and were largely responsible for the most striking thing about all of his fiction: the confluence, in it, of sex, money, and class. In driving these events of 1876 further and further away from the surface of his life as time went on – except, perhaps, to Frederic Harrison, Gissing never spoke to anyone of this passage of his life – the future novelist turned them into vastly influential subconscious forces: obsessions, in fact. He was to make out of them a single, monolithic Guilty Secret, of which the guilt went so deep and the secret of his past became so important to maintain that Gissing found himself trying to exorcise them in everything he did, and in story after story.

The Guilty Secret, as Gillian Tindall has dubbed it, appears and reappears in different guises, but it is usually there in the fiction in one way or another. Sometimes it takes the form of a secret marriage, sometimes a matter of secret identity or birth, sometimes a past indiscretion real or imagined. In Gissing's case the guilt was many-sided – a liaison with an inferior woman, a venereal disease, a crime and a prison term. Such things did not happen to respectable people, and Gissing above all, as a young man without money and, after his expulsion from school, without prospects, yearned more than ever for respectability. How, now, could he ever become respectable? How could he ever live among gentlemen, much less call himself one? Until the last few years of his life, when he was in his forties, he was absolutely convinced, despite his other achievements, that he was unworthy of the love of any respectable woman. And so he came to see himself as his father had seen himself – that is, as an exile, deserving to live among his intellectual peers but fated by circumstances to live below and away from them. Again and again Gissing's fiction portrays the martyrdom of the outsider.

In the years subsequent to 1876 his guilt took many forms, but surely Ms Tindall is right to detect in the stealing episode and its results an indiscretion that seemed to Gissing less moral, sexual, or financial than *social*:

> what Gissing had so calamitously done was to commit a *working-class crime*. He had disgraced his family and himself by doing something not just against the law but utterly out of keeping with the class with which the whole Gissing household fervently wished to be associated. In his temporary abandonment of honesty, he had blundered back through those very social barriers which, by dint of work and scholarships, he had himself so laboriously climbed.

This disaster, which led to others in Gissing's life, though none quite like this, deprived the world, it may be, of a brilliant classical linguist, but it just as surely guaranteed, by forcing him to begin to earn a living almost immediately, that a significant contribution to English fiction would be made instead. Without Nell Harrison we should never have had *The Nether World, New Grub Street* (1891), *Born in Exile, The Odd Women* (1893), *In the Year of Jubilee* (1894), *The Whirlpool, The Private Papers of Henry Ryecroft* (1902).

Let us return to the month of June 1876. The Principal of Owens College put up bail for Gissing, and he was released from prison on the day after he was arrested. The incident caused general astonishment, especially because Gissing was so widely respected in the college community and because so promising a career had been, it appeared, irretrievably ruined. Here was a contemporary tragedy in plain dress. Gissing's mother was quick to blame her eldest son, and this must have hurt too. On 6 June he was sentenced to one month's hard labour, a sentence which he served in Manchester. In those days sentences for first offenders were not suspended. The Owens College Senate committee investigating the matter found the circumstances of the case aggravating rather than extenuating: there could be little sympathy for a man whose mistress was a prostitute on whose behalf he had stolen from his classmates. The Senate committee voted to dismiss Gissing and to rescind his prizes. Years later the University of Manchester would institute a Gissing Prize in English literature.

Upon Gissing's release from prison in July 1876 he returned to Wakefield, but his story was of course well known, and no possibility existed of his getting work there – or of his resuming his studies elsewhere, for that matter. No second subscription would be taken up in the town for the convicted thief. Gissing may have held, briefly, a clerkship of some sort in Liverpool in August, but this is uncertain. In September he became once again the beneficiary of a subscription relief fund, this one raised largely at Owens College at the instigation of its administration. There was some sense that perhaps the College had behaved with gratuitous harshness to this inexperienced, impecunious, fatherless boy of eighteen.

Among the Gissing family and its friends it was decided that the black sheep should be sent, in the manner of British black sheep in those days, to America, where there could be no prejudice against him and where he could become a new man. He would take with him several letters of recommendation; perhaps he would make his fortune. More importantly, he would be out of England, where his shame was known; he would cease to be dependent on his resourceless family, which had been counting on him to help them;

and thousands of miles would be put between him and Nell Harrison. Gissing seems to have observed these plans being made without enthusiasm or much interest, but he did agree to go. He was told that the family and its friends would do whatever could be done to help rehabilitate Nell. And so, using the money raised for him by Owens College, Gissing sailed for Boston in September 1876, having told none of his Manchester acquaintances except Roberts what he was doing. At eighteen he had already cut himself off from virtually all who knew him; he simply dropped out of their lives. It was for Gissing the first of many exiles.

He liked America at first. He moved into a small boarding-house in Boston and almost immediately discovered the local public library, where he went, every day, to read George Sand's novels, and Boswell – whom, like the protagonist of his novel *A Life's Morning* (1888), he admired greatly. His letters to his family during this period make a series of comparisons between England and America unfavourable, in his newfound euphoria, to his native land. Like all of the letters he was to write, then and later, these were full of details about the food and the climate. He was amazed, he wrote, by a new invention called the telephone. Testimonials he had brought with him procured personal introductions to William Lloyd Garrison and William Dean Howells but, as yet, no work.

It seems clear from the early letters that Gissing was hoping now to begin a literary career of some sort – as a journalist, perhaps, or critic, or freelance writer. At Alderley Edge, and again at Owens, he had written a good deal of poetry, and at Owens some of his critical exercises found their way into school publications, but as yet he had produced no fiction, and nothing he had composed had been published outside the world of school magazines. Now, however, his first piece appeared – a critical essay in the *Boston Commonwealth* (28 October 1876) about two paintings on show in Boston. But this was all. He was fascinated by the spectacularly scurrilous presidential election campaign of 1876, by the famous centennial exhibition in Philadelphia, by the optimism and energy of Americans – but still he could find no work. His funds running dangerously low, he moved in December 1876 to suburban Waltham, Massachusetts, where he took a temporary teaching post at the local high school. He taught languages: German, French, and English. One of his students described him then – he was nineteen – as a tall, broad-shouldered figure with a shock of light-brown hair worn rather long, dull light-blue eyes, and a full sandy beard. Probably the latter was a sort of stage prop for the convicted felon to hide behind. At any rate, he did not keep it for long.

Gissing enjoyed teaching – he was a natural teacher, and later a skilled tutor – and the people at Waltham liked him. So that when, on 1 March 1877, he failed without explanation to meet his classes, there was some astonishment in the little town. He was not ill, he was not away for the day: he had packed up and vanished. The reasons for Gissing's sudden departure remain vague. We know he was receiving letters from Nell urging his return to England. At the same time he had made the acquaintance of one of his pupils, an attractive girl a year younger than himself by the name, as Pierre Coustillas has discovered, of Martha Barnes. He began to feel attracted to her. But, considering himself as he did during these days unacceptable to a young girl of good family, and haunted by a strong sense of his various responsibilities, he found flight from Waltham the only way out of an impossible dilemma. Was he entirely cured of his venereal disease? We do not know, and probably Gissing did not know either. We hear of him next in Chicago.

Whelpdale's memorable narrative in *New Grub Street* of his experiences in Chicago, once stripped of its *blasé* humour, is a fairly accurate account of Gissing's stay there, though in later years the novelist's memories of this period of his life were recounted to friends with more painful emotion than appears in Whelpdale's version. Gissing arrived in Chicago with exactly five dollars, immediately paid out almost all of it for a week's room and board, and then set about looking for work. After much hesitation he went to see the editor of the *Chicago Tribune* and offered to write tales of 'English life' for the newspaper's weekend supplement. The editor suggested that he submit some stories; he would see if he liked them. So Gissing wrote his first piece of fiction early in March 1877, literally to keep from starving. The circumstances under which this introduction to authorship took place are vividly described by Whelpdale in *New Grub Street*:

'It was a great thing to be permitted to write a story, but then – *what* story? I went down to the shore of Lake Michigan; walked there for half an hour in an icy wind. Then I looked for a stationer's shop, and laid out a few of my remaining cents in the purchase of pen, ink, and paper ... Then back to the boarding-house. Impossible to write in my bedroom, the temperature was below zero; there was no choice but to sit down in the common room, a place like the smoke-room of a poor commercial hotel in England. A dozen men were gathered about the fire, smoking, talking, quarrelling. Favourable conditions, you see, for literary effort. But the story had to be written, and write it I did, sitting there at the end of a deal table ... I stand amazed at my power of concentration as often as I think of it!'

The story was called 'The Sins of the Fathers'. It was written in two days, and the editor of the *Tribune*, to Gissing's astonishment, gave him eighteen dollars for it, enough to pay his room and board for an entire month. Thus fortified, Gissing immediately wrote another tale, called 'R.I.P.', also accepted by the *Tribune*. His career as a writer of fiction had begun.

'The Sins of the Fathers' is pure autobiography, an accurate portent of what was to be Gissing's usual *genre*. It is about a well-educated, middle-class man who falls in love with and engages himself to a destitute lower-class woman. The hero attempts to help her by getting her sewing to do (Gissing could not get that unused sewing-machine out of his mind). He then quarrels with his father, who opposes the marriage, and goes off to America, where he gets a job teaching in a New England secondary school. Later he hears that the girl is dead; but since he knows that she would not have made an adequate intellectual companion, he is by no means devastated by the news. Soon thereafter he marries a respectable, well-heeled woman. The original fiancée reappears, the reports of her death having been greatly exaggerated. There is a terrible scene, a struggle, and finally the deposed girl drags the man to their deaths in freezing water. The story ends with this double drowning, the first of many drownings in Gissing's fiction and the first of many endings in which a man seeking respectability is dragged down, in this case literally, by an inferior woman. 'R.I.P.' is also about an exogamous relationship which ends in disaster. This time a French nobleman marries a peasant girl; his family drives her out; she kills herself.

For the next several months Gissing earned his living by selling tales to various Chicago newspapers, journals, and magazines. Between March and July 1877 at least seventeen stories of his were published; there are others which may be his but of which the authorship is still disputed – many of Gissing's earliest tales were unsigned. Some of them must be mentioned here, however briefly. 'Too Dearly Bought' is a Dickensian tale about an old man and his granddaughter who, living in the midst of urban squalor, dream of going to the country. Ultimately the grandfather steals some money to get them there; Gissing was to use part of this plot again in *A Life's Morning*. The story is interesting both for its idealization of the country at the expense of the city, a conspicuous theme throughout Gissing's fiction, and its description of the thief's state of mind at the moment of the theft: 'His brain was in a whirl. All his hopes, his longings, his vain schemings, flashed . . . through his mind . . . a cold shudder passed over his body . . . and his tongue felt parched against his palate. He could not reason; he stood a prey to quick succeeding passions and emotions.' Gissing in the Owens cloak-room?

In 'The Warden's Daughter' a man wrongly convicted of theft escapes from prison with the help of the warden's crippled daughter, who has always had great 'compassion for the unfortunate'; later they marry. In 'Gretchen' we learn that to become an artist a man must be brilliant, and starve. In this tale the first of many artist heroes in Gissing's fiction falls in love with a lady he sees in a picture, an idea the mature writer was to use in *Will Warburton*, his last published novel. 'Twenty Pounds', which tells us that 'to be dishonest is worse than going mad', is also about a man who steals money; here the protagonist gets into trouble by having to change a large bill, again anticipating the plot of *A Life's Morning*. 'Joseph Yates' is another story about a theft of money, and also of interest because it contains the first of many idealized wives in Gissing's fiction, the sort of wife he was always to dream about and never to have. This one, Bessie Yates, tells her hard-pressed husband that she can endure 'all things . . . poverty, trial, sacrifice' – but not, significantly, disgrace. Not that she enjoys being poor, of course. The point of the story is that there are worse things: dishonour, for example. 'Brownie' is a grisly Hardy-esque tale of an uncle who murders his niece in order to keep his farm.

Most of these stories revolve around crimes of various kinds, very often theft; Gissing continued to be haunted by the events of the previous year.

In July 1877 he left Chicago. He had had only one story accepted during the last month, he had used up his market and was short of money and out of ideas. Homesick for England, now that he had been away nearly a year, he headed east. In Troy, New York, Gissing found himself in a situation that was to make him, in Jacob Korg's apt phrase, a celebrated case among starving authors – indeed, the plausible protagonist of a Puccini opera, which at various times his life closely resembled. For several days, having no other recourse, he lived on peanuts bought from a street vendor; this too forms part of Whelpdale's narrative in *New Grub Street*. Starvation, for Gissing, came to be seen as one of the initiation ceremonies into the mysteries of authorship. In later years he was often heard to remark of somebody or other, 'How can he write? He never starved.'

Having had enough of Troy, peanuts, and starvation, Gissing decided to go home; whatever his mother and sisters felt about him, at least they would feed him. He wrote to England for money, and apparently borrowed some more in Boston, to which he returned to buy his passage back to Liverpool. For a short time he avoided starvation by working as assistant to a travelling photographer. At some point in his travels he saw Niagara Falls, which was to provide the setting for the final scene of his first published novel. Generally, however, he did not use much American material in his fiction. For a novelist who so often wrote autobiography in the guise of fiction, this suggests among other things that much of his time in America was too unpleasant even to write about.

Gissing embarked for England in September and landed in Liverpool on 3 October 1877. He returned to Wakefield six weeks short of his twentieth birthday, hungry and in debt – by any standards a failure. He had not been expected back, and was not made especially welcome by the Gissing ladies. Algernon was articled to a solicitor and still dependent on his family for support. William was working in a bank but earning barely enough to live on himself. The two girls were at home with their mother. Obviously Gissing could not add to their burdens. Again he packed his bags, determined, like many before him (including Hardy), to make his fortune in the metropolis. His mother was not sorry to see him go; he was a troublesome son whose name was pronounced in the town in a whisper and with knowing looks. In London the young man hoped to earn his living as a writer. He knew that he could expect neither help nor encouragement from his family. He must have been acutely cognizant at this time of the mortgage his past held upon his future.

Gissing arrived in London, took a furnished room in Gray's Inn Road, and began looking about for the means of earning a living. Not much is known about these early months in London – Gissing never said much about them – except that at some point Nell came to live with him. In January 1878 he published his first story ('The Artist's Child') in a major British journal – *Tinsley's Magazine* – and signed his name to it. He moved several times, perhaps because of Nell's alcoholism and the imprecations of landladies. He remained generally secretive about their relationship. His two brothers were permitted to meet her, but Roberts never was allowed to set eyes on her, and there is no mention of her at all in Gissing's letters home to his mother and sisters.

Extant letters written by Gissing early in 1878 (he was now twenty) reveal that he had begun to write a novel. He worked a good deal at the British Museum for the sake of the light and the warmth there and also in order to do the sort of literary hack-work which Alfred Yule in *New Grub Street* is always hoping might be transformed somehow into a permanent meal-ticket. But Gissing apparently failed to sell any critical pieces during this period.

Certainly he was very poor. He complained to Algernon that he could not afford to buy shoes or even a new pair of trousers. He was convinced that no lasting employment would be offered to him because of his shabby appearance, and he was largely right. In February 1878, however, he found some pupils to tutor, and this made things a little better; but he remained in perpetually difficult circumstances during this time. 'My early years in London were a time of extraordinary mental growth, of great spiritual activity,' Gissing was to recall later. 'There it was that I acquired my intense perception of the characteristics of poor life in London.' *The Ryecroft Papers* gives an account, largely autobiographical, though it leaves Nell out altogether, of what life was like for Gissing in those days – the changing of lodgings to save a few pennies (and because Nell's habits were not to the liking of landladies and neighbours), the going without a meal to buy a desired book (or drink for Nell), the gazing through shop windows at food he could not buy, the walking of immense distances to save fares. His clothing was probably ragged. He ate in cheap places when he could afford to eat at all; Nell could cook no better than she could sew. He became, partly through personal embarrassment, a sort of recluse, subject to what Ryecroft calls 'the profound solace of misery nursed in silent brooding . . . I wanted only a little walled space in which I could seclude myself, free from external annoyance. Certain comforts of civilised life I ceased even to regret . . . I just locked my door, and . . . went to bed.' Yet Gissing also managed to do an enormous amount of reading during this period; and he maintained his Greek and Latin, for tutoring was now keeping him alive. Wherever he lived, his precious store of books and the few school prizes he had been able to keep went with him and were proudly displayed. This was the kind of life that George Gissing, ultimately a distinguished man of letters, was forced to live for years. 'Comfortable people talk of his pessimism, and his greyness of outlook, and never understand,' Morley Roberts wrote of him later. 'The man really was a hedonist, he loved things beautiful – beautiful and orderly. He rejoiced in every form of Art, in books and in music.'

During the first half of 1878 Gissing continued to work on his untitled novel. Despite his passion for freedom from domestic annoyances, the conditions of his life during this period could not have been conducive to work. Nell's habits perpetually forced the couple to move; rarely did they stay in the same lodgings for more than a few months. Even the poorest places could not tolerate a woman of her character in the house. She continued to drink, of course; and at intervals she deserted Gissing and went back, for the sake of more drink and the money he was unable to give her, to her old trade on the streets. Again and again she returned in tears; again and again this kindest of men took her in. He made desperate efforts to help her; still, wherever she went, Nell was prone to associate herself with the worst elements in the neighbourhood and eventually to quarrel with everyone around her.

In September 1878 they were living in Gower Place. The autumn of this year was an important period in Gissing's life. On 22 November he was to come of age and would be eligible to receive his share of what little money his father had left: eventually, in April 1879, he got about £300. Also during this autumn he finished his novel and began circulating it to publishers. No one wanted it. Gissing pretended not to be surprised, but he must have been bitterly discouraged. This first novel was never to be published, and it has not survived in manuscript; apparently the novelist destroyed his first offspring. This would not be the last time that a book-length manuscript was destroyed by Gissing; it has been estimated that he threw out about half of what he wrote – quite a lot when one considers that, after Trollope's forty-seven novels, Gissing's twenty-three place him among the most productive of the Victorian novelists, despite the relatively short span of his writing life.

At the end of this year, 1878, Gissing worked briefly as a clerk in a charity hospital, an experience he was to make use of in *New Grub Street* when the novelist Reardon, unable to make a living by writing, 'declasses' himself in the same way, much to the chagrin of his fastidious wife. Nell was less fastidious.

In his second published novel, *The Unclassed* (1884), one of his most underrated and interesting books, Gissing steps aside, as he tended to do from time to time, and describes himself, in the third person, as he thought others saw him. *The Unclassed* is set, very roughly, in 1879.

> He was rather above the average stature, and showed well-hung limbs, with a habit of holding himself which suggested considerable toughness of sinews; he moved gracefully, and with head well held up. His attire spoke sedentary habits; would have been decidedly shabby, but for its evident adaptation to easy-chair and fireside. The pure linen and general tone of cleanliness were reassuring; the hand[s] . . . [were] soft, delicate, and finely formed. The head was striking, strongly individual, set solidly on a rather long and shapely neck; a fine forehead, irregular nose, and rather prominent jaw-bones, lips just a little sensual, but speaking good-humour and intellectual character. A heavy moustache; no beard. Eyes dark, keen, very capable of tenderness, but perhaps more often shrewdly discerning or cynically speculative. One felt that the present expression of genial friendliness was unfamiliar to the face, though it by no means failed in pleasantness. The lips had the look of being frequently gnawed in intense thought or strong feeling. In the cheeks no healthy colour, but an extreme sallowness on all the features. Smiling, he showed imperfect teeth. Altogether, a young man . . . whose intimacy but few men would exert themselves to seek; who in all likelihood was chary of exhibiting his true self save when secure of being understood.

Such is Gissing's picture of himself as he thought he appeared to others in 1879, aged twenty-one. It is an instance, by no means anomalous, of the way in which he wrote himself, physically as well as emotionally, into his books.

In March 1879 Gissing was working on two lectures entitled 'Faith and Reason' and 'The State Church from a Rationalist's Point of View', scheduled to be given at a local working men's club. At this time he felt that the educated poor had an obligation to help the uneducated poor help themselves – an opinion he did not hold for very long. But for a short while he thought he had a mission, and a series of lectures was planned. He wrote to Algernon: 'Scarcely one man in ten thousand is capable of original thought . . . No material advance will ever be effected if we do not take for our earliest watchword – popular education.'

Gissing was quickly disillusioned with this programme of improvement as he became better acquainted with the sort of man he thought he wanted to educate. This bitter experience was to find its way into several of the novels, most notably *Thyrza* (1887), and Gissing's disillusionment was to be translated as time went on into undiluted hatred of the lower classes and of all schemes of educating them. The poor not only disappointed him; by doing so they revealed an apparent error in his own way of looking at things. Such crimes were unforgivable. 'Faith and Reason' was delivered as planned in March 1879, but this was the full extent of Gissing's career on the public platform.

The receipt of his share of his father's legacy in April enabled him to move with Nell from Huntley Street, Bloomsbury, his latest abode, to Edward Street, near Regent's Park. He had been living largely on tutorial fees and eating almost nothing but lentils, rising usually around 5 a.m. for the two-hour walk to his chief pupil's Chelsea home – to be told on arrival there, as often as not, that the man did not want a lesson that day. (Telephones in England were a decade away: Queen Victoria refused to have one.) But the new lodgings seemed to be to Gissing's taste. Despite the utter failure of his first attempt, he now began another novel. The new book was called *Workers in the Dawn*; it was written between May and November 1879, and the 1,234 printed pages of its first edition (1880) addressed, according to Gissing, 'social problems, principally the condition and prospects of the poorer classes'.

The two most important events of these years may now be considered together: Gissing's first marriage and the publication of his first novel. *Workers in the Dawn* is at least in part about Gissing's life with Nell. He finished writing it within a few days of his marriage; in the next decade the publication of *New Grub Street* would coincide with his second marriage, also a disaster. In each case the published work anticipates the fatal nature of the relationship even as the novelist was entering into it.

Why did he do it? Why did he marry Nell? He complained bitterly of her to his friends and wrote mercilessly of her in *Workers in the Dawn*, as we shall see. And yet on 27 October 1879, in the parish church of St James, Hampstead Road, he legalised his relationship with her. None of Gissing's friends or relatives was invited to the ceremony; few were even told of it. His decision to marry, especially considering the difficulties of divorce for a poor man in those days, defies understanding. He took exactly the foolish step which, in *Workers in the Dawn*, he makes his hero take: that is, to try to save a prostitute by marrying and educating her. The novel demonstrates clearly that Gissing no longer could have had any real idea of trying to 'save' Nell, that his few remaining illusions about her had already been shattered. The writer knew more than the man; the man was unable to make proper use of what the writer knew and had actually written. This is only one example of the astonishing relationship between Gissing's work and his life. His fictional protagonists yearn for respectable women while they marry beneath themselves; as a novelist Gissing *knew* what torture this could be for a sensitive man, yet as a man susceptible to women he seems to have forgotten what he knew. Not only was Nell alcoholic, not only did she continue to sell herself in the streets to feed her habit, not only was she ignorant, foolish, wilful, and defiant, but she was also both vulgar and slovenly, two traits which, as Gissing's writings show again and again, he especially abhorred. There is no rational explanation for what he did to himself, though a few clues exist in *Workers in the Dawn*. There are some explanations, of varying degrees of rationality: that the marriage was a masochistic joke he played on himself; that as a highly sexed man he needed a woman and could not be bothered with the elaborate courtship required to get himself into bed with a more respectable woman; that Nell claimed to be pregnant and that he was taken in by her (a character in *The Unclassed* who bears some resemblances to Nell does this to acquire a husband; neither Nell nor her fictional counterpart produced a child); that Gissing simply resigned himself to formalising the existing situation, horrible as it was, feeling that no respectable woman would ever have him anyway (he had no dress clothes, etc.). The fact that Gissing and his first wife were married according to the rites and ceremonies of the Established Church in no way illuminates the question, especially when one considers the novelist's aggressive and oft-repeated assertions of agnosticism.

What does *Workers in the Dawn* have to tell us? Its hero, Arthur Golding, is the first of a long series of fictional self-portraits to come from Gissing's pen. The chief preoccupations of his life are work and love. Should he, he asks himself, dedicate himself to helping others, as Gissing had briefly thought of doing, or to art? Should he devote himself to the drunken prostitute he has made the mistake of marrying (the novel, completed shortly before Gissing's marriage, declares this to be a mistake) or to the 'ideal' woman who both understands and encourages his artistic calling? These questions are asked for over 1,200 pages until Arthur mercifully puts an end to them forever by jumping into the Niagara Falls in the middle of winter (another death by drowning). He was heading in the direction of art and the ideal when the end came. It is possible that Gissing, who must often have wanted to get away from Nell – and did a few years later – and felt guilty in consequence, considered suicide as a solution to his dilemma. The deaths by drowning in the early fiction suggest that this was the means that occurred to him when such thoughts held sway. 'There's a point in the life of every man who has brains, when it becomes a possibility that he may kill himself,' says a character in *The Whirlpool*. 'Most of us have it early.' Gissing probably did.

Arthur Golding's father dies when Arthur is still a boy. Like his author, Arthur has the good fortune to grow up with well-developed sensibilities and a great deal of intellectual curiosity. Like the usual Gissing hero, however, he is condemned by his poverty to a level of existence far below that which he both desires and feels himself fit for. Arthur suffers terribly, even as a child, from feeling *déclassé*. He is brought up by a foster father who, significantly, is interested in literature and botany but not in theology. Like Thomas Gissing, Arthur's foster father keeps a herbarium, the contents of which he has collected himself. He urges his young charge to 'Be a successor of Hogarth, and give us the true image of *our* social dress'. We know that Gissing admired Hogarth, and undoubtedly his first novel is consciously Hogarthian in its examination of the poorer classes. But Arthur Golding instinctively shrinks from the ugly, preferring to contemplate the beautiful instead. We can *see* Gissing in this novel trying to resolve this problem, which was to plague him for the rest of his life. The problem was the fastidious writer's desire to live amid what is soft and gentle, and the necessity of living elsewhere, having constantly in front of him as subject matter for his books only what he loathed. Arthur at seventeen 'felt within himself the stirrings of a double life, the one, due to his natural gifts, comprehending all the instincts, the hopes, the ambitions of the artist; the other, originating in the outward circumstances of his childhood . . . showing him . . . the evermultiplying miseries of the poor amongst whom he lived.' This 'double life' was Gissing's own.

On the subject of Hogarth and his *genre*, Arthur muses:

> The art to which he was devoted was not the same in which Hogarth had excelled. He felt that it would be impossible for him to take up his pencil for the delineation of such varieties of hideousness. Beauty was the goddess that he worshipped at the inmost shrine of his being, and to the bodying forth of visible shapes of beauty his life must be devoted, or he must cast aside the pencil for ever . . . how should he go for his models to the slums and the hovels amidst which his wretched childhood had been passed?

Morley Roberts said later that Gissing's 'very repugnance to his early subjects led him to choose them' (could he have used the same principle in choosing his wives?). 'He showed what he wished the world to be by declaring and proving that it possessed every conceivable opposite to his desires.' One recalls the memorable scene in *New Grub Street* in which Biffen expounds to Reardon his theory of fiction – that novels should deal with human misery as it is, and with nothing else – and Reardon's reply that he could never devote himself to such a task.

Workers in the Dawn also attacks the existence of public houses and examines the evils of drink. Despite its impatient and often unkind account of the poor, it manages to show us many of the worst horrors of poverty. It depicts the lower classes as beyond, in their bestiality, either education or the well-meaning but misguided attempts of philanthropists to help them. And it describes London as a nineteenth-century Waste Land in which it is better not to live. Here is a little Hogarth from Gissing's first novel, Whitecross Street on Christmas Eve: 'Out of the very depths of human depravity bubbled up the foulest miasmata which the rottenness of the human heart can breed . . . stifling a whole city with their infernal reek. The very curs that had followed their masters into the gin-palaces shrank out into the street again, affrighted by the brutal din.'

'Its object,' said Gissing of his first novel, 'is to depict real life,' and certainly the more naturalistic chapters of *Workers in the Dawn* are powerfully written. Much of its second volume is taken up with Arthur's flirtation with a working men's club, described as a nice idea in theory but on the whole irrelevant to the life of a serious artist; this had become Gissing's view in the previous months, as we know. In fact Arthur retraces many of Gissing's steps. From viewing education of the average working man as the only answer, and wanting, in consequence, to help open a working men's library – here is another part of the plot of *Thyrza* – Arthur comes to see the whole thing as a useless exercise. These sections of *Workers in the Dawn* include much discussion, largely unassimilated, of Schopenhauer, Comte, and Shelley, which in turn reflects Gissing's reading in speculative metaphysics through 1879. 'The mystery of life and death begins and ends with a vast doubt . . . boundless conjecture,' the novel declares.

In its focus on the horrors of slum life *Workers in the Dawn* may seem to take a Radical point of view but, in fact, like Gissing's subsequent novels, it adopts a very conservative tone about the poor: it is best to leave them alone because nothing really can be done; give them money and it will be spent on drink; sanity can only be preserved by doing whatever it is that one is destined to do in life; a little learning makes the ignorant more dissatisfied and unhappy. Gissing was to cultivate these themes in book after book.

And the strain in the novel between helping others as the only acceptable morality and personal egotism as the only possible defence against the world's madness is reflected in the story of Arthur's love for two women: Carrie Mitchell, actually Nell, and Helen Norman, between whom and himself 'There is always that horrible difference of caste.' Helen is the first of many unattainable respectable women of education and means who populate Gissing's novels. *Workers in the Dawn* commences the portrayal of Gissing's lifelong sexual schizophrenia: his need for sensual love from, and desire to play providence to, an unsophisticated girl – Pygmalion and Galatea with a twist or two; and his need of the moral approval of a 'respectable' woman in theory his social superior but in terms of education and sensibilities his spiritual equal. This is part of the 'double life' that Arthur talks about in the novel. Was Gissing right to abandon at so tender an age any hope of marrying a respectable, virtuous, educated woman? Was his commitment to Nell's 'salvation' an intelligent decision? Was she beyond help, and was he destroying, by marrying her, whatever hopes he may have held for his own future? Was he, at the age of twenty-one, giving up?

Workers in the Dawn argues that the Helen Normans of this world are always beyond the reach of the Arthur Goldings, and that the Carrie Mitchells will always be the ruination of the Arthurs. The novel also argues that art is a more sacred calling than philanthropy: this is the only aspect of Arthur's 'double life' clearly resolved. Could Gissing have believed that 'art' can be produced only out of misery? *Workers in the Dawn* appears to contradict this idea, one embraced by some commentators on Gissing in recent years. Urging Arthur to give up what she considers to be his foolish notions about helping the unfortunate and to concentrate instead upon his painting, Helen makes an impassioned speech late in the novel.

> 'I bid you give yourself henceforth solely to art, for you are born to be an artist. The feelings of infinite compassion for the poor which work so strongly in your mind . . . you must not allow . . . to lead you astray . . . nothing in this world is more useful than the *beautiful*, nothing works so powerfully for the ultimate benefit of mankind . . . in becoming a pure artist you would do far more to advance the ends [of civilisation] than by wearing away your life in petty efforts to do immediate good. Genius has always had, and always will have, laws to itself.'

The man of genius must have confidence in himself and remain immune to popular ideas. All of this is pure Gissing. He had already decided to take this advice, and was only lecturing himself. Like the hero of Butler's *The Way of All Flesh*, published in the year of Gissing's death, Arthur Golding discovers that he does not love the poor after all.

The Arthur-Carrie relationship is the most autobiographical thing in the novel. Arthur attempts to make Carrie a spiritual as well as a physical companion – the first of many Gissing heroes to undertake this perilous task. Arthur's pitiful efforts to teach his wife to read, write, and speak correctly, all of which she meets with stubborn sullenness, provide the most moving scenes in the novel. On the other hand, a man who sulks on the second night of his marriage because his wife refuses to read Coleridge with him – and because her syntax is anacoluthic – might be less than an ideal husband. Surely Gissing must have been difficult to have around the house. The source of his annoyance is honestly stated, as usual, in the fiction:

> What [Arthur] intensely loved, he could not but wish intensely to respect. The pity which had originated his love was in itself a species of respect; he had convinced himself by force of emotion that Carrie could not deserve the suffering she endured, and he had almost reverenced her as an instance of unmerited misfortune ... He could not believe that such outward perfection could exist with a common-place and sterile nature.

In a sense, this is Gissing the man at his best; here is his desire to respect what he loves, to relieve suffering, to reverse misfortune. It is also Gissing at his silliest: what is physically attractive must be worth saving. The sentimental Golding/Gissing dreams of finding a girl as beautiful as Carrie who has no trouble with her h's. Perhaps listening to a woman is as important as rating her sexuality: Gissing seems never to have learned this. He slept with them first and then worked on their pronunciation. No wonder his inevitable disillusionment sometimes seems bathetic. Predictably, by persistent correction of Carrie's pronunciation, Arthur finally manages to enrage her. The poor girl had not been warned, of course, that her happiness depended on her syntax.

What is additionally fascinating about all this is that Arthur has to marry Carrie to see what she is really like. Gissing, already knowing what Nell was like – they had been together, except for his absence in America, for three years – married her anyway. The account given of Carrie, written *before* Gissing's marriage to Nell, makes this indisputable. Arthur ends up with Carrie primarily because she has no hesitation about sleeping with him. This was a chief reason for Gissing's consistent choice of lower-class partners. They were sexually accessible; he could feel superior to them; he need not worry about being rejected by them; they tended to regard him with some awe (virtually the only things poor Nell Harrison did not pawn before her death were presentation copies of her husband's novels, which she could barely read, and his photograph); his clothes didn't matter. The Helen Normans of the world, who reappear in their inaccessibility in most of Gissing's subsequent novels, were more difficult to approach, more selective, more fastidious, less promiscuous, more virtuous. Indeed, the lives (in terms of marriage) of the Helens, unlike the lives of the Carries, depended absolutely on their virtue. And there was something else, too. The Helens might also inquire into one's past, as Helen inquires into Arthur's, and Gissing's past did not bear looking into.

And yet Arthur hates his life with Carrie. He can have no friends in when she is at home. He thinks of his previous existence without her as a time of 'vanished joys'. Whatever hopes he may once have had for her are short-lived. Soon after their marriage, having become thoroughly acquainted with her cunning ways of obtaining drink, he sums up her character in these terms:

> She seemed to have no innate respect for truth, and had acquired a facility in deception which made it all but impossible to arrive at the truth by questioning her. The knowledge of this terrible flaw in her character gave Arthur many sleepless nights. How could he tell what ruinous schemes were ripening in the brain of the girl who slept so peacefully by his side? . . . his suspicions never ceased to be fed with only too substantial evidence. *Distrust* haunted him like a passion.

Carrie dies of her life on the streets, as Nell was to do. Arthur goes to America to escape his past mistakes but ends up drowning his sorrows in the Niagara Falls. Gissing's epitaph for Arthur sounds like a sorrowing bit of self-portraiture: 'The secret of his life lay in the fact his was an ill-balanced nature, lacking . . . a firm and independent will . . . he was one of those men whose lives seem to have little result for the world save as useful illustrations of the force of circumstances.'

The book may or may not have provided a 'useful illustration' for the rest of the world; apparently it provided none for its author. One might argue that if you see your life as an allegory of unluckiness, then what you do may have the effect of fulfilling the prophecy. This may be one – perverse, to be sure – reason why Gissing married Nell.

Another might reside in Arthur's 'precious sense' of his role in marriage as constituting 'a lofty task which seemed necessary to his existence.' Having given up his working men's clubs and his schemes to improve the literacy of the lower classes, perhaps Gissing's sense of guilt about his own past and the waste he had made of his early years would not allow him to give up philanthropy altogether; he simply transferred it from the lectern to the bedroom. Less complicated clues might be found in Carrie's threat to Arthur – 'I could force you to support me' – and in Arthur's comment about their life together that 'Though we may scorn the world's opinion, we must still fear its tongue.'

When Carrie finally leaves Arthur to get more money for drink, he is intensely relieved – as Gissing would be when, not long afterwards, he gave up on Nell and left her. Arthur thinks of the departed Carrie as a 'weight to which he had immutably bound himself', one which 'was dragging him down, down into the foul atmosphere of a brutal existence'. Arthur perceives his marriage as Gissing perceived his even before he married – as a great error capable of turning 'a moment's folly' into a hellish existence.

Workers in the Dawn chronicles the death of Gissing's love for Nell at the moment he had decided to marry her, just as *New Grub Street* shows Gissing understanding what a disaster his second marriage was going to be while he was engaged in persuading Edith Underwood (another pick-up, marginally more genteel) to marry him. 'Excess of compassion had by degrees developed in him to a feeling which he had mistaken for love,' Gissing says of Arthur. 'My wife? My wife?' Arthur moans to Helen. 'This degraded, horrible, brutalised creature to call herself my wife!' Gissing was about to give Nell the right to do so as he wrote this. Certainly by now he had given up any plans he once harboured for reforming her. The sewing-machine was forgotten. 'All my efforts are vain!' Arthur declares. 'I cannot raise her to my level; but I feel only too well that she has the power to drag me down to hers. It is my fate to suffer.'

Gissing's subjects – sex, money, and class – dovetail in most of his novels and stories into the single subject of marriage, usually exogamous marriage. Perhaps now we can see why this should be so. 'England has produced very few better novelists,' George Orwell has written. 'He does not commit the faults that really matter.' This may be because he knew his subject so well. It was his 'fate to suffer' – and to write. Indeed, no other novelist has written so movingly of the pulverising effects of poverty and the money-race on the sentient spirit, and of the ways in which human feelings can be degraded by economic pressures. It is the focus on the individual confronted by circumstances, social and financial, beyond his control that gives such power to Gissing's best novels – the confrontation of men and economic systems, the brute force of money, the negation of the individual in a money-grubbing system. Scrunch or be scrunched: no other novelist in any language deals so specifically with the consequences of economic systems and failures in the lives of ordinary people. In this context Dickens's work was irrelevant, and Gissing knew it. 'I am constantly astonished to think of the small use Dickens made of his vast opportunities ... in the matter of observation among the lower classes,' Gissing wrote in his Commonplace Book in 1889. 'The explanation ... is, that he did not conceive of a work of fiction as anything but a *romance*. The details which would to me be most precious, he left aside as unsuitable because unattractive to the multitude of novel-readers.' Gissing was no romancer; the 'details' most precious to him were those which most vividly illuminated the ordinary daily existence of the poor. Unlike Dickens, Gissing in his work was brutally honest. Perhaps no other novelist except Trollope evokes so fully the texture, the atmosphere, the feel of daily life in the nineteenth century. Gissing's usual subject is what Biffen in *New Grub Street* in a memorable phrase calls 'the ignobly decent' – the frustration of the normal and reasonable expectations of average people. Gissing never waxed romantic about love in a hut (the famous passage from Keats's 'Lamia' is quoted in the twenty-fourth chapter of *New Grub Street*); healthy relationships, to remain healthy, must be fed with good food and comfortable surroundings. Gissing's idealistic characters who are also impractical always come to bad ends.

No novelist has put more of himself into his novels than George Gissing. The things he wrote about both obsessed him and happened to him. Written directly from life, his books are almost without exception parts of a spiritual autobiography, extracts from the narrative of his own existence. But one can go farther than this. As we have seen in the account given of *Workers in the Dawn*, Gissing sometimes wrote about things he would do later, described people he would resemble later. Most novelists write from experience, describing in their work what they have learned. Gissing was prone to use fiction as a testing laboratory of sorts and then go out into 'real' life and re-enact events he had already written about. Often enough he behaved self-destructively, knowing in advance, by writing about them, what results certain courses of action would lead to.

What can this tell us about the relationship between life and art? We all know the argument about art imitating life – that art is mimetic, that it could not exist without the raw material of life giving it endless situations and themes to work on. But we find Gissing again and again imitating not 'life' but a character he created himself and under his own control. Oscar Wilde's argument that life imitates art, which has seemed merely clever or Delphic to many, is convincingly dramatised in the life and work of his exact contemporary Gissing, who was prone in 'real' life to act out roles and situations he dreamed up as a novelist. To understand his work one must look at his personal life, for consistently he was a 'personal' writer. An interesting feature of Gissing's biography is that he wrote most of his best books during his unhappiest years, and that in his relatively more relaxed final years, when he was earning a sufficient income and had at last achieved some degree of both fame and domestic comfort, there is a marked falling-off in his work. This cannot be explained by the ageing process, for Gissing died in his prime, at forty-six. Though his work was always good, it was great only when he was gloomy – bearing out, perhaps, the idea that art and misery are natural bedfellows after all.

Sounding like a combination of Matthew Arnold and the elder Heyst in Conrad's *Victory*, Gissing wrote to his brother Algernon in 1885: 'Keep apart, keep apart, and preserve one's soul alive – that is the teaching for the day. It is ill to have been born in these times, but one can make a world within a world.' The 'world within a world' is the world of fiction, here less an escape from the 'outer' world than a reflection or extension of it. *The Ryecroft Papers*, in some ways Gissing's most autobiographical volume, ends on this remarkable note: 'May I look back on life as a long task duly completed – a piece of biography; faulty enough, but good as I could make it – and, with no thought but one of contentment, welcome the repose to follow when I have breathed "Finis."' Gissing saw his life as 'a piece of biography', and his novels duly constitute an extended piece of autobiography. The idea of the novelist as biographer or historian is of course a common one in the nineteenth century, reaching a kind of apotheosis in the work of James. In the fiction of Jane Austen, Thackeray, Charlotte Brontë, George Eliot, Trollope, Hardy and many of their contemporaries, the novelist-biographer relates the 'true history' of a fictional personage – plausible, but not really 'real'. Gissing's 'histories' often are in fact case-histories constituting an autobiographical world within a world, and thus really real after all.

Joseph Conrad in 1874, aged sixteen (*Harry Ransom Humanities
Research Center, University of Texas at Austin*)

CHAPTER FOUR

Conrad Alone

A book is a huge cemetery in which on the
majority of the tombs the names are effaced and
can no longer be read. Sometimes on the other
hand we remember a name well enough but do
not know whether anything of the individual
who bore it survives in our pages.

Proust, *Le temps retrouvé*

'Very few sailors can swim,' he said. 'They are
fatalists.'

V. S. Pritchett, 'The Rescue'

Who can be more nerve-racking than a neurotic?

Proust, *La prisonnière*

'She is no bother at all,' Joseph Conrad wrote of his wife Jessie, in
1896, to Edward Garnett. 'As a matter of fact, I like to have her with
me.' They were on their honeymoon.

Conrad was thirty-eight, and had been alone most of his life. As a
child he had been shuffled from one place to another due to the
underground anti-czarist political activities of his father and their
consequences, including the early death of both of his parents. He
went to sea at seventeen, retired from it at thirty-five, and tried the
profession of writing. He set foot in England for the first time at
twenty, and began to learn English properly in his early twenties. He
had, as Edith Wharton was to remark, worshipped the English
language all his life like a lover, but had never romp·d with it in the

nursery; becoming fluent in the language he was to write in turned out to be a lonely and laborious process for him. All his life he was uncomfortable in company with other people – perhaps in part because being with others required him to speak to them, and this he disliked to do. 'I have never been very well acquainted with the art of conversation,' he admitted years later in his autobiographical memoir *A Personal Record* (written 1908; published 1912). 'My young days, the days when one's habits and character are formed, have been rather familiar with long silences.' In English fiction, at any rate, Conrad was to be silent for many years, largely because of the circumstances of his life. He did not attempt any fiction in English until he was twenty-eight, he did not begin to write anything in English that (eventually) got published until he was thirty-one, he did not actually publish anything in English until he was thirty-seven. This is an astonishing story.

Conrad's 'young days' were as solitary as it was possible for them to be. He was born on 3 December 1857 (exactly eleven days after Gissing) in that part of Poland which was then incorporated into the Russian Ukraine, and christened Józef Teodor Konrad Nalecz Korzeniowski. When Conrad was three his father Apollo Korzeniowski was arrested for carrying on clandestine political activities against Poland's Russian rulers; one of the future novelist's first recorded deeds was the sending of pastries baked by his grandmother to his father in prison. In 1862 Apollo, his wife Evelina, and their young son, an only child, were sent into exile at Vologda, north of Moscow, thus effectively depriving Conrad of a childhood. It was here, in 1865, that Conrad's mother died. He was seven. Suffering from tuberculosis and a semi-invalid, Apollo Korzeniowski wrote despairingly to a friend in Warsaw that his boy 'is of course neglected . . . Poor child: He does not know what a contemporary playmate is.' Young Conrad was given some schooling in the Russian exile he shared with his father, now his only 'playmate'. He could read from the age of five, but apparently he never saw a child's book. The father wrote of the son: 'My dear little mite takes care of me – only the two of us left on this earth.' In 1900 the son was to write of the father (and describe himself as well) as 'A man of great sensibilities; of exalted and dreamy temperament; with a terrible gift of irony and of gloomy disposition . . . [and of] mysticism touched with despair.' From an early age Conrad was exposed to that 'terrible gift of irony', long before he understood what it was or meant. In a sense he grew up in a context of 'terrible' irony, to use his own adjective, which undoubtedly contributed something to the 'gloomy disposition' and 'mysticism touched with despair' he attributes to his father but obviously shared with him.

Apollo Korzeniowski worried about their isolation. 'The little mite is growing up as though in a cloister,' he wrote to a cousin when the boy was eight. Is it any wonder that Joseph Conrad was seriously ill during the summer of his ninth year? Later commentators have diagnosed psychosomatic epilepsy, brought on by the painful experiences of his earliest years. Somerset Maugham and Elizabeth Bowen, also deprived early of normal family life and a conventional childhood, developed a debilitating stammer no doubt also psychosomatic in origin. If you are cut off from life long enough, you begin to become allergic to it. The young Conrad, in social terms, may be compared to an invalid who loses the use of his limbs after a long time in bed. Of his first son Borys, Conrad wrote to a friend in 1889: 'I can't confess to any reverential feeling for childhood. I've heard people, more or less sentimental, talk about it but I question whether it is not a rather artificial attitude.' For Conrad, childhood was something that others, even his own son, only allegedly had; he had no intuitive understanding of what the term meant.

At the age of eleven the boy began to write patriotic polemics in Polish, but his health was unsettled and his nerves shaky – indeed, they would be from that time on. In 1869 Apollo Korzeniowski died, and Conrad's nominal childhood abruptly ended. Like Somerset Maugham, he was orphaned early. Like Edith Wharton and George Gissing, he was deprived prematurely of his closest and most sympathetic friend, his father. He was passed now from a friend of his father's to his maternal grandmother to some of her aristocratic friends and finally to a maternal uncle, Tadeusz Brobowski, who was to become the guardian of his adolescent years. Conrad was sent to a series of Polish schools, found that his favourite subject was geography, and began smoking cigars. At fourteen he made two declarations: he disliked the Christian religion, he said – its doctrines, its ceremonies, its festivals; and he wished to become a sailor. Besides Polish, Russian and French, he knew German: he thought he might begin his career as a sailor by escaping to Austria or Germany, for he could not see himself living under the rulers who had murdered his parents. He read travel books by the score, and in one by his compatriot Jan Kubary he found the following passage: 'What today happens on land can evoke nothing but contempt, and seclusion at sea is a hundredfold more pleasant than life among men.' Death at sea, where there is no politics, was preferred by Kubary to life on land because at least, in the former instance, 'you lie in a free grave.'

One of the few friends of Conrad's youth recalled years later that the boy had a habit of spinning fantastic yarns whose action always took place at sea. We know that daydreaming can be a means of escape from an unpleasant existence; Trollope, that most prolific of storytellers, was addicted to daydreaming. Trollope and Conrad may surely lay claim to being among the most internally tormented of authors.

Conrad saw the sea for the first time when he was fifteen, from the Lido in Venice. He travelled for several months in Switzerland, which was bursting with Russian political exiles and, years later, would serve as the setting of *Under Western Eyes* (1911). Like his hero James, Conrad required only the most fleeting impression to recreate subsequently, with the most unerring accuracy, scenes he had once briefly glimpsed.

In October 1874, two months shy of his seventeenth birthday, equipped only with clothes and books and fluency in French, Conrad left the home of his Polish uncle and set off for Marseilles and the career at sea he had been dreaming about. He had learned some Latin and Greek in school; he was fluent in Russian, Polish, German, and French. At seventeen, the homeless son of political exiles, he still knew no English, though he had read English authors in translation and wished to learn the language. He was, of course, on his own, as he had been more or less for years. What was his natural environment? Where were his family and friends? What, indeed, was his nationality, and what was his native language? He seemed to have none of the usual human attachments and possessions. Physically, psychologically, spiritually, he was, and remained, alone.

During the next four years, from 1874 to 1878, Conrad lived in Marseilles. In 1875, as a passenger, he sailed for five months to the West Indies and back. Marseilles, a large and rich and lively place, a centre of trade and smuggling, a meeting place between East and West, fascinated him with its swarming temptations and opportunities.

In July 1876, as a steward in the French merchant marine, Conrad sailed in the barque *Saint Antoine*. The first mate was a Corsican named Dominic Cervoni, later the model for Nostromo. The *Saint Antoine* called first at Martinique and then made for South America, with stops in Colombia and Venezuela. Conrad got off the ship at La Guaira in Venezuela and acquired the small material he needed years later to reconstruct the country of Costaguana in *Nostromo* (1904). Everyone agrees that the South American setting of what is perhaps his greatest novel is as vivid and unforgettable as the setting in any work of fiction; the fact is that the eighteen-year-old Conrad, nearly three decades before *Nostromo* was published, spent only a few days in 'Costaguana' and never strayed far from the coast. It is a remarkable event in the history of English fiction.

There is disagreement about the cargo of the *Saint Antoine*. The ship may well have been involved in smuggling guns to the conservative rebels in Colombia; in later life, at any rate, Conrad enjoyed describing his career as a gun-running smuggler. After stops in the Virgin Islands and Haiti, the *Saint Antoine* returned to Marseilles in February 1877, and Conrad, now nineteen, had completed his first voyage as a seaman, gathering impressions he would never forget.

A year later he supposedly tried to kill himself. There are various accounts of the run-up to this affair, the more romantic ones involving, again, the smuggling of arms – this time to Spain for the supporters of Don Carlos, the Bourbon Pretender to the throne. That is the subject of Conrad's late novel *The Arrow of Gold* (1919). A doomed imbroglio with a girl named Rita adds spice to the story in some of its versions. The facts are that Conrad invested what little money he had in the cargoes of ships sending contraband to Spain, lost every franc, and felt oppressed by this financial catastrophe. He got himself seriously into debt. There were desperate schemes to recoup. He thought of running off to join an American squadron at Villefranche, but this came to nothing. He tried his luck at Monte Carlo with some money he borrowed, and lost every penny of it. Worst of all, it appeared that as – still – a Russian subject, he might have to give up the French merchant marine and serve in the Russian army. 'Rita' may well have been an invention; it is certainly more romantic to say that you are in despair over a woman than to say that you are in debt. In any case, on a pleasant evening in Marseilles,

Conrad invited his chief creditor to tea, and just before the man's arrival shot himself in a fleshy part of his upper body. No organ was touched by this famous bullet, and the addresses of his physician and closest relatives were conveniently left in the clear view of his visitor so that the help he would need, both medical and financial, could be instantly summoned. Conrad's uncle paid his debts; no more was heard of 'Rita' until many years later, when this pathetic episode was transformed by Conrad, in one of his autobiographical volumes, into an interesting attempt to take his life after his first disappointment in love, which occasioned a duel. Conrad never fought a duel. The scars on his body were the result of his deliberately bungled suicide attempt, and the duel was invented because of the scars. But what is important here is what actually happened. Conrad's was the anguished act of a hapless youth who needed help and knew no other way to ask for it. In Marseilles, on the *Saint Antoine*, and back again in Marseilles, though he formed acquaintances, Conrad was still very much a solitary; and this concocted suicide attempt was in fact the gesture of an adolescent at the end of his tether whose chronic loneliness drove him at last to seek attention, affection and help where it was not freely given. Later, writing would become another attempt to create a world around himself and populate it with others, as it had been for Trollope.

The year 1878 was an important one for Conrad, and for English literature. In the spring of this year he sailed as an ordinary seaman from Marseilles to the Sea of Azov and then to Lowestoft in England. He saw England for the first time in June 1878, aged twenty. He joined the British merchant marine that same summer and took the first of his many voyages as a British sailor. In the 1870s over half the ships afloat around the world were British; men were in considerable demand to serve in them, and no special permits were required for enlistees, foreign or domestic. The no-questions-asked policy made things quite simple for Conrad – much simpler, as we shall see, than if he had tried enlisting in the 1880s, by which time steam was considered more economical than wind, and jobs on sailing ships were getting scarce. In later years Conrad was fond of saying that he always intended to be a British seaman, but the process by which he became one could better be described as serendipitous than inevitable.

Indeed, it could hardly be described as anything else, since Conrad, at the time he first reached England, intended to return to France and join the French navy, at least in part to escape Russian conscription. He had no money and he still could not, in 1878, speak a word of English. Despite his later version of events, he became a British sailor in the first instance because he needed the work, the money, and the anonymity, and he happened to find himself in a place where all were to be had for the asking. And so he sailed for two months in the latter half of this year as an ordinary seaman on the *Skimmer of the Sea* between Lowestoft and Newcastle. He got another British ship, this time the *Duke of Sutherland,* and on it, again as an ordinary seaman, he sailed to Australia and back in 1879. In 1880 he served in the *Europa* between London and several Mediterranean ports. During these years he began to learn English.

This is not the place to sketch a contemporary history of the British merchant marine, but something must be said of the sort of life an ordinary seaman in his early twenties was likely to lead on ships in those days. Crews of such vessels, as Zdislaw Najder has described them, were for the most part city riffraff, castaways, vagabonds, and waifs. An ordinary seaman lived in constant danger of disablement or death while doing what was in effect routine work; there was, of course, no disability insurance. The men who sailed before the mast might develop physical courage, or absolute indifference to human life, or perhaps a stoical combination of the two. Certainly courage and cowardice, as well as savage indifference, are depicted in Conrad's many tales of the sea. Excessive drinking among certain classes of Englishmen was as endemic then as now, and so foreigners were routinely sought by ship's masters recruiting manpower. Few people chose the sailing profession, during the latter decades of the nineteenth century, for the sake of adventure, or love of the sea, or to 'gather material'; usually the alternatives such men faced were worse. Sailors with some education enlisted in the Royal Navy; aboard merchant vessels most of the men were there, quite simply, because they needed the miserable remuneration and knew no safer way to earn it; or because they wished to drop out of sight, and this was a good way to do it. Conrad, who feared both debt and Russia, felt relatively secure in the hold of a British ship, though his youthful solitariness was reinforced yet again. His life at this time was not free of problems. In the English service, unlike the French, he later wrote, 'no one is in the least concerned with the crew's comfort,' which was nil anyway; and again, unlike the French service, the British merchant marine required members of the crew to purchase their travelling and working kit out of their own wages. In no sense could it have been an easy life. But, as Conrad said of the English flag, it was 'destined for . . . many years to be the only roof over my head'. In fact he lived at sea or nowhere.

Conrad now took another of those decisions which in retrospect came to seem momentous. The son of exiles, and of an age to be conscripted, theoretically he was now obliged to do military service in Russia or be shot as a deserter should the Russians lay their hands on him. He would be safe from Mother Russia only by climbing out of the ranks of ordinary seamen and becoming an officer. Officers in the British merchant marine traditionally were exempt from conscription. And so he applied to sit the examination for second mate. One of the requirements, of course, was passable English, and this spurred Conrad on to improve his adopted language. Another was a minimum of forty-eight months at sea, a requirement which in fact he was nowhere near able to satisfy. But Russia was calling. Conrad quickly got his friends in the French service to cook up some documents which were then submitted to the British service; he was risking indictment for perjury had the fraud been discovered. In June 1880 he was allowed to take, and passed, the examination for the second mate's certificate. The minimum age for the certificate was seventeen; Conrad was now twenty-two. Probably he never forgot that the first step he took up the ladder of the British merchant marine was founded on deceit and forgery, though of course he never spoke of it in later years.

He obtained his first job as an officer on the *Loch Etive*, in which he sailed not as second but as third mate to Australia and back in 1880–81. This was a ship of the iron clipper class, engaged mainly in the wool trade. Conrad's pay was three pounds and ten shillings per month. In the spring of 1881 he returned from the ten-months voyage with some money saved. His English, which in the previous year had been good enough to get him through the mate's examination, continued to improve. The next examination he would have to take if he wished to advance in his profession was that for first mate, and the reading he did to prepare himself for this next step helped secure his grasp of English. Still, he had not, except in the course of duty or some other necessity such as an examination, *written* a word of English. This man, destined to become one of the acknowledged masters of English literature, remained unable, in his twenties, to compose in the language in which his greatness was to be achieved. And Conrad was to become not only a great novelist but also – and this is not always the same thing – a great stylist as well, renowned for the eloquent way in which he used a language in which now he remained mute. For Conrad would write as beautiful, as descriptive, as evocative, as vivid an English as anyone who has ever put pen to paper; among British novelists his only peers are Jane Austen, Thackeray, and possibly George Eliot (Conrad had the excellent sense, and the modesty, to wish to become, he told a friend in 1897, 'a minor Thackeray'). Compared to Conrad's, the English of Hardy (in his prose) and Gissing, for example, seems sluggish and inert; and yet each of them, in his way, is a wonderful and fascinating writer – and, of course, a native Englishman.

As always, Conrad was bad with money, and soon managed to lose his small savings. And so, back to sea. In September 1881, at £4 a month, he signed on as second mate of the *Palestine*, a ship in which he was destined to serve – more or less, as we shall see – until March 1883. The *Palestine* would take him to the Far East for the first time – its initial destination was Bangkok – and it would become the model for the *Judea* in one of Conrad's earliest literary successes, 'Youth' (1902). Both in the story and in fact the vessel's captain was named Beard and its first mate, Mahon; Conrad often could not be bothered to invent names. The ship's grotesque fate, in contrast to the heroics of the crew keeping her afloat, is faithfully rendered in 'Youth', though other aspects of the tale are wholly fictional, as one might expect. Conrad described 'Youth' later as 'a record of personal experience purely', telling his friend R. B. Cunninghame Graham that he could never 'invent an effective lie – a lie that would sell, and last, and be admirable'. He didn't need to lie: he wrote from life.

The *Palestine* embarked for Bangkok in November 1881, lost a mast, and started to sink before it got out of the Channel. It limped back to Falmouth, where repairs took over eight months. In September 1882 it finally sailed for Bangkok, encountering its final disaster much nearer the shore line than the *Judea*'s end as described in 'Youth'.

The crew of the *Palestine* was taken to Singapore, where in March 1883 a court of enquiry cleared all officials and crew of responsibility for what was in effect the ship's spontaneous combustion. Coal and

grain were the most dangerous cargoes, being so flammable, and the
Palestine had been carrying coal. Conrad waited in Singapore for a
ship. While languishing there he became sufficiently acquainted with
the harbour district to use it later as the setting of several of his
tales, including one of his best, 'The Shadow-Line' (1917). Tired of
waiting, he returned to England in May 1883 as a passenger. He
was now twenty-five. He was living in lodgings in what was still in
many ways a foreign country, he had little money, he knew few
people outside his profession, he had no intimate friends. Little
about his life at this time is actually known, though this has not
prevented a great deal from being written about it. All we can be
certain of is that, as so often before, Conrad was largely by himself.
Few men who have gone on to become successful in any line of
work can have had such an appallingly miserable, nerve-wracking,
and solitary first quarter-century of life.

In 1883, for the first time, the number of steamships exceeded the
number of sailing ships. The demand for sailing officers was
dropping sharply. Conrad, feeling that he was too old a hand to
start learning the principles of navigation by steam – he never did
learn them, but rather retired from the sea around the time sailing
ships became virtually obsolete as long-haul freighters – decided to
study for his first mate's examination; this might make him more
marketable as an officer. In the autumn of 1883 he sailed aboard the
Riversdale as second mate, with a crew composed largely of
Scandinavians, to South Africa and India, places he made little use
of in his fiction. The return journey from India to England (June to
October 1884) was immortalised thirteen years later by his first tale
of the sea, for this ship was called the *Narcissus*. About half the
crew were foreign. There was one negro aboard. His name was
Joseph Barron, and on the crew list he put a cross against his name.
He died, and was buried at sea, three weeks before the *Narcissus*
reached Dunkirk; he was thirty-five. Some of the other characters in
The Nigger of the 'Narcissus' (1897) are based on members of the
crew of the *Narcissus*, and some on men Conrad sailed with
subsequently. Forty years later the novelist commented that 'The
voyage of the *Narcissus* was performed from Bombay to London in
the manner I have described,' though he went on to add, reasonably
enough, 'I do not write history, but fiction, and I am therefore
entitled to choose as I please what is most suitable in regard to

characters and particulars to help me in the general impression I wish
to produce.'

In November 1884 Conrad sat, and failed, his examination for first
mate, an event which goes unmentioned in *A Personal Record*. His
failure was largely the result of a poor performance in the section called
'Day's Work', which consisted of questions about navigation based on
entries in the logbook, the ship's position, speed and so forth. He went
to a crammer and tried again. This time, in December 1884, he passed.
In the same month he turned twenty-seven. As the number of officers'
jobs continued to decline, Conrad began to work for the master's
examination. But the market for ship's officers remained depressed,
with opportunities at all ranks becoming scarcer as more and more
shippers turned to steam. Fewer new vessels were being built; between
1865 and 1894 the total number of ships sailing under the red ensign of
England, still the world's maritime leader, declined by thirty-nine per
cent. One of Conrad's sailing colleagues wrote at this time: 'I know of
no more depressing occupation than that of a capable seaman looking
for a ship as officer.'

After a long search, in the spring of 1885 Conrad found a ship. This
was the *Tilkhurst*, and he signed on as second mate – he could not get a
first officer's position – at £5 a month. The *Tilkhurst* unloaded a cargo
in Singapore and Calcutta, and from these ports Conrad dispatched to
a Polish friend living in England some of his earliest surviving letters.
Interestingly, he wrote in English rather than in Polish; he was by now
more a Briton than a Pole. The letters are full of current British politics:
Conrad had become an ardent Tory. In one of them he declares: 'when
speaking, writing or thinking in English the word Home always means
for me the hospitable shores of Great Britain.' In another letter we may
find a foreshadowing of his retirement from the sea some eight years
later. He wishes, he says, 'to work for myself – I am sick and tired of
sailing about for little money and less consideration. But I love the sea;
and if I could just clear my bare living . . . I should be comparatively
happy. Can it be done?' The Liberal victory in the General Election of
1885 enraged him: 'the International Socialist Association are
triumphant, and every disreputable ragamuffin in Europe feels that the
day of universal brotherhood, despoliation and disorder is coming
apace, and nurses day-dreams of well-plenished pockets amongst the
ruin of all that is respectable, venerable and holy.' He laments the
torrent of 'social-democratic ideas . . . England was the only barrier

to the pressure of infernal doctrines born in continental back-slums
... Socialism must inevitably end in Caesarism.' The mixture of
fatalism, stoicism, and conservatism so recognisable to the reader of
Conrad's fiction was beginning to jell. As he got older he lost
altogether any faith he might once have had in politics as a means for
improving, much less changing in any way, the lives of individuals – a
faith which had deeply animated his father. Eventually Conrad settled
into a sort of stoical nihilism, a point of view seen most clearly,
perhaps, in his great novel *The Secret Agent* (1907). Now, at the age
of twenty-eight, he could still take up causes passionately, as his
father had done – though more fatalistically, to be sure. But where the
father had been a noted liberal, the son took a different line – inspired
in part, no doubt, by the contempt he felt for the only sort of men he
had known well since he went to sea at seventeen, and the urban and
port riffraff he was to describe so scathingly in several of his tales.
For he was a fastidious and ambitious man just now starting to feel in
earnest that he inhabited the wrong world. The son of upper
middle-class parents, he was beginning to feel *déclassé*.

Conflicts with port rabble and a decline in the discipline of work on
the part of sailors must have been among Conrad's reasons, and those
of many of his fellow merchant officers, for a generally unfavourable
attitude not only towards ordinary seamen but also what they
represented potentially and symbolically: incipient trade unions and
socialist agitation. It had not been so long since Conrad served before
the mast as an ordinary seaman. Now he had some position, though
no money, and his views kept pace with his professional status. Like
many self-made men, he could be contemptuous of and unsympathetic to his less fortunate brethren. And like all men, his views grew
more emphatic as he got older. 'I haven't the taste for democracy,' he
would bluntly admit to a correspondent in 1897. Conrad's later
indifference to political forces of any shade – an indifference even
more deeply felt, if possible, than that of his future hero Henry James
– may be foreshadowed in this passage, quoted from a letter written
in December 1885: 'I live mostly in the past and the future. The
present has ... but few charms for me. I look with the serenity of
despair and the indifference of contempt upon passing events.' What
a world of woe is here. He was twenty-eight, poor, unhappy, and – as
so often before in his life – alone. Is it any wonder that he chose to live
in 'the present' as little as possible? Instead he dreamed of the past

and the future. Unhappiness may spur creativity, the desire to assert and express oneself, to restore one's self-esteem. Withdrawal from present actuality is fairly common in the lives of many writers: one thinks again of Trollope. What is unusual here is the 'serenity of despair and the indifference of contempt' with which the future novelist regarded his surroundings. The combination of pessimism and resignation which marks so much of his fiction came directly from Conrad's heart and soul.

In the spring of 1886 the *Tilkhurst* returned to England, and during that summer – indeed, within twenty-two days of one another – two important events overtook Conrad. In July he failed the master's examination. Again he performed poorly in 'Day's Work', and this time also in mathematics. He must have been embarrassed. After all, he had been at sea for eleven years – just six were required for the master's certificate – and the minimum age for a captain in the British merchant marine was only twenty-one. In August a much more important event occurred: Conrad became, officially, British.

His naturalisation papers were approved. He had long since discovered that the first and third of his five Polish names were the easiest for Englishmen to pronounce, and so Józef Teodor Konrad Nalecz Korzeniowski became Joseph Conrad. Now no longer one of the Tsar's subjects living illegally abroad, he was transformed, by the stroke of a pen, into one of Queen Victoria's subjects – indeed, one of her most loyal ones. In connection with this changeover, Conrad had to pay a visit to the Russian Embassy at Chesham House, Belgrave Square – called Chesham Square in *The Secret Agent*, which describes the embassy carefully.

Encouraged now to persevere, he applied himself with greater urgency to his studies for the master's examination, and passed it in November. He had become, at the age of thirty, a British captain, though for the moment one without a ship. But at least he occupied, finally, a recognised position. 'Some insignificant boy, from . . . some place called Poland, became a captain in the British Merchant Marine without any backing' – this is how Conrad saw it from the vantage point of 1914. Certainly he had few if any influential friends. Of the four acquaintances who testified to his good character on his naturalisation application, three were fellow mariners, none had known him for more than five years, and two had known him for two years or less. Though he had been sailing in English ships for a decade now, he had made no close friends. He remained, for the most part, alone.

One other event of the year 1886 – important for Conrad in so many ways – must be mentioned. It was during this year that he turned his hand for the first time to the writing of fiction. The weekly *Tit-Bits*, a popular digest of the sort so unmercifully satirised by Gissing in *New Grub Street*, sponsored a short story competition, and for it Conrad wrote a tale called 'The Black Mate' – probably an early draft of what would become, in 1897, *The Nigger of the 'Narcissus'*. The story, which would be published in 1908, did not win the competition. But it is interesting that, three years before he began to write what he and other commentators have always thought of as his first genuine work of fiction, *Almayer's Folly* (composed 1889–94; published 1895), Conrad drafted a story of life at sea.

'The Black Mate' is significant in at least three other ways. It further helps dispose of the myth, now generally discredited anyway, that when Conrad began to write *Almayer's Folly* he hesitated between English and French. *Almayer* could have been written only in English. Conrad himself was by then thoroughly English; by 1889, when he began to compose *Almayer's Folly*, he had already, in 'The Black Mate', chosen the language of his fiction. 'English was for me neither a matter of choice nor adoption,' he declared some years later in *A Personal Record*. 'The merest idea of choice had never entered my head. And as to adoption – well, yes, there was adoption; but it was I who was adopted by the genius of the language, which . . . made me its own completely.' He wishes to be believed, he adds here, when he says 'that if I had not written in English I would not have written at all.' Surely this is true. And so in 1886 he began to write for publication, though not yet to publish. Also important is the testimony offered by composition of 'The Black Mate' to Conrad's general discontent with the seaman's profession (despite his recent promotion), his frustration with his life as it was, and his need for contacts and activities which might help him to overcome the single most potent fact of the first thirty years of his life: his isolation. Finally, we should note that the story he submitted to *Tit-Bits* was a tale of life at sea. It is not surprising. What else but a sea story could have been the result of his discontent, his desire to enter another world? The world he wished to leave was the world he knew best, found unsatisfactory, and yet was eminently suited to describe. 'Everything can be found at sea, according to the spirit of your quest,' he declared years later: 'strife, peace, romance, naturalism of the most pronounced kind, ideals, boredom, disgust, inspiration – and every conceivable opportunity, including the opportunity to make a fool of yourself – exactly as in the pursuit of literature.' One gets the impression that Conrad wanted to leave the sea in order to write about it. He made use of the only world he knew in order to leave it.

Conrad's maritime appointments always seemed to lag behind his qualifications. Since he had passed his first officer's examination he had served only as a second mate. Now that he had his captain's certificate, he finally found a position as first mate. The salary was £7 a month, and the ship was the *Highland Forest*, to which he was attached throughout the first half of 1887. The *Highland Forest* took him from Amsterdam to Java; the captain's name was McWhir – who, with another *r* in his name, reappears as master of the *Nan-Shan* in the brilliant novella *Typhoon* (1903). Conrad did encounter, while in Singapore, a steamer called the *Nan-Shan*, which was used for transporting hundreds of Chinese, as in *Typhoon*. In the course of the trip to Java, he was injured by a falling spar. He spent some time during July 1887 recuperating in the European Hospital in Singapore – described in *Lord Jim* (1900), whose hero, also hit by a falling spar, is treated for his injury in the same hospital. Jim, while in hospital, hears 'the bewitching breath of the Eastern waters' and intuits 'suggestions of infinite repose, the gift of endless dreams'.

During the short trip (four days) from Semarang to Singapore for treatment, Conrad met, aboard the S.S. *Celestial*, Frederick Havelock Brooksbank, son-in-law of the well-known merchant and sailor William Lingard, the original of Tom Lingard in *Almayer's Folly*, *An Outcast of the Islands* (1896), and *The Rescue* (1920). Conrad never actually met William Lingard, but he was regaled, during the four-day journey to Singapore, with tales about him from two of his nephews, who by chance were travelling with Brooksbank on the *Celestial*. Conrad became friendly with Brooksbank, who introduced him to the master of a small steamer called the *Vidar*. Destined to play a crucial role in Conrad's life, the *Vidar* made regular voyages between Singapore and Borneo, where one of Lingard's nephews had been living for some years as a trading agent.

And so in August, from Singapore, Conrad embarked on what would turn out to be a series of significant journeys. He served as first officer of the *Vidar*, which between August 1887 and January 1888 made four voyages between Singapore and Borneo. The impressions he gathered during these trips were to serve him variously and well and to provide at least some of the inspiration for *Almayer's Folly*, *An Outcast of the Islands*, *Lord Jim*, 'The End of the Tether' (1902), 'The Shadow-Line', and *The Rescue*. (Like Captain Whalley in 'The End of the Tether', Conrad had some trouble with his eyes during these voyages.) The important point here, as Mr Najder has observed, is that these trips on the *Vidar* gave Conrad his first genuine opportunity to see the East at close range, unconcealed by port buildings, hotels, offices, and colonial institutions. The *Vidar* penetrated inland, often steaming miles up the rivers of Borneo to deliver its various cargoes. Here, against the lush tropical background, the isolated trading posts must have impressed Conrad as foolish challenges to invincible and unseen forces, as pathetic proofs, were any needed, of human vanity. Here he met white men, Europeans cut off from civilisation, who sometimes became deranged in their exile. The significance of this kind of experience for the would-be writer will be instantly understood by anyone who has read even a few pages of Conrad.

It was while on one of his journeys up a river in Borneo that Conrad met the Eurasian Dutch trader Charles William Olmeijer, who had lived at his outpost for the past seventeen years. Like Conrad's Almayer, he was married to a woman of mixed caste by whom he had children (not just one daughter), and was constantly engaged in a struggle for power with a local chieftain named Abdulla. 'I [saw] him for the first time . . . from the bridge of a steamer moored to a rickety little wharf forty miles up, more or less, a Bornean river,' Conrad tells us in *A Personal Record*. Having tried, and failed, to get himself started as a writer of fiction with 'The Black Mate', Conrad was seeking, more consciously this time, another subject. 'That morning, seeing the figure in pyjamas moving in the mist, I said to myself: "That's the man." Olmeijer – of which Almayer is a phonetic English transcription – had come down in his pyjamas to the wharf to pick up from the *Vidar* his cargo, which on this trip consisted of a pony for one of his children. Conrad recalled that he did not want to look at his mail: 'I shall never forget that man afraid of his letters.' He adds: 'if I had not got to know Almayer pretty well it is almost certain there would never have been a line of mine in print.'

This final statement should not be taken too seriously. In fact Conrad never got to know the real Olmeijer at all well; and in any case, when someone is ready to write, as Conrad was by 1887–8, there will always be an Olmeijer to hand. And though Conrad, as we know, often used in his work the real names of people, places, and ships, in it they move out of the realm of mere reminiscence, as Olmeijer was to do when he became Almayer. Olmeijer was simply Conrad's excuse to start writing; it could easily have been someone (or something) else. In fact he acknowledges in *A Personal Record* that no artist merely copies what is in front of him. 'Only in men's imagination does every truth find an effective and undeniable existence,' he says in his autobiographical memoir. 'Imagination, not invention, is the supreme master of art as of life.' By this time his imagination was ready to go to work.

Why, one might ask, was it Borneo – rather than Singapore, or India, or Australia, or South Africa, or for that matter England – that drew him at last into the sustained writing of fiction? What, in that Malay Archipelago, touched him into creative life? The answer is not easy; it may be non-existent; but there are clues. The time and the place were right, and the man was now watching out for 'material'. The Malayan scene plays an important role only in his early works (except *The Rescue*, which was written and dropped and picked up again dozens of times over many years, like Gissing's *Veranilda*), up through *Lord Jim*. Conrad, the exile and wanderer without a home except for the British ensign over his head, would have been aware of the lack of almost any cultural background potential readers, British or otherwise, could have found to share with this first of his fictional communities. The subject and the setting provided a safe ground for fiction without risking discussion of matters with which English readers might have been better acquainted than he was himself. Indeed, he may have found himself hard pressed; Almayer and his trading post were a godsend. Conrad's readers, he knew, would have been more familiar with life in Greater Britain, its idioms and its fashions, than he was. Singapore, India, Australia, and South Africa, with their British connections, would be known to a dangerous number of potential English readers. But not the Malay Archipelago; not then, at any rate, before Somerset Maugham and H. E. Bates appropriated it as a setting. Kipling had aroused English interest in exotic locales; but Malaya was still utterly and safely non-English, and writing about it would place Conrad, as Mr Najder rightly reminds us, in a position no worse than that of an author born and bred in England.

Olmeijer/Almayer and his surroundings were perfect for Conrad in other ways. The themes of moral and physical isolation, the dreariness of human life, the paralysis of human will, and the destructive potentiality of physical nature, especially in the face of that paralysis, all accorded with Conrad's mood in the late Eighties; he saw them all as subjects. And along came Almayer. And so it happened that his first novel would be set in Borneo, and that its central character would be isolated there. Conrad knew all about isolation, and he had just seen Borneo and Olmeijer for himself. His imagination took over the Malay motifs, and they began to grow spontaneously in his consciousness.

But the writing of *Almayer's Folly* did not commence immediately. After his four voyages up the Bornean rivers, Conrad signed off the *Vidar* in Singapore in January 1888. While waiting for a boat back to England, he lived at the Sailors' Home there – a stay later described in 'The Shadow-Line'. But, as it turned out, he did not go back to England; not yet. As in 'Falk' (1902), 'The End of the Tether', and 'The Shadow-Line', a ship lying at anchor in Bangkok happened to be looking for a captain to take her over. By sheer chance, Conrad secured the appointment. Instead of returning to England, he signed on as master of the *Otago*, his first and in fact his only real command at sea. The *Otago* sailed from Bangkok to Singapore in February-March 1888, a voyage described in detail in 'The Shadow-Line'. And in March it embarked for Australia with its cargo of timber, arriving in May. The *Otago* made several local voyages during the latter half of 1888. In August-September it sailed to Mauritius; during this trip Conrad had to do some risky manoeuvring through the Torres Strait, of the sort required of the new, untested captain in 'The Secret Sharer' (1912). The *Otago* remained in Mauritius for two months, a period of Conrad's life described in part in his story 'A Smile of Fortune' (1912). The director of the firm which had chartered the *Otago* saw a great deal of its captain while they were both in Mauritius. Many years afterwards he described Conrad, at the time in his thirty-first year, as 'forceful', with 'very mobile features, passing very rapidly from gentleness to an agitation bordering on anger; big black eyes usually melancholy and dreamy, and gentle as well, except for fairly frequent moments of irritation'. He dressed stylishly and well while on land; he was not popular with his sailing colleagues, who found him unfathomable, and nicknamed him 'the Russian Count'. Conrad, said his employer, was 'quite often taciturn and very excitable . . . he had a nervous tick in the shoulder and the eyes, and anything the least bit unexpected – an object dropping to the floor, a door banging – would make him jump.' During the seven weeks Conrad spent in Port Louis he rarely took a walk, was seen only infrequently amidst the local fashionable society, which entertained itself vigorously, and thrust his impeccably correct manners between himself and all others. Even here he remained virtually alone. The author of these recollections concludes, pungently and incisively: 'Today we would call him a neurasthenic, in those days one said a neurotic.' Of course he knew nothing of the circumstances which might have made such a man as Conrad, who would readily have been welcomed into the 'best' houses on the island, remain on board his ship for seven weeks, in splendid isolation. Alone, at least, he had nothing to fear, lonely though he was; in company with others there were too many pitfalls to bear thinking about, much less to skirt. And so he would not come out and play.

The *Otago* sailed back to Australia, this time with a cargo of sugar, from November 1888 to January 1889. More local hauls were undertaken in February and March. In this latter month Conrad signed off the *Otago* after fourteen months of command and embarked as a passenger aboard a German steamer in April, bound for England. He reached Southampton in May and rented a flat in Bessborough Gardens, Pimlico. It was during this summer, the summer of 1889, that Conrad began to write in earnest the tale that would come to be called *Almayer's Folly*. By the autumn he had three chapters drafted. What he could not have known during that first stretch of writing was that this particular task would take him five years to complete. But the beginning was made. For eleven years he had been in daily contact with people speaking English; he spoke and read English, followed English politics, read English newspapers, considered England his home. He sat down now and wrote in English.

In 1903 Conrad told a friend that he 'began writing *Almayer's Folly*, just like that, not thinking much what I was doing, in order to occupy my mornings during a rather long stay in London after a three years' cruise in the South Seas.' But it was both less and more complicated than that. On the one hand, it is clear now, looking back, that what Conrad did in 1889 was to give up one profession for another, though his maritime career was not yet officially over. On the other hand we have the evidence of his autobiography, in which the hesitations and fears, the delays in actually getting started which every writer knows, are described in harrowing and fascinating detail.

'It was in the front sitting-room of furnished apartments in a Pimlico square,' Conrad tells us, that Almayer and his surroundings began to live again for him with vividness and poignancy: 'They came with a silent and irresistible appeal.' Alone, as always, he now found the story of Almayer taking him over. 'Till I began to write that novel I had written nothing but letters, and not very many of these,' Conrad says in *A Personal Record* – having forgotten, or simply buried, 'The Black Mate'. Like most of us, he preferred not to dwell upon his failures. He had been reading one of Trollope's political novels; meanwhile the story of Almayer gnawed away at him. 'I was not at all certain that I wanted to write, or that I meant to write, or that I had anything to write about.' But obviously he had. The landlady's daughter was cleaning his room; he waited impatiently for her to finish. While she worked, he brooded. 'It was ten to one that before [she] was done I would pick up a book and sit down with it all the morning.' She left. Conrad sat down at a table. Up to that moment he had never, he says, 'made a note of a fact, of an impression or of an anecdote in my life. The conception of a planned book was entirely outside my mental range when I sat down.' This declaration has been scoffed at, but it is undoubtedly true. *Almayer's Folly* turned out to be the shortest of Conrad's many novels, though it took him five years to complete. Of course he could not have planned it out to the last detail. During the next five years he found himself writing, rewriting, revising, and then revising the revisions. Some sections were written at least three times. 'There was not a day I did not think of it. Not a day,' he told a friend some years later. The result was to be the first of those astonishing tales Conrad produced in the 1890s which would have secured his fame and his position had he expired along with the nineteenth century. It is worth noting that after this shattering start to his career as a writer, Conrad's literary output, though always hostage to temporary bouts of depressive paralysis, was steady and large for the rest of his life.

'The ambition of being an author had never turned up amongst [the] gracious imaginary existences one creates fondly for oneself at times in the stillness and immobility of a day-dream,' Conrad mused years later. And yet, he went on to declare, 'from the moment I had done blackening over the first manuscript page of "Almayer's Folly" ... from the moment I had, in the simplicity of my heart and the amazing ignorance of my mind, written that page the die was cast. Never had Rubicon been more blindly forded, without invocation to the gods, without fear of men.' And so was born Almayer, 'a man busy contemplating the wreckage of his past in the dawn of new hopes,' as the first chapter of *Almayer's Folly* describes him. Lonely, isolated, and inert, Almayer is the only white man on the eastern coast of Borneo, where he had lived for 'twenty-five years of heart-breaking struggle ... [feeling] like a prisoner'. An 'almost palpable blackness' blots out stars and sky at night. In his coastal retreat, Almayer is subjected to the 'turmoil of leaping waters, driving logs, and the big trees bending before a brutal and merciless force'.

Nature is never placid or passive in Conrad's works, as it often is in those of the Romantic poets. As a sailor he had seen immense masses of water, gigantic storms, exotic islands, tropical archipelagoes. For Conrad nature could have philosophical meaning without the emotional complications and psychological ambiguities of human life. Murderous and murky, the landscape of 'Sambir' (Borneo) in *Almayer's Folly* is ordered upon a principle of struggle so truculent as to make malignancy seem at times a condition of nature. In fact Conrad saw nature as indifferent to man's fate, which is even more frightening than seeing it as malignant, as his characters tend to do. Malignancy, at least, is comprehensible; it can be understood.

Nature in *Almayer's Folly* is an inevitable expression of Conrad's temperament. He conceives of the world in shifting hues of black and grey because, given his history, that is how he was compelled to perceive it himself – as part of a universe impenetrably governed by an unpredictable maniac. Conrad refers in an 1891 letter to 'the inexplicable cruelty of an invisible power which had guided inanimate things toward the destruction of an existence necessary to the happiness of other innocent beings and of a being not yet conscious ... we are the slaves of Fate even before birth, and we pay tribute to adversity even before making its acquaintance.' In portraying such a universe, like Hardy's impervious to human expectations of it,

Almayer's Folly contains the sort of savagely macabre humour that constantly crops up in Conrad's work, as it was so important a part of his outlook on life. If we ask – where did this idea of 'inexplicable cruelty' come from, the answer must be: from the only existence he knew after thirty-one years of life.

Almayer alone is the victim of an acute paralysis of will of the sort Conrad sometimes found himself subject to, especially when composing a story ('I am paralyzed by doubt and have just sense enough to feel the agony but am powerless to invent a way out of it,' Conrad told Garnett in 1896, in the midst of his struggles with the first of many drafts of *The Rescue*). In portraying Almayer as having to face down 'a brutal and merciless force', Conrad indeed was, as he declared, casting his die and crossing his Rubicon. The scene, the situation – the isolation of the individual, subject to the indifferent forces of the universe – were those the novelist would return to again and again in his fiction. But it all began there, on that first 'blackened' page written in the sitting-room of those lodgings in Pimlico one day in the summer of 1889, a few months before Conrad's thirty-second birthday.

Almayer's Folly, it must be said, is by no means one of Conrad's greatest achievements; the achievement is in the writing of the book at all – a first novel by a man in his thirties composed not only in a foreign language but in fact a fifth language. He was a self-conscious foreigner writing in an alien language of obscure experiences; indeed, he never wrote for publication in his native tongue. Conrad had very little opportunity to develop and hone his English through conversation with cultured people; when he started *Almayer's Folly* the English he knew could only have come from books. Edward Garnett later recalled: 'When he read aloud to me some . . . MS pages of *An Outcast of the Islands* he mispronounced so many words that I followed him with difficulty. I found then that he had never once heard those English words spoken, but had learned them all from books!' As late as October 1897 we find Conrad admitting to a friend: 'I always mistrust my ear; I am never sure even in my own miserable prose.' Here was a man writing a novel in a language he could not even speak properly. No wonder one of Conrad's favourite criticisms of his work remained, to his dying day, a review of *An Outcast of the Islands* in the Aberdeen *Free Press* in 1896 which went out of its way, as Conrad said, to 'extol my English – and that is a real, a great pleasure; for I *did* try to earn that kind of notice.'

Earn it he certainly did. In the story of these three decades we can see at least some of the origins of Conrad's characteristic vein as a writer of fiction. In all of his works – all, without exception – an individual or a small group of people find themselves in isolated circumstances, physically or spiritually, whether in Africa or the Far East or England, whether at sea or in a city or on an island. Life appears both fragile and cheap, easily lost and easily undervalued. Conrad's characters are almost all of them *strangers* in one way or another – foreigners, intruders, anomalies, exiles. No matter what they do or where they go, they remain psychologically isolated. Conrad lived almost all of his first thirty-two years by himself. If his characters are solitaries, in one way or another, it is not hard to see why this might be so. The novelist drew from his terrifying ordeal by loneliness the knowledge that isolation – such as that of Decoud in *Nostromo*, for example – can make you mad; Decoud, Conrad's most vivid solitary, is driven, by his involuntary disjunction from his fellows, to the ultimate act of self-destruction.

In part Conrad's decision to write must have been an attempt, ultimately successful, to break out of the iron circle of his own loneliness, to communicate with others. Isolation corrupts: it is one of Conrad's most famous themes. Men alone cannot be trusted. No other writer is so certain of this – so certain that human intercourse, society of some sort, is required to keep men both sane and good. It is a measure both of Conrad's solitariness as a boy and young man and of the pessimism about life which was one result of it that this should be the case. No one else argues so eloquently as Conrad does, indirectly though it may often be, how important it is for people to live together peaceably and honestly. It is the tragic fate of many of his protagonists to be unable to do so; the characters of *Victory* (1915) and those of *The Secret Agent*, one group on an island and the other in the heart of London, come to grief because they are unable to bridge that distance between human beings seen by Conrad as unavoidable. They remain prisoners of consciousness and of life, unable to merge their identities with those of others.

The vicissitudes of Conrad's early years seem to have made these themes inescapable. He possessed, at the time he began to write, few of what we might consider the normal foundations of psychological stability. He had no parents, no siblings, no friends, no home; his nationality was borrowed. When he was thirty he declared that the quality he felt he most lacked was self-confidence. It is not surprising. As a boy he had once broken in on the conversation of adults with the question, 'And what do you think of *me*?' No wonder the mature man was renowned among his contemporaries for a mercurial temperament, for 'nerves'. No wonder that, throughout the rest of his life, he was sometimes prostrated by psychological depression so acute he was unable to lift a pen. Again and again he sought relief in hydrotherapy; he would take himself off for 'treatment' every few years. And yet his work, gloomy as it is, is marked by a moral strength and sanity that demonstrate the power of his personality and his will in overcoming these potentially crippling debilities, largely traceable from his appallingly solitary youth.

We do not become less what we are as we get older, and Conrad was no exception to this rule. The novels and stories he wrote after *Almayer's Folly* continue to place his characters in harrowing spiritual and physical isolation. He finds more ways than any other writer to quarantine his people. Almayer, standing in his pyjamas alone on that Bornean quay, was just the beginning. Nor did Conrad ever reach a more optimistic view of existence: his early years assured that. He could never be wholly secure, nor could he ever bring himself to believe in the benignity of the universe. He developed and articulated in his work the inherent fatalism of his own character, and combined this with the stoical indifference to tragedy he had developed in order to stay alive and sane in Poland, in Russia, at sea. Things, in Conrad's fiction, are fated to turn out as they do, and there is nothing to be done about it. Yet this is not necessarily a cause for despair. Why worry about the unavoidable?

'Each act of life is final, and inevitably produces its consequences despite all the weeping and gnashing of teeth, and the sorrow of feeble souls who suffer the terror that seizes them when confronted by the results of their own actions,' Conrad told a correspondent in 1891. And to the same, in 1892: 'to make plans is a thankless business. It is always the unforeseen that happens.' (This is not so very different from the message of Hardy's *Jude the Obscure*, which appeared in the same year as *Almayer's Folly*.) To the same correspondent, in 1893: 'Life is upside down. I have made this an article of faith, and I am resigned to it.' In 1896 Conrad told his publisher, Fisher Unwin: 'Everything is possible – but the note of truth is not in the possibility of things but in their inevitableness.

Inevitableness is the only certitude. . . . You cannot escape. Our captivity within the incomprehensible logic of accident is the only fact of the universe.' Few pessimists are so uncomplicatedly 'resigned' to 'the incomprehensible logic . . . of the universe'. But for Conrad, understanding and accepting the way things were, or seemed to him to be, was a requisite of sanity. Indeed, the only consoling aspect of this nihilistic, absurdist philosophy is that it relieves us from worry, which is irrelevant and self-destructive. Resign yourself to 'the incomprehensible logic of accident' and you will survive. This message, in various forms and formats, Conrad was to repeat again and again. He believed in not thinking too much – that salvation, if there is any, lies not in thought but in action. Better not to know too much, better to have some illusions left, better to remain a little innocent if possible. The alternative is madness and despair. Where ignorance is bliss, 'tis folly to be wise.

'The habit of profound reflection . . . is the most pernicious of all the habits formed by civilized man,' Conrad wrote in his second (1920) preface to *Victory*, a novel whose story bears out this philosophy. 'Would you seriously, of malice prepense cultivate in . . . unconscious man the power to think?' he asked a friend in 1897. 'Would you seriously wish to tell such a man: "Know thyself"? Understand that thou art nothing less than a shadow, more insignificant than a drop of water in the ocean, more fleeting than the illusion of a dream? Would you?' The great test of mankind is to remain sane in a senseless world. 'I have arrived at the conclusion that *there* lies the sole chance for happiness,' Conrad wrote to a friend in 1895: 'In a task accomplished, in an obstacle overcome – no matter what task, no matter what obstacle.' The great test is to retain our humanity in an 'incomprehensible', contingent universe.

Conrad believed that we cannot escape this testing of our souls; the test comes in various guises, and his characters are forever passing or failing it. What counts in a world without meaning? Actions, not philosophies. So we find Conrad writing in 1895 that 'To live means to struggle, and for me the pleasure consists in the struggle itself – never the victory, or the results of the victory. I never think about it.' Substitute 'salvation' for 'the pleasure' and we gain some insight into Conrad's moral philosophy. Victories and defeats are meaningless in a world without poetic justice, or any other kind. The 'struggle' – the testing – is doubly important in such a situation. Henry James believed that we must conduct ourselves as though what we do matters, because there is no alternative to such conduct; clearly Conrad believed something like the same thing. His own testing continued. Just as he once stalked the deck to keep his ship afloat in an inimical ocean, so the older Conrad found himself struggling for survival as a writer of fiction. 'You must do it so that at the end of your day's work you should feel exhausted, emptied of every sensation and every thought, with a blank mind and an aching heart, with the notion that there is nothing – nothing left in you.' His younger son recalled that Conrad, when encountering a particularly knotty problem in his work late at night, would wake him up for a game of chess until his mind had cleared, the problem was solved, and the novelist was ready to return to his desk. Like his own admirable characters, Conrad fought against his terrors rather than giving in to them. 'People die – affections die – all passes – but a man's work remains with him to the last,' he wrote to Unwin in 1896. For him, no matter what others thought of it, his work was potentially 'the only lasting thing in the world', and so he went on torturing himself well into his sixties with his characteristic brand of perfectionism. It was his own way of passing the only test that mattered.

We should not be surprised to find that those of his characters who think too much in isolated circumstances – like Decoud, or Kurtz in 'Heart of Darkness' (1902), or a dozen other Conradian protagonists – go mad. Things do not bear much looking into, as Winnie Verloc discovers, to her horror, in *The Secret Agent*. Like James, whom he came to admire more than any other novelist – *Chance* (1913) reads at times, uncannily enough, as if it actually were a novel by James – Conrad was endlessly fascinated by the balance between innocence and knowledge, by the question of how much it is good for us to know, whether or not we are better off having a few illusions left to us. In the work of both writers the process by which knowledge is acquired and innocence lost is a tragic one; one cannot go back, one cannot unknow what one learns. Knowledge seems to bring neither solace nor understanding – only disappointment and disillusionment, and the realisation that it has come too late to be of use in guiding us toward the answer to the all-important question of how to live. Indeed, the real subject of his work, Conrad said in 1897, in connection with *The Nigger of the 'Narcissus'*, was exactly that: 'how to live'. In a world in which results are always bad, progress is what counts; the journey not the arrival matters. In any case, for James and Conrad the cost of knowledge is always too high; a little ignorance can be consoling. James, perhaps, like another of his disciples, Elizabeth Bowen, saw innocence as potentially more destructive than Conrad ever did; for Conrad, there are many saving virtues in an illusion which muffles. Avoid metaphysics, he believed, and you have a chance. The greatest danger of isolation is that it leads to thought, and thought is the enemy of mankind. 'That's my view of life,' Conrad wrote to a correspondent in 1895, 'a view that rejects all formulas, dogmas and principles of other people's making. These are only a web of illusion . . . Another man's truth is only a dismal lie to me.' It may not be surprising to find this view adopted by a man who spent the first three decades of his life by himself; one can only wonder how excruciating Conrad found his loneliness. As a young man he had ample opportunity to work out for himself this highly individual philosophy. It is inseparable from his biography, and probably a logical result of it.

Everyone who wrote down his impressions of Conrad after he had become famous emphasises certain qualities in the mature man deducible, perhaps, both from his books and his youth: a mercurial temperament; nervousness to the extent of neurasthenia; chronic hypochondria; conservatism, both in personal relations and in politics; lifelong Russophobia; alternating moods of despair and calm, almost manic-depressive in their virulence (Conrad in 1895 referred to 'attacks of melancholy which paralyse my thought and will'); fascination with the English language and at the same time astonishing gaps in his reading and in his education generally (in his fifties he amazed H. G. Wells by demanding to be told, 'What is all this about Jane Austen? What is there *in* her? What is it all *about*?'); great capacity for affection but a pronounced disinclination to show it; the feeling that he was always being stretched, tested, measured up in some way; compulsive perfectionism; and so on. Who else but Conrad could have complained (in 1890) that it was impossible 'to make a human being happy for an *entire hour*'? 'I have long fits of depression, that in a lunatic asylum would be called madness,' he told Garnett in 1896. 'I do not know what it is.'

Conrad rarely changed his mind about anything. In 1897, in a letter to a friend, he constructed an astonishing metaphor for existence as he saw it. It is sufficiently vivid and interesting to quote at length.

There is a – let us say – a machine. It evolved itself . . . out of a chaos of scraps of iron and behold! it knits. I am horrified at the horrible work and stand appalled. I feel it ought to embroider – but it goes on knitting. You come and say: 'this is all right; it's only a question of the right kind of oil. Let us use this – for instance – celestial oil and the machine shall embroider a most beautiful design. . . .' Will it? Alas no. You cannot by any special lubrication make embroidery with a knitting machine. And the most withering thought is that the infamous thing has made itself; made itself without thought, without conscience, without foresight, without eyes, without heart. It is a tragic accident – and it has happened. You can't interfere with it. The last drop of bitterness is in the suspicion that you can't even smash it. In virtue of that truth one and immortal which lurks in the force that made it spring into existence it is what it is – and it is indestructible!

It knits us in and it knits us out. It has knitted time, space, pain, death, corruption, despair and all the illusions – and nothing matters. I'll admit however that to look at the remorseless process is sometimes amusing.

The stoical resignation of the early years persevered. In the Preface he wrote to *A Personal Record*, Conrad says:

The sight of human affairs deserves admiration and pity. They are worthy of respect, too. And he is not insensible who pays them the undemonstrative tribute of a sigh which is not a sob, and of a smile which is not a grin. Resignation, not mystic, not detached, but resignation open-eyed, conscious and informed by love, is the only one of our feelings for which it is impossible to become a sham . . . Those who read me know my conviction that the world . . . rests on a few very simple ideas; so simple that they must be as old as the hills. It rests notably, among others, on the idea of Fidelity.

Substitute resignation for despair and one can go on living. Take seriously the universe, which does not take us seriously, and one goes mad. Be true to oneself, do honest work; this is what Conrad means by 'Fidelity.' He goes on in *A Personal Record* to say this:

The ethical view of the universe involves us at last in so many cruel and absurd contradictions, where the last vestiges of faith, hope, charity, and even of reason itself, seem ready to perish, that I have come to suspect that the aim of creation cannot be ethical at all. I would fondly believe that its object is purely spectacular; a spectacle for awe, love, adoration, or hate, if you like, but in this view – and in this view alone – never for despair! Those visions, delicious or poignant, are a moral end in themselves.

It was this meaningless spectacle that he wished to record in his books. Like the universe as he perceived it, they were 'a moral end in themselves': his work became, until his death in 1924, 'the only lasting thing in the world', all that could 'remain' with him 'to the last'.

And so it did. Ancient mariner that he was, Conrad felt 'compelled', he said, positively 'compelled, unconsciously compelled, now to write volume after volume, as in past years I was compelled to go to sea, voyage after voyage.' Each new volume was, in a sense, another voyage, on which he travelled alone. He tells us in *A Personal Record* that he became at last a prisoner of his memories – a prisoner, that is, of his past, of his own biography.

I catch myself in hours of solitude and retrospect meeting arguments and charges made thirty-five years ago by voices now for ever still; finding things to say that an assailed boy could not have found, simply because of the mysteriousness of his impulses to himself. I understood no more than the people who called upon me to explain myself. There was no precedent. I verily believe mine was the only case of a boy of my nationality and antecedents taking a, so to speak, standing jump out of his racial surroundings and associations.

Did he feel guilty as an expatriate and a conservative? Were the 'voices now for ever still' those of his liberal Polish parents? Conrad does not say. Writing this in his fifties, he remained bound in perpetual memory to the story of his youth.

Conrad believed that 'a novelist lives in his work. He stands there, the only reality in an invented world, among imaginary things, happenings, and people. Writing about them, he is only writing about himself . . . A writer of imaginative prose (even more than any other sort of artist) stands confessed in his works . . . Indeed, every one who puts pen to paper for the reading of strangers . . . can speak of nothing else' but himself. This is clear enough. Conrad understood – indeed, few novelists, if any, have understood it better – that fiction grows out of life: that, writing ostensibly of others, in fact you continue to write primarily of yourself. He always found it almost impossible to revise his work because, as he told Garnett in 1895, 'I cannot meddle with what is within myself.' And while his life changed dramatically in its outward circumstances after the summer of 1889, when Conrad sat down in those London lodgings to write the first chapter of *Almayer's Folly* – he married, had two sons, published books, earned money, became famous, met and befriended the leading literary men of the day, was offered a baronetcy, and all the rest of it – the inner man never changed. Being, as he said, 'the only reality in an invented world', the same hopes, fears, and memories got themselves translated again and again into his fiction. They were those which, after the first thirty years of his life, Conrad found he was unable to escape, either in fiction or in reality; indeed, the two became for him inseparable, as he tells us himself. Writing about what was in his mind, he continued to write about himself.

It is impossible to explain, to assess, to annotate his work without knowing what happened to him as a youth. 'My later life has been so different, so unlike the life that I began,' he wrote to a friend in 1890, 'that those earlier impressions, feelings and memories have in no way been erased.' Quite the contrary. 'I am devoted to Borneo. What bothers me most is that my characters are so true,' Conrad wrote in 1894, describing *Almayer's Folly* and *An Outcast of the Islands*. 'I know them so well that they shackle the imagination.' Tied so completely to himself as a subject, he found it difficult to invent.

As late as 1897, after explaining that up to that moment 'Most of my life has been spent between sky and water', Conrad, then forty, wrote to a friend: 'I live so alone that often I fancy myself clinging stupidly to a derelict planet abandoned by its precious crew.' By this time he had published *Almayer's Folly*, *An Outcast of the Islands*, *The Nigger of the 'Narcissus'*, 'An Outpost of Progress', 'The Lagoon', and 'Karain', and was well launched on his new career; he had become the friend of John Galsworthy, Edward Garnett, T. Fisher Unwin, Henry James, Stephen Crane, R. B. Cunninghame Graham, William Blackwood, and A. T. Quiller-Couch, among others; and he had married. And yet he continued to live, as he put it, 'so alone' that it seemed as if he inhabited an empty planet. He remained imprisoned within himself. His life from an early age was a series of adaptations to odd circumstances that kept him perpetually off balance, as Frederick C. Crews has observed. In a very real sense, Conrad's discomposure was his passport to distinction.

Why, the critic Q. D. Leavis asked, does Conrad 'rub in so intolerably the inescapable isolation of every man'? Surely now we know. The little boy who wanted so badly to hear what the adults thought of *him* had grown up to become, in a phrase familiar to readers of *Lord Jim*, one of them. And still he was alone.

Edith Wharton, *ca.* 1880, aged about eighteen (*Manuscripts Department, Lilly Library, Indiana University, Bloomington, Indiana*)

CHAPTER FIVE

Edith Wharton's Drawing-Room

For 'to make tongues wag,' that phrase which in
every sphere of life is applied to a woman who
has a lover, could also be used in the Faubourg
Saint-Germain of women who write books and
in the respectable society of Combray of those
who make marriages which, for better or for
worse, are 'unsuitable.'

Proust, *Le temps retrouvé*

Survivors of the older generation assured me that
society had completely changed and now opened
its doors to people who in their day would never
have been received.

Proust, *Le temps retrouvé*

The savages I have met on my travels have all
been formidably overdressed.

Evelyn Waugh, 'Work Suspended'

Looking back in the 1930s to her life in New York in the 1870s, Edith
Wharton said: 'When I was young it used to seem to me that the
group in which I grew up was like an empty vessel into which no new
wine would ever again be poured. Now I see that one of its uses lay in
preserving a few drops of an old vintage too rare to be savoured by a
youthful palate.' Mrs Wharton was a woman divided, attacked in her
emotions by opposing influences; this began early, and is apparent in
one way or another in practically everything she wrote. She loved Old

New York because she understood it so well, because it supplied the material for most of her best work, because it was the source of everything she was and had become. She also resented its limited imagination, its lack of emotion, and its failure to interest itself in anything that interested her. But as time went by, and she grew to hate the age in which she was growing old, she felt anew the importance of roots in an increasingly rootless world.

The tension created by this double vision runs through all of her best work, which is her work about New York, and is the mainspring of that work. 'Her life had been so carefully guarded, so inwardly conventional in a world where all the outer conventions were tottering,' she writes of the protagonist in a late story, 'Atrophy' (1930). As a result of ambiguities in her own childhood and youth, Mrs Wharton was always fascinated as an artist by the balance between old and new, reactionary and progressive, ancient and modern. Like James and Conrad, she became an expatriate, after hesitating between cultures. Like Gissing and Maugham, she died in France, having lived her last years there. Recognising the sources of her spiritual schizophrenia, a result of the lifelong influences and contradictions of her early years, may help us to understand the fiction which became their byproduct.

'You will tell me that the rules I was striving to maintain were merely social ones. But for all their apparent frivolity they might have prevented many excesses,' Proust makes a character declare in *Le temps retrouvé*. He and Mrs Wharton both found plenty to despise in the manners of the Old Guard, yet both came to see these manners – outdated, stultifying, and hypocritical as they could be – as preferable to social conduct in the Age of No Manners at All which came next. Proust's vivid characterisation of the actress 'Berma' (Bernhardt) at the end of her life might apply as well to Edith Wharton during her last years: 'conscious of her own genius and having learnt at a very early age the meaninglessness of all . . . decrees of Fashion, she for her part had remained faithful to Tradition, which she had always respected and of which she was herself an embodiment, and which caused her to judge things and people as she would have judged them thirty years earlier.' Its contempt for 'Fashion' and respect for 'Tradition' is still the most striking thing about Mrs Wharton's autobiographical memoir *A Backward Glance* (1933), from which the opening quotation about new wine and old vintage is taken.

Edith Wharton's great subject was Old New York, the city in which she was born in 1862 and which provided the setting, the background, and the inspiration for her great trilogy of social chronicles, *The House of Mirth* (1905), *The Custom of the Country* (1913), and *The Age of Innocence* (1920). The first made her famous; the last won the Pulitzer Prize and became a bestseller. It was this group of books to which the next generation of American writers, most notably Sinclair Lewis (who dedicated *Main Street* to her) and F. Scott Fitzgerald, turned in their search for a native tradition in the novel of manners. They found more of it in Mrs Wharton than in Henry James, who seemed to them more European than American. Her importance in the history of American letters, not to mention her brilliance as a novelist of the very first rank, has never been properly appreciated outside the United States; and even in her native country she is often given short shrift by those who know only her classic stories of New England life, *Ethan Frome* (1911) and 'Summer' (1917), and by left-wing academics who find the rarefied air of her drawing-rooms alien and undemocratic and feel more comfortable with the passionate socialist mutterings of such contemporaries of Edith Wharton as Jack London, Upton Sinclair, and Frank Norris. But the American writers of the 1920s and 1930s who count for anything all read Edith Wharton, admired her, and learned from her. Indeed, she may well be the most influential American novelist of them all. For she showed that Americans *could* write novels of manners set in America – that they need not transfer their settings to Europe, that there was a home-grown social tradition for them to draw on, that they could go far beyond the historical novel and the romance so beloved of Nathaniel Hawthorne, if only they would write about what they knew at first hand, no matter where they lived.

Looking at that old bottle of wine, Mrs Wharton saw it half-empty at some moments and half-full at others. This is the source and the heart of her unique double vision. She wrote a great many first-rate novels and stories on other subjects; perhaps the most notable of these is indeed *Ethan Frome*, set in the Berkshires of western Massachusetts, where Edith Wharton had a home – a tale which has become one of the few indisputable American classics. Like James and Conrad, she felt comfortable on the slippery slope of the novella, producing over the years a series of superb works in that form, of which one might mention 'The Touchstone' (1900), 'Madame de

Treymes' (1907), 'Bunner Sisters' (1916), *Xingu* (1916), 'Summer', and the brilliant stories which collectively make up *Old New York* (1924) – 'False Dawn', 'The Old Maid', 'The Spark', and 'New Year's Day'. This latter tetralogy of tales together forms yet another 'history' of Edith Wharton's New York.

Between 1899 and 1938, the year after her death, twenty-one novels or novellas by Edith Wharton appeared in print, as did eleven collections of short stories, nine works of non-fiction of astonishing variety, three volumes of poems, and nearly three dozen uncollected essays, articles, and reviews. She wrote a great deal; from the turn of the century onward, she averaged a book a year. And yet, as these dates suggest, Edith Wharton did not begin to publish until she was well into her thirties; of the forty-four books which appeared during her lifetime, only four were in print before she was forty. Why this happened, why she was thirty-five when her first volume *The Decoration of Houses* (1897) was published (this is not counting her juvenile poems, privately printed in 1878), why she wrote about the things she did, why she wrote at all, are related questions which may largely be explained by an account of her early years. So too can the theme, also inseparable from these questions, of the thwarted life that runs through all of her best work. In the same way the sometimes ambivalent moral perspective of her fiction, that curious double vision of which mention has been made, may also be traced back to a youth both cosseted and difficult, happy and restless, complacent and rebellious.

As a newly published author, still very much a member of New York's upper crust, into which she had been born and in the midst of which she had always lived, Edith Wharton was more flattered than otherwise to be invited to what was being advertised by her conventional hostess as a 'Bohemian' dinner-party. The evening arrived, and Mrs Wharton saw no one at the gathering she had not seen before at dinners identical to this one. It was only later that she discovered the 'Bohemian' element of the party was considered by her hostess to have been represented by herself.

Having by tireless industry developed into precisely the kind of woman who would have been most out of place in the New York society of her early days, in time she came to share the 'outside' view of herself as a person of experience, understanding, and imagination – the sort of person a well-bred woman of her time and place was presumed incapable of becoming – and this too contributed to the interesting multiplicity of her vision of things past. Her complicated view of herself, her lack of certainty as to just where, exactly, she belonged, the desperate unhappiness of her marriage, the new and different pressures of the beginnings of authorship – these things, before she was able to express them overtly in books, in her divorce, in her flight from America, and in her decision to live in France, undoubtedly were at least some of the causes of her two crushing nervous breakdowns in the 1890s, when she was in her thirties. The consideration of her, by elements of Old New York, as 'Bohemian', gave way to tight-lipped reticence as she began to publish more and the subjects of her stories became unmistakable even to those who did not read. New York society grew wary of her; it did not wish to be her material. Had her New York contemporaries read her early stories with any care, they would have noticed that among the major themes is that of the thwarted exit: the desire but the ultimate impossibility of achieving any real escape from the conditions which have formed one's life and character. However deeply, as an author, Edith Wharton might have longed to break free of the old proprieties and restraints, a part of her was forever and inexorably bound to them. What she managed to do was to convert her sense of imprisonment into art, and in this way to overcome the emotional instability that had struck her down. Nor did she ever lose her sense of humour or perspective. In her tale 'Writing a War Story' (1919), a young poetess goes to 'a bohemian dinner in New York' consisting of herself, a clergyman, and the editor of a weekly journal.

Her parents were leaders of the fashionable and conservative society into which she was born and about which she would write 'shocking' novels – novels about illegitimacy, adultery, hypocrisy, and the wounding, sometimes mortally, of those who failed for one reason or another to measure up to the exacting standards of their social environment. It was a rarefied milieu which, as Edith Wharton later put it, had been formed by three hundred years of social observance, 'the concerted living up to long-established standards of honour and conduct, of education and manners'. It was the age of Longfellow and Lincoln. The unfashionable Abraham was president, and New York disliked him and his war against the South. Edith Wharton would know two American presidents, Chester A. Arthur and Theodore Roosevelt – the latter, also a New Yorker, invited her to lunch at the White House after *The House of Mirth* was published to talk about books, for he too, of course, was an author – and she lived long enough to deplore the re-election of Franklin D. Roosevelt, whom she had known as a boy in Old New York and whom, in her old age, she condemned as a dangerous socialist. In her last years she befriended Aldous Huxley, declared Trollope her favourite novelist, worshipped Henry James, and thought the claims made for Joyce's *Ulysses* exaggerated, though she liked the book. For the last twenty-five years of her life she lived in France, mostly in Paris, visiting America only once during these years and knowing it, after the Great War, only by hearsay. Leaving her husband in 1913, at a time when divorced women were often shunned by polite society in her native land, she chose, quite simply, to stay away from it. Her last novels are shrilly critical of America, but her lack of first-hand observation, so often her strong suit in the books down through *The Age of Innocence* and *Old New York*, is betrayed when she attempts contemporary assessments of the place it had become.

When Edith Wharton is writing about Old New York she is, as a novelist of manners, a social historian, and an observer of fashions, peerless. The three great New York novels show what happened when the newly rich from the industrial West – from Pittsburgh, say, or Chicago – began to infiltrate New York society after the Civil War. At first, in the latter decades of the nineteenth century, those who bought their way into it – the *nouveaux riches* thrown up by the war and Reconstruction – did not affect the old customs, since, as Mrs Wharton says, 'the dearest ambition of the newcomers was to assimilate existing traditions. Social life ... went on with hardly perceptible changes till the [first world] war abruptly tore down the old frame-work, and what had seemed unalterable rules of conduct became of a sudden observances as quaintly arbitrary as the domestic rites of the pharoahs.' These post-war phenomena were of course not restricted to the United States. But by then Edith Wharton had begun to remember America rather than to see it with her own eyes.

As a social historian, the change that struck Mrs Wharton most forcefully in her New York over the years is described in these terms in *A Backward Glance*:

> in my youth, the Americans of the original States, who in moments of crisis still shaped the national point of view, were the heirs of an old tradition of European culture which the

country has now totally rejected. This rejection . . . has opened a gulf between those days and these [the 1930s]. The compact world of my youth has receded into a past from which it can only be dug up in bits by the assiduous relic-hunter; and its smallest fragments begin to be worth collecting and putting together before the last of those who knew the live structure are swept away with it.

As an heiress of the old tradition – her mother's family was Dutch – Edith Wharton, not surprisingly, became more solicitous of her past as it began to fade away. Thus a relatively early novel like *The House of Mirth*, the book which made her reputation and shocked her friends, sides with the individual and against the pressures on him or her of a cloistered, cultureless, and reactionary society; while *The Age of Innocence*, published fifteen years later, after the Great War had 'torn down the old frame-work', takes a tender view of the old ways, and declares that after all there was some good in them. 'The small society into which I was born,' Mrs Wharton declares in her autobiography, 'was "good" in the most prosaic sense of the term, and its only interest, for the generality of readers, lies in the fact of its sudden and total extinction, and for the imaginative few in the recognition of the moral treasures that went with it.'

Herself one of its 'moral treasures', she was born, during a critical period of the Civil War, on 24 January 1862, the daughter of George Frederic Jones and Lucretia Rhinelander Jones of New York City and Newport. Three months later, in Manhattan's Grace Church, she was christened Edith Newbold Jones; Newbold was the name of a maternal uncle. There were two older brothers, the youngest twelve years her senior. She was a late child: her father was forty, her mother thirty-seven.

Property values declined sharply in New York after the Civil War, and Edith's father decided to lease his homes there and in Newport – the fashionable summer watering-place of the rich in Rhode Island – and take the family to Europe. For Edith, as for Henry James, this early trip abroad was absolutely crucial. The Joneses remained away for six years, from 1866 to 1872. By the time Edith returned to America she was ten – old enough to realize, like James before her, that the world offered many more choices than seemed to be available in New York, New York. There was a year in Rome, a trip to Spain, then two years in Paris. Here, where she would live the last third of her life, Edith first began what she called 'making up' – that is, creating 'stories' about 'real people'. She was taught by tutors how to read, and she read voraciously. The Joneses went on to Germany, where Edith contracted typhoid fever and almost died (again, the parallel with James's early history is striking), then to Florence, and finally back to New York. Eventually, she was to spend abroad half of the sixteen years between the ages of five and twenty-one. Europe presented her with a vast array of experiences, impressions, and memories; and one result of encountering a wide variety of comparative manners would be to make it possible for the young girl to look with a more discerning and critical eye at the manners of her own society. 'Perhaps, after all,' she wrote in her autobiography, 'it is not a bad thing to begin one's travels at four.'

During her adolescent years in New York, Edith had ample opportunity for observation. In the beginning, like many young girls with means, she was simply frivolous. 'What would you like to be when you grow up?' she was asked by an aunt. Her answer was unhesitating: 'The best-dressed woman in New York.' This ideal began to fade as she looked more carefully at those who ruled New York society in the 1870s. And yet she never lost entirely her reverence for her parents' generation and what it represented. 'Their lives, as one looking back,' she wrote later, 'certainly seem lacking in relief; but I believe their value lay in upholding two standards of importance in any community, that of education and good manners, and of scrupulous probity in business and private affairs.' Though during her middle years she was often prone to scoff at these achievements, she came to value them more as they seemed to be disappearing. The first duty of her parents' class, she commented in *A Backward Glance*, 'was to maintain a strict uprightness in affairs; and the gentlemen of my father's day did maintain it.' Any irregularity in business matters excited both horror and relentless social ostracism. 'I should say that the qualities justifying the existence of our old society were social amenity and financial incorruptibility; and we have travelled far enough from both,' she wrote in 1933, 'to begin to estimate their value.'

The double vision of the later Edith Wharton was present in embryo in young Edith Jones, who noted that, as she described it later, 'the weakness of the social structure in my parents' day was a blind dread of innovation, an instinctive shrinking from responsibility.' In polite conversation, art and music and literature – 'unless Trollope's last novel were touched upon': he was safe – were 'timorously avoided.' Even in her teens Edith found this small world claustrophobic and reactionary. 'Conformity,' she declared later, 'is the bane of middle-class communities'; and though she was to break through its iron circle, it would be at great cost to herself – not least, as she admitted, because of 'the old obediences that were in my blood.' It was all very 'useful – for a novelist'. While it might be less 'useful' than bewildering for a sensitive, shy young girl, the future chronicler of Old New York had as an adolescent a subject under her hand: the society of her youth, which fascinated and repelled her, which she admired and loathed, whose good opinion she craved and scorned. So she 'made up' stories about 'real people'. Looking back, Mrs Wharton recalls the latter as 'grown-up people, resembling in appearance and habits my family and their friends', doing things that might or did happen to them. The habit of constructing tales about Old New York began early: 'Happy misfortune, which gave me, for the rest of my life, that background of beauty and old-established order!' After her youthful European travels, she was to come of age in Manhattan and Newport, and acquire by experience there that sharp observation of comparative manners for which she became justly famous.

After Europe, New York seemed ugly to her. The description in Edith Wharton's autobiography of her putative feelings upon returning, at the age of ten, to her Manhattan home, is chilling.

> What I could not guess was that this little low-studded rectangular New York, cursed with its universal chocolate-coloured coating of the most hideous stone ever quarried, this cramped horizontal gridiron of a town without towers, porticoes, fountains or perspectives, hide-bound in its deadly uniformity of mean ugliness, would fifty years later be as much a vanished city as Atlantis or the lowest layer of Schliemann's Troy, or that the social organization which that prosaic setting had slowly secreted would have been swept to oblivion with the rest. Nothing but the Atlantis-fate of old New York, the New York which had slowly but continuously developed from the early seventeenth century to my own childhood, makes that childhood worth recalling now.

It was fascinating because it was gone. She could not, of course, have felt or known this at ten. What as a girl she hated so much – and this passage clearly demonstrates hatred – became fascinating to her later, when it had been murdered by outsiders, by the new money and the new standards of conduct acquired by those who had gotten rich, through 'trade', during and after the Civil War, which created an instant new class of millionaires.

Like most of us, Edith Wharton felt free to criticise what belonged to her, but could not tolerate criticism by others – those who had not belonged to her world, and offered nothing better. She came especially to cherish two golden rules of her time and place: '"bad manners" were the supreme offence'; and '"Never talk about money, and think about it as little as possible."' These were among the rules consistently broken by the *nouveaux riches* who began to plunder New York society in the 1880s, represented in Mrs Wharton's fiction by Rosedale in *The House of Mirth*, Beaufort in *The Age of Innocence*, and others like them.

One of the advantages of her return to New York in 1872 was that it gave young Edith the run of her father's well-chosen library. During the next years she largely educated herself, while sprawled upon the Turkey carpet of this quiet room. 'Whenever I try to recall my childhood it is in my father's library that it comes to life,' she declared in her seventies. The library in question consisted chiefly of the historians, both ancient and modern, the great European poets, the English and French dramatists and diarists, various works of philosophy and art history, and the Bible. She was especially struck by the Elizabethan playwrights and the Romantic poets. There was not much fiction. Mrs Wharton remembers reading, early on, Walter Scott, Washington Irving, and Thackeray, but not much more. Apart from Irving and Longfellow she read nothing by Americans; Melville was excluded because of his alleged 'bohemianism'. Thus the American idiom of the time contributed negligibly to her formative education; and indeed, reading her, one is reminded of the great nineteenth-century British novelists rather than of Poe or Hawthorne or Emerson.

When she was not reading, Edith was watching her parents and their friends. Like James, she quickly developed a capacity for quiet observation. Her parents entertained a great deal, and she found ample opportunities for espionage. It was a safe, monotonous, and, as Mrs Wharton has told us, a rigidly circumscribed society. Conversation was usually about food, houses, travel; gossip of a personal nature fell under the heading of Bad Manners. Her mother loved to shop; Edith remembers seeing her father, often enough, seated at his desk agitatedly going over the household accounts. She came to believe that her father was an imaginative man whose 'buds of fancy' were stifled by her unimaginative, matter-of-fact mother. Certainly her perception of her parents' relationship, accurate or not, prefigures some of her familiar themes as a mature novelist, themes equally dear to Henry James: the defeat of a larger spirit by a pettier one, of strength by weakness; the subduing of imaginative needs by a more powerful prosaicness, the thwarting of intellectual life by the forces of safety and dullness.

While in her teens Edith on a number of occasions tried to elicit from her mother what today are called the facts of life – only to be told crisply that 'It's not nice to ask about such things.' Her parents believed, Mrs Wharton observed later, not so much in God as in good breeding. Her adolescent years were not happy; but whose are? 'If I ever have children,' she declared when still a young girl, 'I shall deprive them of *every pleasure*, in order to prepare them for the inevitable unhappiness of life.' As R. W. B. Lewis has surmised, her adolescent nature contained a great many contradictions, not uncommon in young persons, of intelligence, imagination, and incipient talent. She could be a creature of great vivacity, given to bursts of enthusiasm, harmless vanities and great physical activity. She could also experience chills of self-doubt and embarrassment. By nature she was shy with strangers. But all the while her inner life continued to expand. Beautiful objects and great poetry made her senses race. And yet at times she found herself overcome by what seemed to her the mysterious and dreadful sadness of life. She took nothing calmly.

At the age of eleven, in 1873, Edith, in the throes of the 'secret ecstasy' she enjoyed amidst the books in her father's library, decided to write a story. In a very real sense this was an act of defiance: 'In the eyes of our provincial society authorship was still regarded as something between a black art and a form of manual labour.' Her story began with some dialogue: ' "Oh, how do you do, Mrs. Brown?" said Mrs. Tompkins. "If only I had known you were going to call I should have tidied up the drawing-room." ' Commencing, character-istically, on a note of social realism – the unexpected call – the story, when completed, was submitted to Mrs Jones, who read only the first sentence. 'Drawing-rooms are always tidy,' she remarked, and handed back the composition. Edith reports a 'sudden drop of my creative frenzy'. This chilling, crushing experience turned her away from the writing of fiction for a few years; she tried her hand at poetry instead. Her path to fame was not an easy one. Nobody in her immaculately appointed home would give Edith any writing paper, and there seemed to be no scraps of it lying around. To satisfy her creative ambitions she was driven to beg for the wrappings of parcels delivered to the house; there were plenty of these. 'After a while [they] were regarded as belonging to me, and I always kept a stack in my room . . . I used to spread them on the floor,' Mrs Wharton recalls, 'and travel over them on my hands and knees, building up long parallel columns of blank verse.' She began to send her poems to magazines and newspapers. But her first and most lasting interest was in what, more prosaically, went on in her mother's tidy drawing-room, an interest that never flagged from the age of eleven.

That poetical composition had been only a temporary substitute for the writing of fiction became plain enough when Edith turned fifteen. In January 1877 she completed a thirty-thousand-word tale called 'Fast and Loose'. The narrative moves between England and the Continent; the young author had already begun to find a subject in comparative manners. Though it is, not surprisingly, sentimental and melodramatic, 'Fast and Loose' introduces the first of many Whartonian protagonists – this one called Georgie – whose chief desire is to obtain material comfort through a fashionable marriage. At the end she dies, and the story concludes, on a note of mournful resignation, with these words: 'And every year when April comes the violets bloom again on Georgie's grave.' In her story 'April Showers' (1900) Mrs Wharton made some gentle (but private) fun of her unpublished adolescent novella by using its last line as the conclusion of an insipid short story by a silly girl addicted to writing. And in her story 'Expiation' (1904) she continued the private joke, giving the title 'Fast and Loose' to a successful, scandalous novel cynically written by one of the characters to make money.

Despite the flaws perhaps inevitable in any juvenile effort, Edith's first sustained piece of composition is nonetheless literate and clearly written, and bears traces of the cool satirical perspective character-istic of the later work. Georgie's mother is described as 'one of those weak, shrinking women who seem always overwhelmed by her clothes.' There is an impressive account of an artist's studio in Rome. Most significant is the theme 'Fast and Loose' underscores: the defeat of human aspiration by more powerful social forces.

Her penchant for mockery and mimicry led the fifteen-year-old writer to write a review of 'Fast and Loose' in the didactic style of *The Nation*, where Henry James's first youthful reviews had appeared in the 1860s, and which came to be called 'the weekly Day of Judgment' by some unhappy authors. 'It is a false charity to reader and writer to mince matters,' declared Edith in her *Nation* voice. 'The English of it is that every character [of "Fast and Loose"] is a failure, the plot a vacuum, the style spiritless, the dialogue vague, the sentiment weak, and the whole thing a fiasco.' Nonetheless, she kept it; it was found among her papers after her death. In her seventies, while composing *A Backward Glance*, she looked at it once again, noting that it was 'beautifully written out in a thick copy book'. Its title-page quoted Meredith's 'Lucile':

> Let Woman beware
> How she plays fast and loose with human despair,
> And the storm in Man's heart.

In 1878, when Edith was sixteen, her mother made a selection of the poems written by her daughter during the previous few years and had them privately published by a Newport printer. *Verses* reveals in its author, as Mr Lewis observes, technical competence and verbal assurance, and a fairly wide range of reading in English and German poetry, but little vitality or originality, even in a sixteen-year-old girl. The influence of Browning, one of Edith's favourite poets, is clear. Also clear is the young author's sensitivity to her physical surroundings and her interest in history, traits which were to develop markedly later. Edith's copy of *Verses* carried a frivolous but amusing inscription in her own hand:

> Who wrote these verses, she this volume owns.
> Her unpoetic name is Edith Jones.

Some Newport friends of the Joneses dispatched *Verses* to Longfellow, telling the poet that the young author had been 'brought up in fashionable surroundings little calculated to feed her taste for the Muses'. Longfellow sent the volume, along with a friendly word, to William Dean Howells, editor of the *Atlantic Monthly*. Howells published one of the poems; two others appeared in the *New York World* newspaper in 1879. It was a promising start to a long career; but nothing else of Edith's was to appear in print for another decade.

She made her official social 'debut' in 1879, a little early at the age of seventeen. Commenting on the insularity of New York society at this time, Mrs Wharton characterised it in old age as 'indifferent to anything outside of its charmed circle', but she added that 'no really entertaining social group has ever been anything else.' She concluded: 'I doubt if New York society was ever simpler, gayer, or more pleasantly sophisticated, than it was then.' This was the same woman who wrote novels tearing it limb from limb. Even in her last years she was divided: her memoirs are nostalgic, her fiction savage. At any rate, her debut took place in the private ballroom of a millionaire friend's Fifth Avenue house; Mrs Wharton described the event later as 'a long cold agony of shyness'. She was too self-conscious to dance, and hated the evening. Nonetheless she was 'launched', officially declared by her parents to be of marriageable age. They were telling the world they would now entertain suitors for their daughter's hand. Is it any wonder that the accomplished society hostess of later years was at this moment neither self-assured nor sure-footed?

Initially, the chief significance of this passage in Edith Wharton's life is that it opened society's doors even wider to her, allowing for greater observation. She saw that her parents lived in the most exclusive layer of New York society. Though not nearly so wealthy as some of their set, the Joneses had an impeccable pedigree; they were among the most fashionable and exclusive people of their day. The set their daughter was born into valued breeding and tradition and looked askance at 'mere' wealth, and especially at its display. These themes would haunt Mrs Wharton's novels. Like Henry James, she was a born observer and historian: she *watched* everything. Inevitably it was the most conservative rather than the most progressive element of her milieu that shaped the early vision of things against which she would ultimately rebel. Finding her contemporaries, as a young woman, overly cautious and small-minded, she would also see them, in middle age and after, as 'singularly coherent and respectable' in comparison with those harbouring a 'chaos of indiscriminate appetites' – her characterisation of the 'modern tendencies' taking over New York society in later years. Such discriminations were always important to her. Like the rest of

her tribe, Edith Jones valued restraint, dignity, integrity, fidelity –
moral coherence, in short. But hers was not a world in which an
artistic bent was encouraged; food, clothes, and security continued to
be its dominant concerns.

Though Edith's book-loving father was a notable anomaly among
his immediate contemporaries, he nonetheless observed the usual
custom of providing no formal education for his daughter; indeed,
the few years Jane Austen spent in school gave her more formal
education than Edith Wharton, born eighty-seven years later, ever
had. The rector of the fashionable Trinity Church of Manhattan
declared that a woman's role was 'to be to the man all that he needs'
and 'to keep her home pure and sweet'. So the boys went off to
Harvard and Columbia, Oxford and Cambridge, and the girls went
nowhere. Staying at home, however, gave Edith, observing more
sharply than her contemporaries the life around her, an opportunity
to store up material that later would serve her well.

Outwardly at least Edith Jones conformed to the clothes-conscious,
party-conscious, security-conscious ideal of the New York debutante,
circa 1880. Her mother's job was to make her marriageable; Edith's
job was to get married. The mother said nothing about life after
marriage; the daughter knew nothing about it. Now suitably
launched, Edith went to balls and dinners. Occasionally she attended
one of the regular Monday and Wednesday performances of the
opera at the Academy of Music – the venue of the brilliant opening
scene of *The Age of Innocence*, where society has come to display
itself rather than be ravished by culture and by Christine Nilsson
singing Marguerite in *Faust*, as in fact she did during New York's
1877 season.

Edith had her admirers when she was eighteen, but her shyness plus
her apparent penchant for the safely conventional put some people
off, and there remain on record, as applied to her, phrases such as 'icy
cold' and 'youthful hauteur' and 'ultra fashionable'. Her occasional
bursts of intellectualised conversation may also have made some
uneasy.

The summer of 1880 was divided by the family between Newport
and Bar Harbor, Mount Desert Island, in Maine. Bar Harbor gave
Edith her first taste of northern New England, a setting she would
come to love and go on to use in various guises in several of her
stories. In November 1880 the Joneses went abroad again, largely in

an attempt to repair the failing health of Edith's father. Of her return to Europe, Mrs Wharton recalls: 'What were society and dancing and tennis compared to the rapture of seeing again all that, for eight years, my eyes had pined for?' Looking back, the older woman seems to think that the seeds of revolt were always there in her younger self. Perhaps they were. The family went to London, then to Cannes, then to Venice, and back to Cannes, where George Frederic Jones died in March 1882, two months after his daughter's twentieth birthday. 'I am still haunted by the look in his dear blue eyes, which had followed me so tenderly for nineteen years, and now tried to convey the goodbye message he could not speak,' Edith Wharton wrote in 1933.

She spent the summer of 1882 in Newport, almost getting engaged to an assiduous admirer named Harry Stevens, whose mother, a leading hostess of the time, lent her home for a dinner-party given by Julia Ward Howe for Oscar Wilde; later that season Mrs Stevens gave a huge reception for President Arthur. She did not approve of Edith Jones as a prospective daughter-in-law. 'An alleged preponderance of intellectuality' and the fact that Edith was described as 'an ambitious authoress' were said to be among Mrs Stevens' objections, but the plain fact seems to have been that the Joneses and the Stevenses were in different and rival 'sets'. And the Stevenses were very rich, while the Joneses were not. Edith was taken by her mother to Paris to 'recover', which she quickly did. While available evidence suggests that she was never in love with Harry Stevens, the experience of rejection must have been deeply wounding for the shy twenty-year-old, whose first 'romantic' passage this was.

When the winter season of 1883 came around, Edith was back in New York, twenty-one and still – indeed, for four years now – an eligible bride. A friend of those days recalls how she used to tremble whenever she entered a room full of observant people; being 'fashionable' did not come easily to her. The year passed in the familiar rounds of Manhattan, Newport, and Bar Harbor, the only difference being that Edith was now in possession of $20,000 of her own, left in trust for her by her father. Her mother had inherited a very large sum from a Rhinelander relation, and it began to become clear that Edith would some day be rich in her own right.

It was in Bar Harbor, in July 1883, that Edith met Walter Van Rensselaer Berry. Three years older than she, he was a graduate of Harvard and about to embark upon a distinguished career as a lawyer. Tall, thin, with probing blue eyes and an aristocratic mien, the possessor of a cultivated and discriminating literary mind, and a veteran of eighteen months' travel abroad, Berry found Edith's company invigorating; she seems to have hung on his every word. They bicycled, hiked and canoed together. Yet again Edith failed to get her man, though she and Berry were to become lifelong friends. He was by nature promiscuous, and never married; there is some evidence to suggest that, with his roving eye, he wearied quickly of Edith's persistent intellectuality. Later, she attributed the anticlimax of their relationship in 1883 (they were not to meet again for fourteen years) to her own ignorance: she did not, she said, know how to interest a man. What is clear is that for the second time in two years she was privately humiliated by 'the word not spoken', in Mr Lewis's apt phrase – a theme one finds everywhere in her fiction, perhaps most spectacularly in the last pages of *The House of Mirth*.

So it was in this context that, 'quivering with pain and bewilderment', she met, at Newport during the following month (August 1883), Edward Robbins Wharton. 'Teddy' Wharton, a friend of one of Edith's brothers, was thirty-three, twelve years older than she. A Bostonian, he was said to be the handsomest man in his class at Harvard, where he was admonished more than fifty times for absences from class and chapel. He was totally dependent on an elderly mother and spinster sister, who together provided him with an allowance to live on. He had no profession, then or later. He was a comfortable bachelor dilettante, interested chiefly in food, wine, and his own comfort. He was not so much selfish as superficial, shallow; in any case, he was no thinker. He and Edith had one thing in common: they both loved to travel. The autobiographical late story 'Atrophy' characterises the heroine's husband as weak, vain, bad-tempered, pitiful, forlorn, and comic.

They were together again briefly during the winter season in New York in 1884. They became engaged a year later, in March 1885. The engraved wedding invitations sent by Lucretia Jones to her friends and relations managed to omit the bride's name: 'Mrs George Frederic Jones requests the honour of your presence at the marriage of her daughter to Mr Edward R. Wharton, at Trinity Chapel, on Wednesday April Twenty-Ninth at twelve o'clock.' There were no bridesmaids. Instead of the usual bouquet, Edith was given a gilt-bound prayer-book to carry. The affair struck many contemporaries as a classic example of a conscientious mother getting a difficult daughter off her hands. After the wedding the couple went immediately to Newport and began to participate with great gusto in the kinds of social activities traditionally favoured by their families.

Why did she do it? In *A Backward Glance* Teddy Wharton is never mentioned by name, and the marriage is not discussed; such reticence is equalled only, perhaps, by Trollope's failure in his *Autobiography* to say anything about his wife. Mrs Wharton merely tells us that 'at the end of my second winter in New York' – after returning from Europe, she means – she was married, her husband 'was thirteen years older than myself' (she adds a year), and that he was from Boston. The chapter in which her marriage is mentioned is called 'Friendships and Travels'. In a private letter written in 1907 she describes marriage as one of the most painful of human experiences.

After meeting Teddy, Henry James was to call the marriage 'inconceivable'. But in light of the Stevens and Berry disappointments, Edith's unhappiness at home, especially after her father's death, and the appearance of an apparently 'safe' older man upon the scene, the marriage is not quite so inexplicable, disastrous as it certainly turned out to be. Edith, after all, was twenty-three in the year of her marriage, dangerously close to being on the shelf by the standards of those days. A New York debutante was *supposed* to get married – that is what her existence aimed at – and Edith by that time had been 'out' for six years, a long time; in *The House of Mirth* Lily Bart sees her chances of marriage diminish in direct proportion to the passage of time. It may well be that Edith thought herself, for the third time, in love, if the testimony of some of her contemporaries is to be trusted. Certainly she was on the rebound – indeed, doubly so. Teddy was handsome, pleasant, educated, attentive, a close friend of one of Edith's brothers – and his family had money, which would have been no mean consideration for Edith's domineering mother. People liked Teddy. He was popular in society, where Edith was shy and uncertain. He was well-bred, conservative, and gregarious. He seemed a plausible husband for her. She could not have gone into the question very deeply; it was her fate and her job to get married.

A few days before the wedding, Edith plucked up the courage to ask her mother yet again 'what marriage was really like'. Mrs Jones replied that this was a ridiculous question. 'I want to know what will happen to me,' Edith persisted. Her mother referred her to paintings and statues and noted that men and women were made differently. She would entertain no more 'silly questions. You can't be as stupid as you pretend,' she told her daughter.

If the sexual side of the relationship between Edith and Teddy was a disaster, it may not, under the circumstances, be surprising. The marriage was not consummated for three weeks. Whatever happened on the first fumbling occasions had the effect, as Mr Lewis has noted, of sealing off Edith's vibrant but untutored erotic nature for years. As an older woman she would blame her mother's reticence for 'falsifying' and 'misdirecting' her life.

Like the rest of their set, the Whartons divided their time between New York and Newport. Marriage did not quench Edith's capacity for observation or her appetite for knowledge. But she was disappointed. She and her husband were establishing a relationship that could be described as amicable – so long as Edith got her way, which turned out to be most of the time. But where was the passion she had always looked forward to? Where was the intellectual stimulation?

By the late 1880s she had found a few men who were her equals in intelligence and cultivated friendships with them. She thought that the homegrown American intellectual, hard to locate, led a 'starved existence . . . compared to what . . . might have been in England and France.' In her autobiography Edith Wharton comments on these years in New York, those of her late twenties:

> As in most provincial societies, the scholars, artists and men of letters shut themselves obstinately away from the people they despised as 'fashionable', and the latter did not know how to make the necessary advances to those who lived outside of their little conventions. It is only in sophisticated societies that the intellectual recognize the uses of the frivolous, and that the frivolous know how to make their houses attractive to their betters . . . In every society there is the room, and the need, for a cultivated leisure class; but from the first the spirit of our institutions has caused us to waste this class instead of using it.

Mrs Wharton goes on in this section of *A Backward Glance* to refer to her indifference to the fashionable world of the day, her 'disregard of society'. But early in her married life, at least, she continued to play many of the social games her mother's generation played. At the same time we find her reading Darwin, Spencer, and Huxley, whose discussions of the power of the environment over individuals impressed her.

The Whartons took the first of their many trips abroad in 1888, a cruise through the Aegean. But Italy was to become Edith's greatest love, and by study and application she began to acquire expertise on things Italian, especially the painting, architecture, and furniture of eighteenth-century Venice. The interconnections in this lost world between art, intellect, and social life fascinated her, and probably contributed to her growing feeling of alienation from America and American culture. Without knowing it, she was also acquiring the materials for her first novel, *The Valley of Decision* (1902), set in northern Italy, and two other studies, *Italian Villas and Their Gardens* (1904) and *Italian Backgrounds* (1905). The couple returned to America to discover that Edith had been left a fortune by a reclusive relation she not only never had met, but never had heard of. This money, added to the money from her father's trust fund, made Edith financially independent – a fact that would have a role to play some years later in her decision to leave her husband and her country.

Feeling, in 1889, more secure than she had been for years, Edith Wharton, now twenty-seven, began to write again. At first she turned to verse and quickly published poems in *Scribner's*, *Harper's*, and the *Century*. During the spring of 1889 she decided to try her hand at fiction. On 26 May 1890 she was informed that *Scribner's Magazine* would publish her story 'Mrs Manstey's View', and it duly appeared in July 1891. During the next ten years Mrs Wharton was to write approximately two-dozen stories, many of which were collected in two volumes published by Scribner's, *The Greater Inclination* (1899) and *Crucial Instances* (1901). Some exuberant reviewers compared the author of these volumes, in her subtlety and her understanding of social forms, to Thackeray and James. She would also compose two of her greatest novellas, 'Bunner Sisters' (written 1891–2; published 1916) and 'The Touchstone' (1900) – and, with her architect friend Ogden Codman, Jr., the surprisingly popular and enduring study, *The Decoration of Houses* (1897).

A word should be said, before turning to the fiction, about the last of these – the first of Edith Wharton's many volumes to appear in print. Among other things, it is an interesting indictment of her New

York background as represented by its habitual living conditions; it manages indeed to pay off scores against the physical surroundings in which one of its authors grew up. The old New York town house of Edith Wharton's youth is exactly the sort of cold, ugly, uncomfortably cluttered building *The Decoration of Houses* was written to demolish. In such chilling, repellent places, this book declares, no one can live. It is rather the homes of France and Italy which epitomise taste, comfort, and beauty. Here was one of Mrs Wharton's opening shots across the bows of Old New York.

As her stories began to come out with increasing regularity, 'I continued to live my old life,' Edith Wharton tells us, 'for my husband was as fond of society as ever, and I knew of no other existence, except in our autumnal escapes to Italy. I had as yet no real personality of my own, and was not to acquire one till my first volume of short stories was published.' According to Mrs Wharton, then, she was not a person until she was a writer, and she was not 'officially' a writer until 1899, when she was thirty-seven and her life had run half its ultimate course. She decided that her very earliest tales were not good enough to go into *The Greater Inclination*. As a result, 'Mrs Manstey's View', 'The Fullness of Life' (1893), 'That Good May Come' (1894), 'The Lamp of Psyche' (1895), 'The Valley of Childish Things, and Other Emblems' (1896), 'April Showers' (1900), 'Friends' (1900), and 'The Line of Least Resistance' (1900) – some of them very good indeed – were omitted, and remained unreprinted in any collection until 1968.

By the mid-1890s, now in her early thirties and convinced that she was alive only with a pen in her hand, Edith convinced Teddy to do something unusual. They abandoned Newport to the conventional snobs who inhabited it and began to spend their summers in Lenox, a magnificent venue in the Berkshires of western Massachusetts, where Edith, less fettered by social duties, found herself better able to write (indeed, she found the setting for *Ethan Frome* here). *A Backward Glance* makes clear how important her work was to her during this period of her life, when she was just beginning to make a name for herself as an author.

At last I had groped my way through to my vocation, and thereafter I never questioned that story-telling was my job, though I doubted whether I should be able to cross the chasm which separated the *nouvelle* from the novel. Meanwhile I felt like some homeless waif who, after trying for years to take out naturalization papers, and being rejected by every country, has finally acquired a nationality. The Land of Letters was henceforth to be my country, and I gloried in my new citizenship.

I remember once saying that I was a failure in Boston (where we used to go to stay with my husband's family) because they thought I was too fashionable to be intelligent, and a failure in New York because they were afraid I was too intelligent to be fashionable.

Unable to reverse these so-called 'failures' – due largely to a life of irresolution, stretched between different systems of values – Edith Wharton was to abandon both New York and Boston, and ultimately choose French citizenship. It was during this period of her life that she suffered from nervous disorders, and undoubtedly the tensions of her 'double' life – tugging her towards 'fashion' and towards 'intelligence', towards marriage and towards art – at times were too much for her. Eventually marriage, fashion, and America would all be the losers in the tug of war going on within her for the allegiance of her heart and soul. Publication of *The Greater Inclination* at last 'broke the chains which had held me so long in a kind of torpor,' she recalls. 'For twelve years I had tried to adjust myself to the life I had led since my marriage . . . but now I was overmastered by the longing to meet people who shared my interests.' Marriage and sharing her interests with likeminded others had come to seem to her mutually exclusive activities; the astonishing thing is that she did not leave her husband for another fourteen years. People, she complained – and she meant society people – could never understand 'my longing to break away from the world of fashion and be with my own spiritual kin.' Spiritual kin for her were other writers, 'people who were thinking and creating.'

Perhaps one reason her contemporaries found it hard to see why she did finally break with her past was that she was prone to write so obsessively about it, about fashionable New York. But, as in the case of Joyce and Ireland, the parting of author and subject helped save the subject for the author. Years had to pass before the unequivocal rebellion, but it is clear now that Mrs Wharton's dissatisfaction with her life was of long standing at the time of her break with America in 1913. 'The reception of my books gave me the self-confidence I had so long lacked,' she wrote afterwards, 'and in the company of people who shared my tastes, and treated me as their equal, I ceased to suffer from ... agonizing shyness.' Such people were not easily found in Old New York.

Looking back at the slow, stammering beginnings of her literary life, Edith Wharton wondered, in her autobiography, whether or not it is a good thing for a writer to grow up in an atmosphere in which the arts are non-existent. 'Was it helpful or the reverse to have every aspiration ignored?' She decided, upon observation of a number of fellow-artists, that those who had their ways made smooth for them from the cradle – 'geniuses whose families were prostrate before them before they had written a line' – had a tendency to dry up in middle age, sitting in ineffectual ecstasy before the blank page or the empty canvas; 'the baffled, the derided or the ignored', on the other hand, battled through to achievement. In her own case, she says, 'a development ... naturally slow was ... retarded by the indifference of every one about me ... I had to fight my way to expression through a thick fog of indifference.' Thus Edith Wharton. Combative by nature, she fought; and the fight she fought gave her her great subject. 'The *soul* of the novel,' Mrs Wharton observed, 'is the writer's own soul.'

Unlawful attachments and illicit passions were considered in some places in the 1890s unfit subjects for fiction – Hardy's *Jude the Obscure* (1895) was burned in public by the Bishop of Oxford – and Edith Wharton often had to battle her way into print, especially before she became famous. Referring in her old age to her reputation for conservatism and conventionality, a reputation she despised and thought unfair, as indeed it was, Mrs Wharton complained in 1933 that 'we who fought the good fight' against censoring editors 'are now jeered at as the prigs and prudes who barred the way to complete expression.' Her early stories – some of which, as we have seen, were not published until three decades after her death – are remarkable for at least two things: in terms of subject matter and treatment, they break many of the rules of Mrs Wharton's day; and they speak, in the clearest possible tones, of concerns of her own in the 1890s. During this decade, as Mr Lewis has shown, much of her energy, both imaginative and physical, was directed toward the attempt to liberate herself from the anti-intellectual social world in which she had grown up and which she continued to inhabit. Now in her thirties, she had achieved a considerable degree of independence, but found genuine liberation not possible, at least in New York; she was, quite literally, a child of her time and place. She began to do what she would so often do when conflict threatened: poised between the rebellious and the traditional sides of her nature, she vacillated. The tension runs through the early tales as surely as it runs through the later ones. The connections between herself and the old world of values from which she had been trying to distance herself could never be entirely sundered. Part of Edith, like her mother, believed instinctively that, by definition, drawing-rooms are always tidy. Another part of her, very unlike her mother, was prone to peek under the carpet. She was Edith Jones, and she was Edith Wharton. This spiritual schizophrenia must have been a contributory cause of the nervous disorders she suffered in the 1890s; equally, it must have inspired her to find some release from them in the writing of fiction. For Edith Wharton, perhaps, neurosis and literary composition were symbiotic. Writing kept her sane. It allowed her to express herself – or her selves. Had she been unable to do so, her submerged conflict might have taken her over; instead it took over her work.

In her first story, 'Mrs. Manstey's View', the opening line – 'The view from Mrs. Manstey's window was not a striking one, but to her at least it was full of interest and beauty' – underlines the tension of two points of view simultaneously held. Estranged from her daughter – significantly, mother and daughter represent mutually exclusive values – Mrs Manstey wishes to get away from New York and live in the country, in a house with a garden. Mrs Wharton's houses, in later life, were famous for their gardens. Gardening was one of her passions; like the heroine of her first published story, she found she could not indulge it in New York. Like her author, Mrs Manstey has a keen sense of interior decoration. The proposed construction of a new building threatens to destroy the view from Mrs Manstey's window, to obliterate from sight a large magnolia tree on which she dotes. As so often in Edith Wharton's fiction, 'progress' squares off against taste. Mrs Manstey is a vintage Wharton heroine, the first of many who complain, 'I never had what I wanted.' The opposing forces of old and new are introduced here; the old values are defeated, the new ones treated contemptuously. 'Mrs. Manstey's View' examines the same theme which, three decades later, would flash through Edith Wharton's greatest novel, *The Age of Innocence*: the collision between different values. Early as it is, the first story indicates directions never abandoned afterwards by its author.

'Bunner Sisters', written next (1891–2) and published many years later in *Xingu*, is also set in New York. It touches several veins – in part autobiographical – Edith Wharton was to mine successfully again and again throughout her long career: the struggle of the individual against an impersonal environment (New York); thwarted passion; the agonising self-knowledge experience of the world can bring; the sensitive woman tied to an inferior partner. At the end of 'Bunner Sisters', Ann Eliza reaches conclusions reached over the years by a long succession of Whartonian protagonists:

> For the first time in her life she dimly faced the awful problem of the inutility of self-sacrifice. Hitherto she had never thought of questioning the inherited principles which had guided her life. Self-effacement for the good of others had always seemed to her both natural and necessary; but then she had taken it for granted that it implied the securing of that good. Now she perceived that to refuse the gifts of life does not insure their transmission to those for whom they have been surrendered; and her familiar heaven was unpeopled.

'Questioning the inherited principles which had guided her life' is the sort of thing many of Edith Wharton's heroines are driven to do; Ann Eliza merely happens to be the first of them.

'The Lamp of Psyche', set in 1891 and published in 1895, is the most interesting of the four other 'uncollected' stories Mrs Wharton wrote during the mid-Nineties (the others are 'The Fullness of Life', about an unsatisfactory marriage; 'That Good May Come', about the moral compromises often made in order to succeed; and 'The Valley of Childish Things, and Other Emblems', about a woman who grows more thoughtful and a man who grows more childish with the passage of time). 'The Lamp of Psyche' offers some interesting comments on marriage, a subject about which the author found herself growing cynical. Delia, the protagonist, married her husband for love, but 'was well aware that the sentiment she had once entertained for him had nothing in common with the state of mind which the words now [represented] to her. . . . She had married him at nineteen, because he had beautiful eyes and always wore a gardenia in his coat.' Delia wishes both to hide her unhappiness and to do something about it – that desperate double vision again. 'How many of us could face each other in the calm consciousness of moral rectitude if our inmost desire were not hidden under a convenient garb of lawful observance?' Mrs Wharton's characters go on tensely asking themselves this question in tale after tale. 'It could hardly be expected that a woman who reasoned so dispassionately about her mistakes should attempt to deceive herself about her preferences,' the author writes of Delia. The dilemma of many of Edith Wharton's heroines is self-knowledge for which too high a price has been paid, or which has come too late; here, certainly, there are similarities to James's great tragedies, and some of Conrad's.

The point is that the theme of the thwarted life is as ubiquitous in the obscure early tales as in the later, more famous ones. 'The great secret of living,' Mrs Wharton declares in 'The Lamp of Psyche', is 'to be thoroughly alive.' The only character in it who is indeed 'thoroughly alive' turns out to be Delia's Aunt Mary, conveniently unencumbered with husband or family, a law unto herself, who does what she likes regardless of current fashions; 'thoroughly alive' would seem to mean here 'thoroughly emancipated' from family and social life. For Delia, ultimately, the solution is expatriation from America: she goes to live in France. Another theme of 'The Lamp of Psyche' repeated later on is the weakness and cowardice of men, represented here by Corbett, whose dilettantism is punctuated by our discovery of his cowardly refusal to fight in the Civil War (one could find a substitute, or pay $300 in lieu of going). Mrs Wharton's generation did not approve of shirkers; it is perhaps fortunate that (so far as we know) she never discussed the subject with Henry James.

The Greater Inclination, Edith Wharton's first volume of stories, contains eight tales written during the middle Nineties. 'The Muse's Tragedy' is about a woman, insufficiently loved, who has wasted her life as a result of male indifference and selfishness. 'A Journey' focuses on the death of a husband; Mrs Wharton kills husbands off with consistency and some zest in her fiction of this period. In 'A Journey' the husband, once again, is said to be 'childish'; of the wife: 'Life had a grudge against her . . . she was never to be allowed to spread her wings.' The woman is the stronger character, yearning for experiences the weaker man can hardly imagine. In 'The Pelican' a widow pays for her son's education by going on the lecture circuit.

'Souls Belated', one of the most interesting stories in this volume, concerns another unhappy marriage. This one ends in Divorce; Mrs Wharton capitalizes the word as if it were one of the Deadly Sins, and no doubt most of her friends and acquaintances thought that it was. The divorced woman, in another of those inspired prophecies which seem to dot Edith Wharton's early fiction, takes up residence in France – and a lover. To Lydia, the heroine of 'Souls Belated', divorce means 'freedom'. Lydia's mother-in-law (like Lucretia Jones) 'dreaded ideas as much as a draft in her back ... to do anything unexpected' is considered by the mother-in-law's generation both foolish and rude. 'One of the chief advantages of being rich was that one need not be exposed to unforeseen contingencies: by the use of ordinary firmness and common sense one could make sure of doing exactly the same thing every day at the same hour.' Thus Edith Wharton on Old New York. What discomforts Lydia most about her irregular private life is 'the necessity of having to explain herself'; for conventional girls 'explanations' are extraneous. The story advances the argument that 'no ceremony is needed to consecrate ... love,' that weddings exist to gain for individuals, whether they want it or not, 'the esteem of ... people [of] conventional morality'.

'Souls Belated' argues unambiguously for the smashing up of stale social conventions, especially those surrounding marriage. A silly woman who nonetheless is allowed by her peers to play the role of social arbiter remarks that if 'nothing is known' about people it must go 'against them. It's infinitely worse than any actual knowledge.' Thus Mrs Wharton comments on blind, reactionary social prejudice. Lydia comes to feel that she is not strong enough to flout convention altogether, that she cannot ignore it and hold up her head. This was the sort of debate Edith Wharton was increasingly likely to have with herself during the nerve-wracking 1890s. 'Souls Belated' is a chilling account of the fear and loathing the conventions can inspire in the frail psyche of an individual who is brought up to believe in them and yet who finds all the arguments of 'real life' ranged against them. Convention is tweaked; still, its safety net seems to be valued. Here again is that double vision we encounter whenever Mrs Wharton writes about Old New York.

She must have been reading some of the major British novelists of the 1880s and 1890s. The most important names at the moment were Meredith, Hardy, and Gissing, all of whom had written books, from varying points of view to be sure, on the position of women and the great question of marriage. Specifically, *Jude the Obscure* and Gissing's *The Odd Women* (1893) and *In the Year of Jubilee* (1894) address themselves to matters relating to the marriage ceremony and the free union. Meredith's *The Egoist* (1879) and *Diana of the Crossways* (1885) and Gissing's *The Emancipated* (1890) and *Denzil Quarrier* (1892) also take up many of the themes that interest Mrs Wharton in 'Souls Belated'. In the 1890s she sometimes told people that Meredith (rather than Trollope) was her favourite novelist; one could not help, at this time, connecting Meredith's name with the Marriage Question, both because of the subjects of his novels and the notorious 'irregularities' – by contemporary standards – of his personal life. Though she says little of Gissing, she read him carefully, as *The House of Mirth* demonstrates; its famous ending is taken directly from his brilliant novel *The Whirlpool* (1897).

'A Coward', one of the other stories in *The Greater Inclination*, portrays yet another weak husband. Like much of Mrs Wharton's subsequent fiction, it also contains substitute or surrogate parents. Indeed, the number of times aunts, for example, bring up children can be equalled in the pages of no other writer. If Edith Wharton tended to see mothers as unsympathetic, she found a way in her fiction to get rid of them. 'A Cup of Cold Water' is another tale of the collision of values inside sensitive minds. Captives of a System which promotes 'participating in the most expensive sports, eating the most expensive food and breathing the most expensive air' must try to resolve, in this story, the struggle for dominance between the power of convention and the advantages of spiritual freedom. The author sides with those who would be rebels if they could. As so often in Mrs Wharton's work, convention here stifles and thwarts honest feeling. Woburn, the hero of 'A Cup of Cold Water', muses:

> Was it to live among such puppets that he had sold his soul? What had any of these people done that was noble, exceptional, distinguished? Who knew them by name even, except their tradesmen and the society reporters? Who were they, that they should sit in judgment on him? . . . Was not all morality based on a convention? What was the staunchest code of ethics but a trunk with a series of false bottoms? Now and then one had the illusion of getting down to absolute right or wrong, but it was only a false bottom – a removable hypothesis – with another

false bottom underneath. There was no getting beyond the relative.

The image of conventional ethics as a false-bottomed trunk is a vivid one. Only someone whose rebellion was already far advanced against the values of a society in which he or she had grown up could declare that, in moral matters, there is 'no getting past the relative'.

The last story in this collection, 'The Portrait', declares that in painting, as in life – Mrs Wharton's stories of artists, like James's, are often meant to be taken allegorically – 'the point of view is what gives distinction to either vice or virtue.' In only slightly revised terms, that is, she tells us again that in important matters there is no getting beyond the relative.

Despite the usual view of her as an austere Defender of the Faith, *The Greater Inclination* shows that from the beginning of her career as a writer of fiction, Edith Wharton questioned rather than defended conventional values and took a relativistic view of human behaviour. She does not, of course, always reject the conventions, because she sees that sometimes they have their uses; but she never blindly accepts them. This questioning is what gives a cutting edge, a bite, to her social tragedies – for stories which describe, as hers do, the muffling of honest feeling must be tragedies. Few of her characters learn from their mistakes or overcome their early training in time to carve out happy lives for themselves. That is what tragedy means.

Written in the year *The Greater Inclination* was published (1899), 'The Touchstone' was the first of Edith Wharton's great novellas to appear (1900). Beautifully written and constructed, it is a fascinating performance. Like Lily Bart in *The House of Mirth* a few years later, Glennard in 'The Touchstone' has the entrée to good society but not the means to sustain it. In order to acquire these means, he anonymously sells for publication the letters of a famous novelist, a woman recently deceased who had once loved him but whom he had never loved. Since 'genius is of small use to a woman who does not know how to do her hair', Society paid scant attention to the lady; her fame was posthumous. She 'had stored . . . her rarest vintage for [the] hidden sacrament of tenderness' revealed in the letters to Glennard. After their sale – ironically, they are bought up at a brisk pace, when published, by the very people who had taken no interest in their living author – Glennard is beset by guilt; the social position he is now able to maintain derives, financially, from an unknown act of treachery. Having purchased respectability foully, he cannot enjoy its lustre. He is another of Mrs Wharton's weak men who want what is not worth having and pay too much to get it. The society he covets is frivolous and trivial. 'The Touchstone' concludes memorably: 'We live in our own souls as in an unmapped region, a few acres of which we have cleared for our habitation.'

Before the publication of her first novel in 1902, Edith Wharton wrote another ten stories, seven of which appeared together in her second book, *Crucial Instances* (1901), a collection oddly inferior in quality to *The Greater Inclination*. In these later tales there are some familiar, or at any rate not wholly unexpected, themes: thwarted ambitions, disappointed expectations, wasted lives ('Friends' and 'The Angel at the Grave'); the hollowness at the apex of society, this time Newport's, and the fatal weakness of its men ('The Line of Least Resistance'); the superiority of French culture to American ('The Recovery'), in which Paris, Mrs Wharton's future home, is described as having 'a sensibility so delicate, alert and universal that it seemed to leave no room for obtuseness or error.'

The Valley of Decision, her first novel, published when she was forty, was written mostly at Lenox. While by no means an auspicious debut, by being an historical novel of panoramic scope the book undoubtedly helped the author to find the path she was to follow so much more successfully in her greatest works, in which the social history of New York was incomparably written. Her subject in *The Valley of Decision* is northern Italy in the eighteenth century. And though the book fails by being too dense, too detailed, too descriptive, too worked-up, too 'pictorial' and insufficiently 'scenic', to borrow some terms from Henry James – still, in her attempt to recapture an entire society, Edith Wharton displays the anthropological side of her talent. She also demonstrates in this first novel her remarkable eye for, and ability to describe and vivify, the details that make places and people come alive in fiction: dress, food, gardens, houses, furnishings. Among the Anglo-American novelists of manners, she is an unrivalled poet of the interior; no one else is as good as she is at making us see a room.

The talents on show in *The Valley of Decision* are those of an author who was shortly to find her true and inevitable novelistic subject. For a woman for whom the past was inseparable from the present, a part and a determinant of it, the similarities between the social order of pre-Risorgimento Italy and that of nineteenth-century New York, with its European flavouring, must have been interesting. Sketching hedonistic, extravagant, narrow-minded, and anti-intellectual Italian aristocrats was good practice before moving on to *dramatis personae* known at first hand. Slow and irresponsible, with 'a kind of fat commercial dullness, a lack of that personal distinction which justifies magnificence', the cast of *The Valley of Decision* prepares the way for the subject and the mood of *The House of Mirth*, published three years later. 'Fine living should be but the flower of fine feeling,' Edith Wharton writes in *The Valley of Decision*, 'and . . . external graces, when they adorned a dull and vapid society, were as incongruous as the royal purple on a clown.' This philosophy and this indictment were soon to be applied to the ornately hideous sixty-room mansions on Fifth Avenue built by the founders of America's post-Civil War dynasties and to the empty social ideals of which they were emblems. Characteristic too is this first novel's pessimism, its disillusionment with the possibilities of a human nature freed from the discipline of a stable social hierarchy and the manners of an established culture. By the time she wrote *The Custom of the Country* and *The Age of Innocence*, both produced in her fifties, it was the discipline of a stable social hierarchy and the manners of an established culture we find Mrs Wharton mourning the loss of and wishing to recover. As a progressive, she hoped people would unfetter themselves from social dogma; as a conservative, she felt dogma was often useful in curbing destructive, anti-social behaviour. She saw both the Civil War and the Great War as catalysts, each in its own way, of a deplorable revolution in manners.

A brief account, finally, of some of the great works which come later and of the ways in which their focus, subject matter, and philosophy may be seen as, among other things, inevitable products of Edith Wharton's formative years.

The House of Mirth, *The Custom of the Country*, and *The Age of Innocence* compose together a history of New York society from the Grant era to Woodrow Wilson. They tell stories of rebellion against society, attempted or accomplished; mindless conformity with moral convention; failures of communication within apparently intimate circles. They note and comment upon the conflict between young and old, and compare the values of America and Europe. These novels chronicle a half-century, Edith Wharton's half-century, in New York; for she did not expatriate herself until she was fifty-one.

When the novelist was young, good conversation, good taste, and good form were New York's reigning deities – worshipped by people who, Mrs Wharton declared in *The Age of Innocence*, 'dreaded scandal more than disease . . . placed decency above courage, and considered that nothing was more ill-bred than "scenes" except the behavior of those who gave rise to them.' Toward this society and these people Edith Wharton, characteristically, cherished both grieving affection and protective impatience. The novels, accordingly, teem with harsh rejection and haughty defence. It was, after all, *her* world, by that time gone, that she was writing about.

More than that of any other twentieth-century cultural historian's, Alfred Kazin's lifelong scrutiny of American society resembles Mrs Wharton's in the brilliance of its language, the depth of its detail, and the sophistication of its conclusions. Mr Kazin writes shrewdly of Edith Wharton:

> she was not so much interested in the accession of . . . new [classes] as she was in the destruction of her own, in the eclipse of its finest spirits . . . She . . . was one of its fine spirits; and she translated effortlessly and pointedly the difficulties of her own career into the difficulties of young aristocrats amid a hostile and alien culture. It is the aristocrat yielding, the aristocrat suffering, who bestrides her best novels; the sensitive cultivated castaways who are either destroyed by their own class or tied by marriage or need to the vulgar nouveaux riches. She had accepted all the conditions of servitude to the vulgar new order save the obligation to respect its values, and she could read in the defeat of her characters the last proud affirmation of the caste quality. She could conceive of no society but her own, she could not live with what she had.

She could imagine no other society, she could not accept the one she knew; like the narrator of Matthew Arnold's 'Stanzas from the Grande Chartreuse', she found herself wandering between two worlds, one dead, the other powerless to be born – with nowhere to rest her head. Thus the double vision of the novels, both condemning and protective; thus the 'beautiful losers' theme revivified, and her veneration of Henry James. Edith Wharton herself was, in Mr Kazin's apt terms, 'The aristocrat yielding, the aristocat suffering,' before she got away – becoming, ultimately, a 'sensitive cultivated castaway' who refused to be tied to what she could no longer respect or reverence. As she grew older, the novelist came to see some value in convention not always associated with it. Negative and opportunistic as it might often be, its faults, she came to see, were sometimes outweighed by certain inestimable advantages. At its best, convention could represent the accumulated experience of the race, its experimentation with cause and effect, human need and fulfilment. Thus her later novels are more conservative than earlier ones. But the tension between the two views runs through them all.

The House of Mirth is a novel about the stratification of society – an indictment, written in Edith Wharton's early forties, whose moral texture and complex accuracy grew out of its author's simultaneous understanding of her native social group and her unwavering presentation of its evils. 'Fate had planted me in New York, and my instinct as a story-teller counselled me to use the material nearest to hand, and most familiarly my own,' she says in her autobiography. She does not say that her old friends never forgave her for writing *The House of Mirth*, which took an uncompromising line on the dullness, snobbery, pretentiousness, and hollowness of Old New York, and made her famous – also, obviously, unforgiveable. Mrs Wharton's reply to her friends was written years later in *A Backward Glance*: 'a frivolous society can acquire dramatic significance only through what its frivolity destroys. Its tragic implication lies in its power of debasing people and ideals.' Her answer, in short, was her heroine Lily Bart, and what happens to her.

Edith Wharton had become convinced, by the time she wrote *The House of Mirth*, that the old society of her ancestors was being destroyed. In the novel, set in New York at the turn of the century, this is translated into the destruction of the heroine. The tale provides a full-scale portrait of a lovely young woman trapped between her own crass ambitions, her disabling refinements of sensibility, and the sheer need to survive. A natural result of having low and sordid standards, but not enough tenacity to pursue them avowedly, is a defeat by the circumstances that created those standards, and a miserable end, which is Lily's fate. But, since *The House of Mirth* is by Edith Wharton and not Theodore Dreiser, there is no overt suggestion in it that the social order requires amendment. The problems cannot be solved by getting rid of the upper class; one can only hope that this class might come to its senses some day and make proper use of its resources. The novel is not a blanket indictment of New York; it is an indictment of an environment which makes it impossible for people like Lily Bart, sensitive but weak, intelligent but squeamish, and without resources, to live.

We can see here Edith Wharton's precarious relation to the material of which she felt herself a part at the same time that she was in resistance to it. This helps give the story its dramatic tension. The novelist never made any pretence of not identifying herself with the world portrayed in *The House of Mirth*. As a writer – indeed, as a woman – Mrs Wharton was painfully divided: distraught, self-critical, torn by opposing impulses. The account of her early life may help us to see why. A confrontation of values is present in all of her best fiction. As in *The House of Mirth*, the vital, the graceful, the instinctive are always at odds with the discipline and responsibility that life seems to demand if it is to escape confusion and failure. Like Lily Bart, Edith Wharton was doomed to live a life divided against herself, and to know she was living it.

The Custom of the Country, published in the year (1913) in which Mrs Wharton divorced her husband and moved to France, portrays New York just before the Great War. In the foreground of this novel, as nowhere else in her work, are the moneyed barbarians who, lacking both a moral and a social code, are attempting to acquire the latter via mimesis. Whereas Old New York, by keeping to itself, had evolved a culture of sorts, New New York is portrayed as trying to construct an imitation of European culture by copying its social surface, purchasing it by marriage, buying up its antiques and its artifacts (as in *The Golden Bowl*, published a decade earlier), and attempting to reproduce its architectural masterpieces at home. It is a picture of New York in the grip of the invaders – the Goths, the Vandals.

The Custom of the Country chronicles the conflict between the old ways of Old New York and the new ways of people who have just arrived there from elsewhere. To the women of this new class she gave names like Looty Arlington and Indiana Frusk; their home towns were called Pruneville, Nebraska, and Halleluja, Missouri. Need anyone wonder where Sinclair Lewis found the courage to name *his* towns Gopher Prairie, Minnesota, and Zenith, Indiana?

In *The Custom of the Country* the point of view is already French. Undine Spragg, the Mid-Western anti-heroine, finds herself being addressed in these memorable terms by Challes, one of the novel's few admirable characters:

'You come among us from a country we don't know, and can't imagine, a country you care for so little that before you've been a day in ours you've forgotten the very house you were born in – if it wasn't torn down before you knew it! You come among us speaking our language and not knowing what we mean; wanting the things we want and not knowing why we want them; aping our weaknesses, exaggerating our follies, ignoring or ridiculing all we care about – you come from hotels as big as towns, and from towns as flimsy as paper, where the streets haven't had time to be named, and the buildings are demolished before they're dry, and the people are as proud of changing as we are of holding to what we have – and we're fools enough to imagine that because you copy our ways and pick up our slang you understand anything about the things that make life decent for us!'

The anti-Americanism of this book grew out of the rejection – the humiliation, as Mrs Wharton saw it – of her Old New York by the barbarous invaders from points west. By the time she left it for good, New York was ceasing to be a place where a descendent of the Dutch gentry could feel at home. 'Breeding' gave way to money; all the barriers came crashing down. The more New York changed, the more the novelist regretted the city that was dead and could not live again.

The Custom of the Country is an expression of love and rejection both, and of nostalgia for the author's own past. Even the defects of Old New York began to seem precious to Edith Wharton when compared with the clang and chaos of a new civilisation which not only had no centre, but no conception of what a civilisation with a centre meant. The new civilisation is represented in the book by Undine Spragg, who is materialism incarnate – the 'international cocktail bitch' whose nature is a wasteland, impervious to a thousand years of Western culture. For Mrs Wharton, the appearance of Spraggses signalled the death and burial of Old New York and its people – 'the Aborigines,' as Ralph Marvell, one of the few nice Americans in *The Custom of the Country*, affectionately describes them. Speaking for the novelist, he likens the old families to other 'vanishing denizens of the American continent doomed to rapid extinction with the advance of the invading race', like the American Indians. Ralph calls Washington Square the 'Reservation', and prophesies that 'before long its inhabitants would be exhibited at ethnological shows, pathetically engaged in the exercise of their primitive industries.'

The Age of Innocence, published when Edith Wharton was fifty-eight, returns to the New York of the 1870s, the New York of her adolescence. Even more than *The Custom of the Country* or *The House of Mirth*, it is an exercise in anthropological reconstruction. The war had made Mrs Wharton's New York thoroughly extinct; her greatest novel is an exercise in loving resurrection. Nowhere else in her work is her nostalgia for the world from which she came so finely blended with her criticism of its genteel timidities and evasions. It is a distillation of the lifelong double vision she had of the world of her youth. For the novel is both an act of love and an act of satire. Though Edith Wharton laughs at the deification of 'form' by her old families and the tyranny of their rigid social taboos, she also reveres all this too much to let it be entirely forgotten or scorned by the new generation.

In *The Age of Innocence* the first families of Old New York simmer gently in their own dullness; the novelist laughs at their charades, at what she calls 'the Pharisaic voice of a society wholly absorbed in barricading itself against the unpleasant.' At the same time she half regrets an age still capable of an innocence which, as she puts it, 'seals the mind against imagination and the heart against experience'. For, in *The Age of Innocence*, we find Mrs Wharton absorbed in the logic and comfort of rules and conventions, even when they deny spontaneity and stifle honesty. The social rebel Ellen Olenska, who has divorced her husband and gone to Europe, tells the conventional hero, Newland Archer: 'It was you who made me understand that under the dullness [of New York] there are things so fine and sensitive and delicate that even those I most cared about in my other life [in Europe] look cheap in comparison.' Thus does Edith Wharton pay homage to the New York of her youth. Society cannot simply be abandoned, the novel argues; society stands for and defends domestic order, something worth preserving – even, it may be, at the cost of personal happiness. The fragile flower of patient altruism can thrive only under the glass of moral convention. To conclude that Newland Archer has wasted his life is to miss the point of *The Age of Innocence*. The very qualities in the characters of Newland and Ellen which make their love for each other sensitive and intelligent also make it impossible for them to be happy at the expense of anyone else. The novel argues against taking your pleasure no matter what the cost; it argues against mere appetite. The price of a delicate sensibility can sometimes be the sacrifice of 'the flower of life' which only this sensibility allows one to glimpse. *The Age of Innocence* suggests, in good Jamesian fashion, that self-sacrifice, renunciation, may be the only way to save a life from waste.

Convention is vindicated at the end of the novel when Newland, who does *not* leave his wife and outrage society, muses:

> Something he knew he had missed: the flower of life. But he thought of it now as a thing so unattainable and improbable that to have repined would have been like despairing because one had not drawn the first prize in a lottery ... Ellen Olenska ... had become the composite vision of all that he had missed ... He had been what was called a faithful husband, and when [his wife] had suddenly died ... he had honestly mourned her. Their long years together had shown him that it did not so much matter if marriage was a dull duty, as long as it kept the dignity of a duty: lapsing from that, it became a mere battle of ugly appetites. Looking about him now, he honoured his own past, and mourned for it. After all, there was good in the old ways.

Like Newland Archer, Edith Wharton honoured her own past, and mourned for it, finding that, 'After all, there was good in the old ways.' But, however guilty her escape from 'the old ways' may have made her feel, there is no evidence that she ever seriously considered returning from France to live in the America she had left. She was talking about the 1870s here, her own past as well as America's. It was gone forever. *The Custom of the Country* shows that she knew it.

Old New York was published in 1924, in four volumes. The second of these, 'The Old Maid' – along with *Ethan Frome*, one of the few tales of Mrs Wharton's to be successfully filmed – was written in 1921, on the heels of *The Age of Innocence*, and takes as its setting an even older New York, that of the 1850s. 'New Year's Day', the fourth volume (the others were 'False Dawn' and 'The Spark'), written in 1922, is set in the 1870s. These are among Edith Wharton's most revealing tales, and among her most brilliant. They were composed when her literary reputation, after the best-selling *Age of Innocence* captured the Pulitzer Prize, was at its height. Both, interestingly enough, were nonetheless rejected by several magazines because of what one editor called their 'powerful but unpleasant' subjects – illegitimacy in the case of 'The Old Maid', adultery in the case of 'New Year's Day'. Mrs Wharton, who had reached the age of sixty in 1922, may have been amused: this was the same objection that had been levelled by her own generation against *The House of Mirth* two decades earlier.

In 'The Old Maid', New Yorkers of the 1850s are characterised as people with 'sluggish blood' who regard 'heroism as a form of gambling'. Edith Wharton observes:

> Those well-fed slow-moving people, who seemed irritable and dyspeptic to European eyes only because the caprices of the climate had stripped them of superfluous flesh, and strung their nerves a little tighter, lived in a genteel monotony of which the surface was never stirred by the dumb dramas now and then enacted underground. Sensitive souls in those days were like muted key-boards, on which Fate played without a sound.

Edith Jones of New York and Newport, half a century earlier, had been one of those 'sensitive souls' – a 'muted key-board' muffled by 'genteel monotony'. It is all there in the fiction.

'The Old Maid' is another tale of thwarted passion, this time the passion of a mother for her illegitimate daughter, a love which cannot be expressed openly without scandal. The narrator of 'New Year's Day', a story which treats adultery with some tolerance, looks back upon the author's youthful days in New York and sums up in these terms:

> Among the young women now growing up about me I find none with enough imagination to picture the helpless incapacity of the pretty girl of the 'seventies, the girl without money or vocation, seemingly put into the world only to please, and unlearned in any way of maintaining herself there by her own efforts.

No one else, from another time, could have told Edith Wharton's story for her. She writes of herself and of women who were like herself when very young – of men and women of her own generation. She always valued 'imagination' and deplored its low place in the hierarchy of values among those who formed her youth. She never forgot her own shy, 'helpless incapacity' upon entering society in 'the 'Seventies'. She may have been 'put into the world only to please', but by great effort she shook herself free of those who expected her to think as little as possible, and learned to 'maintain herself . . . by her own efforts'.

Edith Wharton's literary apprenticeship was unique. The indifference of her husband and their friends to her work represented only one part of her spiritual isolation. She was denied free communication with other members of her craft, as a young writer, by the combined timidity and disdain which characterised the attitude of her class towards art and its creators. Indeed, in this sense she was as definitely isolated as a young writer in the midst of her New York society as Jane Austen was in her country parsonage. Edith Wharton's contemporaries – those she met – feared innovation, distrusted literature, and scorned ideas. She had no encouragement from *anyone*. Jane Austen, at least, had a father and siblings interested in literary questions; Edith Wharton's mother and brothers – and, later, her husband – cared nothing for books. In a very real sense she had much farther to go than Jane Austen to get where she got. Like Gissing she lost, at an early age, the parent who would have encouraged a career in letters.

'No doubt we ourselves may change our social habitat and our manner of life,' Proust reminds us in *Le temps retrouvé*, 'and yet our memory, clinging still to the thread of our personal identity, will continue to attach to itself at successive epochs the recollection of the various societies in which, even if it be forty-five years earlier, we have lived.' We began this discussion of Edith Wharton by quoting Proust: they were, after all, contemporaries interested in many of the same things. Through both their lives runs a stream of snobbishness and conservatism, from which they periodically drew back. Both saw the social barbarities of their younger days with kinder eyes as they grew older and those days became more remote – and more appealing by comparison with what followed them in New York and Paris. Both came from upper middle-class families of social position. Proust's valued the arts and Mrs Wharton's did not, and here their backgrounds are very different indeed; perhaps this helps explain why she settled in his country. Certainly they would have understood each other well had they become intimate. Proust's characterisation, at the end of his final volume, of the elderly Duchesse de Guermantes might also describe Mrs Wharton in later life: 'while well-bred people bored her to tears, she was at the same time horrified by any departure from good manners.' Proust's great duchess has an affinity for bohemian company; he understood the type well.

It was once said of Mrs Wharton – and she liked and repeated the remark – that she was a 'self-made man'. It was also said of her that she was essentially the daughter of Old New York, something she never attempted to deny. Socialite and rebel, historian and critic of the *ancien régime*, arbiter of manners and fierce intellectual: such was the double life of Edith Wharton. Never, to the end of her days, would she abandon her great subject: the needs and desires of the individual, the expectations and requirements of society, and the inevitable collision between them. This subject, for which she is justly famous, grew out of a dilemma that dominated her youth and obsessed her for the rest of her life. Writing about it, she continued to write about herself, about her own youthful responses to her environment, about her later perception of how that youth and that environment shaped her as an artist, and as a woman.

One of the most interesting results of Edith Wharton's fortunate penchant for self-expression in fiction is the oft-quoted story 'Autre Temps' (1911), a striking piece of anticipatory autobiography appropriate, perhaps, to end with. Mrs Lidcote, coming back to New York after a divorce and a long absence abroad, sees her native city as a 'huge menacing mass' which she nonetheless 'understood' and 'knew how to reckon with'. She finds that nothing has changed. As a divorced woman, twenty years after the fact, she is still cut out: 'Society is much too busy to revise its own judgments.' Her ultimate verdict was probably Edith Wharton's: 'There's no old New York left ... It's as if an angel had gone about lifting gravestones.' Only 'new' New York remained.

Somerset Maugham, *ca.* 1895, aged about twenty-one (*The late Mrs Clarissa Farrell*)

CHAPTER SIX

Maugham in Bondage

'Happy! Which of us is happy? Which of us is
not utterly wretched?'

Trollope, *The Bertrams*

But were our wish to be granted, the stinging
pain of an affront, the anguish of being
abandoned would have remained for us lands
which we should never have known, lands whose
discovery, painful though it may be for the man,
is nevertheless invaluable for the artist.

Proust, *Le temps retrouvé*

Yet what also remains is a sense of the man, the
complex human figure, whom nothing in the end
can conceal, and it is that relation which modern
criticism prefers to avoid, seeking a text in which
the author is no longer relevant. Maugham's
personality may be, must be, perpetually relevant.

John Bayley,
in the *Times Literary Supplement* (1987)

Shortly before his death in 1965, the ninety-one-year-old Somerset
Maugham was asked to name the happiest passages of his life.

'I can't think of a single moment,' he replied.

For about one-third of the twentieth century Maugham was the
most famous and the most financially successful of all living writers,

the Dickens of his day. His novels and short stories made him, as he once said ruefully, the poorest millionaire on the French Riviera. The various film versions of his tales earned him another fortune, and his many successful plays yet another. Administering the Maugham estate remains virtually a full-time job for the Royal Literary Fund.

When Maugham died his collection of paintings, mostly of French Impressionists and post-Impressionists, was pronounced literally invaluable by the National Trust of Great Britain, to which they were bequeathed. He lived in luxury at Cap Ferrat for the last forty years of his life – like Edith Wharton and Gissing, dying in France. Like Mrs Wharton, he had made France his home; like Henry James, he lived the last half of his life outside of his homeland, though here we have to make the disclaimer that William Somerset Maugham was actually born in France – at the British Embassy in Paris on 25 January 1874 – so that in fact England was not his native country except by diplomatic technicality. But though, like Conrad, Maugham's first language was not English, there was never a question of his writing in any other one. Coming to England as an orphaned child to live with an uncle, he was called by his first playmates 'the little French boy' and had to learn English before he could be sent to school.

Maugham lost his parents early; his childhood was unhappy, his schooldays miserable. He also made a brief and unsuccessful experiment in marriage. He started writing novels in the 1890s and got respectable notices, though he was primarily known for many years as a playwright. Like Oscar Wilde, he once had four plays running simultaneously in the West End. His novels have been read by more people than those of any other modern novelist.

Maugham was only sometimes taken seriously by contemporary critics – that was one reason for his chronic discontent – and though he professed to care solely for his readers' opinions (every letter he received was answered and signed), the critics' lack of enthusiasm hurt him deeply. They could not forgive, he felt, his success. Forgetting perhaps that in the middle of the nineteenth century in England many of the most talented novelists of the day – among them Thackeray, Dickens, George Eliot, Trollope, Collins – were also the most popular and the richest, Maugham's critics sometimes assumed, with a modern cynicism the Victorians would (rightly) have found absurd, that whatever sells must be second-rate. 'When clever young men write essays about contemporary fiction they never think of considering me,' Maugham grumbled in *The Summing Up* (1938). The critics, he complained, do not 'take me seriously'. Maugham was a late Victorian novelist who lived long enough to be reviewed by 'modern' critics before the Victorian revival of the mid-twentieth century made Victorian literature acceptable again; his most important books were published during and between the two world wars, at a time when Victorians were still in bad odour: that too was a part of the problem.

Maugham often thought of himself as a failure, but much of the explanation for his pessimism and unhappiness lies elsewhere, as we shall see. That pessimism and that unhappiness gave shape, form, and substance to his greatest works. For Maugham surely is one of the greatest writers of fiction in the twentieth century. The critics attacked him for writing *entertaining* fiction, light stuff. But his work is deeper, more philosophical, more profound than critics even today have cared to admit. This is one reason why people continue to read and enjoy it: it is not merely topical, written to appeal to a contemporary audience. Much of Dickens's work was in eclipse during the seventy years following his death. Maugham will probably achieve the status of a classic author in the twenty-first century; he will never cease to be read, so long as people read. His books and stories give unmatched insights into human nature and society – motives and desires, self-destructiveness, selfishness, meanness, monomania. He knew many of these human traits from the inside.

The Moon and Sixpence (1919) is one of the twentieth century's greatest achievements in fiction. The other famous novels are *Of Human Bondage* (1915), *Cakes and Ale* (1930), and *The Razor's Edge* (1944). Tales by Maugham which were bestsellers in their day but seem now unjustly forgotten include *Liza of Lambeth* (1897), written when the author was a twenty-two-year-old medical student; *Mrs Craddock* (1902), a vivid account of a failed marriage; and such mature works as *The Painted Veil* (1925), *Theatre* (1937), and *Christmas Holiday* (1939) – all, for various reasons, underrated productions. Millions of people have read Maugham's stories; 'Rain' and 'The Letter' are perhaps the best known among hundreds. It can hardly be disputed that Maugham is one of the finest writers of short stories in the English language. And a great many people have seen on the stage such famous Maugham plays in revival as *Lady Frederick* (1907), *Our Betters* (1917), *The Circle* (1921), *The Constant Wife*

(1926), and *For Services Rendered* (1932), a fierce anti-war piece that turned out to be one of Maugham's few failures when first presented to the public. *The Circle*, deservedly much anthologised and often revived, may be one of the greatest comic dramas in our language, as good as anything by Congreve, Wilde, or Orton.

It has been said that many people see London with Dickens's eyes, whether they have read him or not, so pervasive has his image of the metropolis become; one might say of Maugham that many people who have never been to, say, the Far East, or the South Pacific, see them with Maugham's eyes, so vivid are his renderings of them.

Why was this man who travelled the world, who wrote so marvellously, who lived so comfortably during the last six decades of his life, who loved and knew so much about art, so unhappy? Maugham's melancholy is the key to understanding the nature of his life and the significance of his work. What made him so sad? How could such a man be so productive? How was his work affected by his personality? And how was that personality formed?

'I have put the whole of my life into my books,' Maugham wrote in *The Summing Up*, his highly selective autobiography. 'In one way or another I have used in my writings whatever has happened to me in the course of my life . . . Fact and fiction are so intermingled in my work that now . . . I can hardly distinguish one from the other.' This was Maugham in his sixties. He appends here an admission that Gissing also could have made but never did: 'I have at times fallen victim to a snare to which the writer is peculiarly liable, the desire to carry out in my own life certain actions which I made the characters of my invention do.' He concludes this confessional section of *The Summing Up* by declaring, 'I have always worked from the living model . . . It is the universal custom. From the beginning of literature authors have had originals for their creations . . . the practice of drawing characters from actual models is not only universal, but necessary.' When a writer 'fashions a character that does not carry conviction it is because there is in himself nothing of that person; he has had to fall back on observation, and so has only described, not begotten.'

Let us return to the nineteenth century. The novelist's father, Robert Ormond Maugham, was a lawyer. His firm was situated in Paris, where among other things he served as solicitor to the British Embassy. Somerset Maugham's maternal grandmother, the widow of an East India Company official, had settled in Paris to have her two daughters educated at a convent school there. So it was in Paris that Robert Maugham met Edith Snell. He married her in 1863; he was forty, she was twenty-three. The Snells, much to Somerset Maugham's later joy, could trace their ancestry back to the line of Edward I and Eleanor of Castile. After their marriage the Maughams lived luxuriously in a huge flat then at 25 Avenue d'Antin, now Avenue Franklin D. Roosevelt. There were Dorés on the walls, Tauchnitz editions on the shelves, a billiard room – overall a sense of wealth and solidity. Robert Maugham's law firm was in the Faubourg Saint Honoré, across the street from the British Embassy.

The Maughams were known affectionately as the Beauty and the Beast among their large circle of stylish friends. Edith was an acknowledged beauty while her husband was quite ugly. In later years Somerset Maugham told a niece that his father, whom he admired but rarely saw, and who was always kind to him, 'was an ugly old toad.' The young Maugham also remembered asking his mother, whom he adored, why she loved his father so much. 'Because he has never hurt my feelings,' she replied. It was a relationship Maugham would always idealise – not only because both his parents died when he was quite young, but also because, as he said on several occasions, 'I have never known requited love,' and he saw a rare example of it in his parents' relationship. On the few occasions when, later, he could be persuaded to talk of his childhood, he always spoke of his mother and his earliest years in Paris; rarely would he talk of the English years which followed. We will see why.

Somerset Maugham had three surviving brothers. Robert, born in 1864, died in infancy. Charles, born the following year, was nine years older than Somerset, and from all accounts turned out to be a dull, dreary man with whom his younger brother had little in common. Frederic, the future Lord Chancellor, was a year younger than Charles; his relationship with Somerset was always a stormy one, perhaps in part because, as a well-known lawyer, sportsman, and politician, his name was also before the public, and thus he remained the only brother with whom the novelist felt competitive. Harry, born in 1868, became an aspiring but unsuccessful writer, a homosexual, and went to an early and sad end. All three were teenagers when they were orphaned. In any case they had been shipped off for their schooling to Dover College in 1877, leaving the youngest brother alone in the field with his parents. After years of having his parents' affection all to himself, the young Maugham was singularly unequipped for the tragedy that awaited him.

In 1879 Edith Maugham gave birth to another child, this one stillborn. On 25 January 1882, the eighth birthday of her youngest son, she died at forty-one in the attempt to bear yet another child, who lived only a few hours. The situation is reproduced in *Of Human Bondage*, in which Philip Carey's mother dies a few days after giving birth to a stillborn child. Shortly before her death, when she felt she could not live much longer, Edith Maugham became convinced that her sons were too young to remember her. She had herself dressed by her maid in formal evening clothes and staggered off to the nearest photographer. This is also described in *Of Human Bondage*. The photograph was one of the few things she was able to bequeath to her eight-year-old son. Meanwhile Robert Maugham's legal practice had been mortally wounded by the Franco-Prussian War; many of his English clients decamped and did not return.

As a schoolboy in Paris one of Somerset Maugham's favourite tricks was to gull local shopkeepers by using counterfeit sous – an early sign, perhaps, of interest in money. Summers were spent at Deauville; in Paris he played on the Champs-Elysées with his friends. Indeed, Maugham's earliest years were not unlike those of another contemporary French boy, Marcel Proust, born in 1871.

His mother's death was the first great tragedy of Maugham's life, and by no means the last. In some ways it caused a wound from which he never recovered. He was a boy who desperately needed to feel loved, and from this moment until the end of his days he would never feel unreservedly loved again. He was left alone with his bereaved, financially strapped father, now nearing sixty and ailing. 'Few misfortunes can befall a boy which bring worse consequences than to have a really affectionate mother,' he observed years later in *A Writer's Notebook* (1949). 'My soul seemed a stringed instrument upon which the Gods were playing a melody of despair.'

When Robert Maugham died two years later of stomach cancer, several things were immediately revealed to his youngest son: he now lived in a world in which he loved no one, and no one he could think of loved him; and he was not, as he had been brought up to believe, a little rich boy after all, for his high-living father hadn't left much behind him. This sudden reversal of fortune, so familiar as an event to readers of Gissing's and Hardy's books and so largely the result, as we have seen, of those writers' own experience, marked in Somerset Maugham the onset of a disability that was to plague him, in private and public, for years: he began to stammer – a physical result, no doubt, of his new emotional insecurities. It is interesting to note that while Gissing never developed a stammer, the terrible reversals of fortune that overtook him in his early years stimulated in him, as in Maugham, what turned out to be a lifelong feeling of unlovableness.

Each of the surviving Maugham brothers inherited an income of £150 a year, which meant they had to earn their own livings when the time came. The older brothers were finishing school or starting work; Somerset Maugham was left without a family or a fortune, not to mention a home of his own. It was decided that the boy should be sent to England to live with his father's only brother, Henry MacDonald Maugham, a Church of England clergyman. So the future novelist not only was orphaned and uprooted from the only home he knew; he was sent to live with an unsympathetic (as it turned out) uncle in a small town in another country.

Henry Maugham was the vicar of the parish of All Saints in Whitstable (the Blackstable of *Of Human Bondage* and *Cakes and Ale*), situated on the Kentish coast six miles from Canterbury. Henry's wife was German. They were in their fifties, and childless. It was in 1884 that Somerset Maugham crossed the Channel to start his new life.

As soon as the boy got to Whitstable, Henry Maugham dismissed his French governess, and the last tie to his happy French childhood disappeared. Nor did he see much of his brothers. Charles took over the family's tottering French law firm, assisted by Harry; Frederic was at Cambridge, the recipient of two scholarships. There was little money for the youngest brother's education. Somerset Maugham's sudden poverty and dependence upon the inimical uncle and aunt he had never seen before made him feel rootless and depressed, a state of mind that was to be endlessly replicated in subsequent years. The little English he knew when he arrived in Kent was the result of his French tutor's practice of making him read aloud the police court reports in the London newspapers.

No one who knows *Of Human Bondage* will be surprised by Maugham's assertion in later years that he wrote the novel to rid himself of intolerable obsessions. Nor did he go back to Whitstable once he left it. If there was ever an example of someone who never got over his childhood, Somerset Maugham is that example. 'To destroy the prejudices which from my youth have been instilled into me is in itself an occupation,' he wrote some years later in his *Notebook*. It reminds one of Gissing's declaration that he had to spend much of his adult life shedding what he considered to be the pernicious influences, moral and religious, of his youth.

According to his novelist nephew, Henry Maugham 'was a vulgar lout who would never have been tolerated in my mother's drawing-room.' The vicar of Whitstable was certainly unlucky in his nephew, but there can be little doubt that he was a strict disciplinarian, and often mean; the allowance to the boy of one half of a boiled egg – and the top half of it at that – on Sundays, as described so vividly in *Of Human Bondage* (and confirmed by Maugham's Notebook), is indicative. No wonder Maugham at Cap Ferrat would employ the most famous chef on the Riviera and take great pride in the food he offered his guests, though he sampled only a little of it himself. Also drawn from life is the pressure on the nephew exerted by the uncle to become a clergyman. Maugham's account in *The Summing Up* of how he began to lose his faith will be familiar to readers of *Of Human Bondage*:

> I had not been long at school before I discovered, through the ridicule to which I was exposed and the humiliations I suffered, how great a misfortune it was to me that I stammered; and I had read in the Bible that if you had faith you could move mountains. My uncle assured me that it was a literal fact. One night, when I was going to school the next day, I prayed to God with all my might that he would take away my impediment; and, such was my faith, I went to sleep quite certain that when I awoke next morning I should be able to speak like everybody else. I pictured to myself the surprise of the boys . . . when they found that I no longer stammered. I woke full of exultation and it was a real, a terrible shock, when I discovered that I stammered as badly as ever.

So much for God. 'I put into it everything I then knew,' Maugham remarked later of his most famous book, sections of which are almost indistinguishable from passages which appear in his various autobiographical reminiscences.

Maugham's earliest student days, first at a Faversham grammar school in the home of a local physician and then at the King's School, Canterbury, were not enviable. He was laughed at by his schoolmates not only because he stammered but also because his English was so poor. Like Conrad in England in the 1880s, he had difficulty making himself understood. 'I had many disabilities,' Maugham admits in *The Summing Up*. 'I was small; I had . . . little physical strength; I stammered; I was shy; I had poor health. I had no facility for games.' These disabilities were not likely to excite the sympathy of his schoolmates. Maugham concludes: 'I knew that suffering did not ennoble; it degraded. It made men selfish, mean, petty, and suspicious. It absorbed them in small things. It did not make them more than men; it made them less than men.' He learned what Gissing learned, and both put it into their books.

From this period of Maugham's life also originated the assertion, repeated over and over again both in print and in private communications, that he had never known requited love. 'The love that lasts longest is the love that is never returned,' he wrote sadly in the Notebook. Already his French childhood was beginning to fade from his consciousness; children have short memories. Only the unpleasant present could be 'real' to the young Somerset Maugham.

Unlike Philip Carey in *Of Human Bondage*, born with a club foot, Maugham was not born with a stammer, though Philip's impediment obviously stands in for Maugham's. The stammer became more rather than less acute under the stern, hard regime of his insensitive Uncle Henry. Years later, writing in a preface to *The Old Wives' Tale* about the stammer of his friend Arnold Bennett, Maugham declared: 'Few knew the humiliations it exposed him to . . . and the minor exasperation of thinking of a good, amusing or apt remark and not venturing to say it in case the stammer ruined it. Few knew the distressing sense it gave rise to of a bar to complete contact with other men. It may be that except for the stammer which forced him to introspection Arnold would never have become a writer.' Maugham added: 'We do not write because we want to; we write because we must.' Clearly he thought that his stammer was at least partly responsible for his becoming a writer – which is another way of saying that he was driven to write out of misery. Again there is a parallel with Gissing, who saw misery as the driving force of the artist. It is no accident that both novelists began their careers by composing depressing tales of life in the slums.

One of Maugham's favourite occupations as a schoolboy was keeping track in his *Notebook* of the foibles of his detested uncle. Under the heading 'Maxims of the Vicar' we find such entries as these:

'A person is paid to preach, not to practise.'

'Only ask those people to stay with you or dine with you who can ask you in return.'

'Do unto others as you would they should do unto you. An excellent maxim – for others.'

Maugham noted that Uncle Henry preached temperance and kept himself well supplied with liquor, which was locked up. And he comments on one of the sermons he heard:

> The Vicar expounded twice on Sunday the more obvious parts of the Scriptures, in twenty minutes or so, making for the benefit of the vulgar a number of trite reflections in a slovenly language compounded from the Authorized Version and the daily version. He [has] a great facility for explaining earnestly and at decorous length texts which [are] plain to the poorest intelligence.

Henry Maugham was having at least two effects on his young nephew: by his personal example he was putting into disrepute the whole foundation of religion; and he was providing a providential opportunity for the boy to improve his use of language by the negative example of his own. So Somerset Maugham early on became a critic. The Notebook shows that his English improved rapidly, ultimately settling into that diamond-hard, clear prose for which even his detractors have had to praise him.

According to the portraits in *Of Human Bondage* and *Cakes and Ale*, Henry Maugham was a monster of selfishness and hard-heartedness. He lit the coal stove only when *he* was cold. When his wife died he argued for economy in the matter of the tombstone but hoped she would receive more floral tributes than those received by another recently deceased vicar's wife. According to his nephew, he was a hypocrite and a bigot. He made the future novelist hate the Bible by attempting to get him to memorize large parts of it. He would seem to have played Theobald Pontifex to Maugham's Ernest.

Nor would he let his nephew play, or read for pleasure, on Sundays; the latter became a secret indulgence to which the young Maugham soon became addicted. He had read all of Walter Scott, he tells us, by the time he was twelve, as well as the *Arabian Nights* and *Alice in Wonderland*. Reading became a refuge from distress, as it did for Henry James and Edith Wharton. The vicar, Maugham declares in *The Summing Up*, 'was incredibly idle and left the work of the parish to his curate and his church-wardens.'

Undoubtedly there is some special pleading here: one looks better in middle age, as Dickens knew, if one exaggerates the horrors of one's early years; one seems to have overcome more, to have travelled further. Still, some of this must be true. Even Somerset Maugham's brother Frederic, who rarely agreed with the novelist about anything, in later years described their Uncle Henry as 'very narrow-minded and far from intelligent'.

Maugham lived with his overbearing uncle and his well-meaning but weak aunt for seven years altogether. Whitstable in those days was a thriving harbour; it is still famous for its oysters. The young Maugham spent many hours watching ships come and go, and loved to swim in the Thames Estuary, which made him feel closer to his old French life. Uncle Henry had status in the county. He lived in some comfort in the large ivy-covered vicarage (now torn down), which also possessed a garden, stables, coach-house and servants. Summers were spent at various German spas, partly in deference to his aunt. Somerset Maugham was taught most of the usual middle-class prejudices of his day. 'I was a very respectable youth,' he says of himself in *Cakes and Ale*. 'I accepted the conventions of my class as if they were laws of Nature.'

When, at the age of eleven, he was sent to the King's School, united by tradition to Canterbury Cathedral, it was assumed (by others) that he would eventually be ordained. He begged the vicar to let the Headmaster know in advance that his new pupil stammered: it was that aspect of himself of which he was most conscious, like Philip Carey of his club foot. Let us consider for a moment that source of special consciousness. Ted Morgan has written perceptively of Maugham's stammer and of some of the reasons why the novelist waited until he was in his sixties to seek therapy for it. Stammers, he argues, are 'self-inflicted. The stammerer has some quarrel with himself, he sets up his own roadblocks. Stammering becomes a self-fulfilling prophecy. The stammerer knows he will be made fun of, and he is. Stammering is a way of guaranteeing the situation you foresee.' The stammerer is usually ambivalent about oral communication: he wishes not to reveal himself. Stammering is also an appeal for sympathy – and also, perhaps unconsciously, an appeal for attention. Maugham is on record as having believed that his life was 'greatly influenced' by his stammer, that it remained the most important fact about him. He could not be a clergyman, a lawyer, or a politician; he must find another way to express himself. Without the stammer, there would have been no club foot for Philip Carey; indeed, there would have been no *Of Human Bondage*. Maugham's stammer made him reserved and shy. Like Henry James, and perhaps for some of the same reasons – for Maugham turned out to be homosexual – he felt forced to become an onlooker instead of a participant, in life as in games. Once again the detached observer stayed on the sidelines, biding his time. Should he give of himself, or hold back? Which part of himself, if any, was worth giving? The emotional stress on Maugham in early years may be compared with that which caused the youthful James's constipation and bad back. Both men, in various ways, asked themselves the same question: What am I?

Though modern psychologists and speech therapists will tell you that there must be some connection between early grief and stammering, they cannot tell you what it is; they can only observe and record it, they say. Maugham liked to psychologise, and when he said in later years that the most important fact about himself was his stammer he was undoubtedly right, for by then he had made himself right. The relentless stammer afflicting him reflected and demonstrated the persistence and penetration of the past into his mature years.

Maugham was a student at the King's School, which calls itself the oldest school in England, from May 1885 until July 1889 – that is, between the ages of eleven and fifteen. Standing upon the ground of the cathedral of Canterbury, the school is connected to one of the most ancient places of Christian worship in England, dating back to the time of St Augustine. As at the other public schools, the boys wore straw boaters and black uniforms with wing-tip collars. The masters wore mortar-boards and gowns. In *Of Human Bondage* Maugham's account of the school is given with photographic detail. Indeed, the physical descriptions of the masters are so accurate that all have since been identified. Maugham was teased unmercifully at King's, and hated the place. He dreamed of waking up to find himself at home in Paris with his mother.

But he applied himself, especially to Greek and Latin, and was first in his class in 1886. The next year he became a scholarship student in the Senior School and won the prize in music. In 1888 he was awarded prizes in divinity, history, and, not surprisingly, French. As *Of Human Bondage* suggests, his pre-eminent academic position in the school gradually freed him from bullying, he became happier, and his stammer was turned from a source of ridicule to a source of forgiveness on the part of his fellow-students. One reason he ceased to be teased was the barbed wit he had developed as a defence against it. This made him no more popular with his classmates, though it saved him from some of their cruelties. He longed for genuine popularity as a schoolboy but never achieved it, as *Of Human Bondage* tells us, and resorted to daydreaming to blot out reality. 'He would imagine,' Maugham writes of Philip Carey, 'that he was some boy whom he had a particular fancy for; he would throw his soul . . . into the other's body, talk with his voice and laugh with his heart . . . in this way he enjoyed many intervals of fantastic happiness.' As the novel also suggests, Maugham fell in love with one of his classmates, an eventuality from which no one at an English public school is immune, then or now. At Harrow in the nineteenth century the 'prettiest' younger boys routinely were given feminine names and each was considered the personal sexual property of one of the older boys.

During the winter of 1888–9 Maugham came down with pleurisy and was sent to an English tutor at Hyères on the French Riviera. (Here, some years later, Edith Wharton was to have a home.) The spring of 1889 was his last at King's. Now fifteen, Maugham told his uncle he would not go back to the school again, he would not go to Oxford, he would not be ordained. He spent the winter of 1889–90 again at Hyères and returned to Whitstable without specific plans. His German aunt suggested that he spend a year in her native land. After a little research she found a Heidelberg professor who took in boarders. And so at sixteen Maugham went off to Germany, eschewing the university scholarship certain to be his had he stayed at King's. Gissing's cancelled university scholarship turned a classicist into a novelist; Maugham's resignation of a university career just as certainly turned another potential scholar in the direction of fiction. In later years Maugham wondered how things might have turned out had he gone to university. The narrator of *The Razor's Edge*, who is named 'Maugham' and resembles the author temperamentally, comments that he 'had the chance' of a university education but 'refused it. I wanted to get out in the world. I've always regretted it. I think it would have saved me a lot of mistakes.' At the time, though, the 'real' Maugham was delighted to get away from Kent – from Whitstable and from Canterbury. And so at sixteen he found himself in the home of the von Grabaus in Heidelberg.

He was relatively happy there. For the first time in years he had genuine freedom, including the opportunity to read and study and talk about virtually anything he liked. His chief interests were art and literature, and he indulged them wherever he could. And one of the von Grabaus' boarders, a twenty-six-year-old Englishman named John Ellingham Brooks, took Maugham to bed with him between discussions of aesthetics and taste. Maugham was drawn to Brooks both physically – he was always moved by affection shown to him – and intellectually, for Brooks preached flouting the conventions, living a life of letters, and devoting oneself to 'beauty'. In *Final Edition*, the last volume of E. F. Benson's memoirs, Brooks is described as a dilettante 'who, partly from a flawless mental fastidiousness, made less of fine abilities and highly educated tastes than anyone I have ever known. He was short in stature and clumsy in movement, but his face was very handsome.'

During the winter of 1890–91 Maugham attended some lectures at Heidelberg University and began to read Schopenhauer, that dour philosopher so admired by Gissing, who read him in German as he was published, and by Hardy, who could not read German and had to wait for the English translations of the 1880s. As Mr Morgan has shown, the young Maugham found Schopenhauer's pessimism comfortable. Schopenhauer argues among other things that no *reason* for existence can be identified, that free will is a mirage, that the afterlife is merely a pleasant illusion to help us get through this one. This fitted Maugham's adolescent mood. His mother's death, the miserable time since, his growing atheism, his newfound sexual identity all caused in him a monolithic guilt that could now be at least somewhat assuaged by Schopenhauer's idea that the universe lacked logic and that human tragedy could have no reasonable explanation and therefore no reasonable cause. Only truly exceptional beings such as artists and philosophers, Schopenhauer argued, could be 'free' – that is, unbound by the restrictions and beliefs of the past. Of course we can see these ideas at work in Maugham's novels – most patently, perhaps, in *The Moon and Sixpence* and *The Razor's Edge*.

In Heidelberg Maugham saw some of Ibsen's plays performed, and this too had an impact on him, for Ibsen was another who expressed contempt for the conventions of the present day. Public productions of his plays were still banned in England, though translations of them could be read. Indeed, while Maugham was in Germany soaking up new ideas, the British Parliament was passing a series of reactionary measures, one of which made homosexual acts between consenting adults in private a crime – a law which stood until 1967 in England. This law, which was to become known as the blackmailer's charter, drove many Englishmen abroad in ensuing years; Somerset Maugham was to be one of them.

In the spring of 1892, now eighteen, Maugham returned to England. The country which had declared the fulfilment of his sexual inclinations illegal now seemed to him, after the liberation of his intellect in Germany, even less alluring than it had been two years earlier. The unhappy young man renewed his determination not to go to any British university. The teachings of Schopenhauer were now very much present to him, as he tells us in *The Summing Up*:

> I believed that we were wretched puppets at the mercy of a ruthless fate; and that ... we were doomed to take part in the ceaseless struggle for existence with nothing to look forward to but inevitable defeat. I learnt that men were moved by a savage egoism, and that love was only the dirty trick nature played on us to achieve the connection of the species, and I decided that ... it was impossible for them to aim at anything but their own selfish pleasure.

Seeing love as nature's 'dirty trick' is cynical enough. Maugham goes on here:

> if there was no God who could consign me to eternal flames and no soul that could be thus consigned ... I could not see that there was any meaning in good .... I came to the conclusion

that man aimed at . . . his own pleasure . . . and . . . it was only common sense to seize every pleasure that the moment offered . . . right and wrong were merely words and . . . the rules of conduct were no more than conventions that men had set up to serve their own selfish purposes.

Despite Maugham's observation of the surface proprieties, we can see here the origins of his lifelong contempt for what he often referred to as bourgeois convention: it consisted for him in 'the rules of conduct . . . that men had set up to serve their own selfish purposes.' He lived his life and wrote his novels accordingly, always keeping a special eye out for social hypocrisy and moral pretentiousness.

As for England – Maugham felt, he said, 'attached' to England, but not 'very much at home there'. These feelings were to persist into old age. The English, he would complain later, are 'not an amorous race. Love with them is more sentimental than passionate . . . they cannot control the instinctive feeling that the sexual act is disgusting.' He formed a succinct theory of conduct, expressed by Philip in *Of Human Bondage* and repeated word for word in *The Summing Up*: 'Follow your inclinations with due regard to the policeman round the corner.' He began to feel that, unlike Continental Europeans, the English despised art and were in fact more interested, as he puts it in *The Summing Up*, 'in works of information'. Maugham's rating of the cultural level of the English resembles Gissing's. It may also remind us of Henry James and Edith Wharton in America. What they perceived as a lack of culture there, and the absence of values that routinely embraced it, played a part in their expatriations.

The entries in the Notebook Maugham always kept by him now began to grow harsher and more querulous:

Men are mean, petty, muddle-headed, ignoble, bestial from their cradles to their death-beds; ignorant slaves now of one superstition, now of another, and illiberal; selfish and cruel . . . Everything in life is meaningless, the pain and the suffering are fruitless and futile. There is no object in life . . . The thought of living for ever is horrible.

The young Maugham became a cynic. 'In the perusal of books men are able to lead artificial lives which are often truer than those circumstances have forced upon them,' he observes in *A Writer's*

Notebook. He was now heading in the direction of literature and the search for spiritual peace that would consume the next five decades of his life. But not yet. At eighteen he wrote a biography of the German composer Meyerbeer, whose French operas he had never heard. He tried, unsuccessfully, to find a publisher; the manuscript was burned.

When Maugham returned to England from Germany his uncle found a job for him in the office of an accountant in Chancery Lane, an ordeal described vividly in *Of Human Bondage*. Living in London for the first time, Maugham, like Hardy in similar circumstances, was lonely and depressed, and bored by his work. He lasted only a month, then went home to Kent. When the local physician suggested medicine as a career Maugham agreed, fearing to let his uncle know he wanted to be a writer. It occurred to him, further, that as a medical student he could gain some of the direct experience of life he needed to have if he was going to write and that he could go on with his course of reading in the privacy of lodgings. So he was sent to a 'crammer' to pass the medical entrance examination, which was the only barrier in those days to any man who wished to go into medicine. In Maugham's time, as in Jane Austen's, physicians need not have a university education, and it was largely for this reason that they remained relatively low in the social scale. You could be a doctor without being a 'gentleman', just as any other tradesman could.

On 27 September 1892 Maugham registered as a medical student at St Thomas's Hospital in Lambeth Palace Road. Here he would spend a large part of the next five years, between the ages of eighteen and twenty-three. During this period of his life, among other duties, he would deliver sixty-three babies in the slums of Lambeth, not surprisingly the setting of his first published novel. He never intended to practise medicine for a living, though every now and then early in his writing career he would talk about signing on as a ship's doctor if he failed with the reading or the play-going public – and indeed, ship's doctors figure in many of his stories.

Maugham took lodgings in furnished rooms at 11 Vincent Square, Westminster. Years later, in *Cakes and Ale*, he immortalised the Cockney landlady who looked after him there. Like all first-year students at St Thomas's, Maugham began with anatomy and gynaecology. He never forgot the first words he heard a medical school lecturer speak: 'Gentlemen, woman is an animal that micturates once a day, defecates once a week, menstruates once a month, parturates once a year and copulates whenever she has the opportunity.' There were, of course, no women in his class; the professions were not yet open to them.

As we know, Maugham thought that being a medical student was going to give him that invaluable 'experience of life' which, as an embryo writer, he felt in need of. In a practical sense he was right, as *Liza of Lambeth*, published when he was twenty-three, would show. What he was not prepared for was the pain and sorrow doctors and would-be doctors routinely encounter. He enjoyed his anatomy classes; corpses did not bother him. What did bother him was the *process* of dying, to which he was all too often a witness. So far as he could see, a human being died 'as a dog dies': there was nothing noble or inspiring about death. Reading about it in Schopenhauer had not prepared him for seeing it in Lambeth. He wrote in the Notebook: 'in the great majority of cases, pain, far from refining, has an effect which is merely brutalizing. An example in point is the case of hospital in-patients: physical pain makes them self-absorbed, selfish, querulous, impatient, unjust and greedy; I could name a score of petty vices that it generates, but not one virtue.' Like Gissing, he saw that those tested by pain and suffering were made worse, not better, by such testing, and his instinctive cynicism grew. Was there any nobility in human life? That Maugham was deeply affected by his experience at St Thomas's may be seen, to take just one example, in a pathetic *Notebook* passage in which he describes a Caesarian he observed on a patient who had set her heart on having a baby even though she had been told the chances were no better than even that she would come through it alive. The woman and her husband decided to take the gamble.

> The operation appeared to go very well and Dr C's face beamed when he extracted the baby. This morning I was in the ward and asked one of the nurses how she was getting on. She told me she'd died in the night. I don't know why, it gave me a shock and I had to frown because I was afraid I was going to cry. It was silly, I didn't know her, I'd only seen her on the operating table. I suppose what affected me was the passion of that woman, just an ordinary hospital patient, to have a baby, a passion so intense that she was willing to incur the frightful risk; it seemed hard,

dreadfully hard, that she had to die. The nurse told me the baby was doing well. That poor woman.

The tender-hearted young man who considered himself a cynic and yet wanted to see more of life was especially affected by a death in childbirth; this was how his own mother had met her end. It was almost too much for him. Nowhere in Maugham's many volumes, however, is there a suggestion that he regretted his decision to become a medical student and 'see life'.

Maugham kept to a regular schedule for the next few years. He did what was required of him at St Thomas's. He read a great deal, wrote a bit, carefully kept his *Notebook* current, like Hardy in London visited art galleries exhaustively, like Gissing went to the theatre whenever he could afford it. One evening, as another experiment in life, he picked up a girl in Piccadilly; gonorrhoea, for him as for Gissing in Manchester, was his reward. Meanwhile he continued to study the pathology of human beings, a better education for a budding novelist, he was certain, than anything he could have learned at university. Indeed, none of the novelists discussed here even began a university career; among the great Victorian novelists not a single university degree may be found. 'If you want to be a novelist, work in the wards,' Walker Percy, a qualified physician, has remarked. This is what Maugham was about to do. It was not, of course, unprecedented. Among other writers who at one time or another have studied medicine one could list Keats, Francis Thompson, Conan Doyle, Céline, Chekhov, William Carlos Williams, and undoubtedly others.

After the biography of Meyerbeer was rejected and destroyed, Maugham tried writing plays in the manner of Ibsen. He got nowhere. 'It occurred to me,' he recalled later, 'that my best plan was to write two or three novels that would give me sufficient reputation to induce managers to look on my plays with favour.' This decision, as it turned out, was the right one.

In 1894, now twenty, Maugham again went abroad, this time to Italy. He saw travel as part of his literary education; his lifelong peripatetic intercontinental wandering, however, was also a symptom of restlessness, unhappiness, loneliness – and his feeling that there was something to learn, greener grass, more interesting people, elsewhere. He travelled, almost manically, until his last years. In this, as in many other things, especially in his continual search, through movement, for 'peace' and 'meaning', he resembles the hero of his last great novel, *The Razor's Edge*.

In the autumn of 1894, back at St Thomas's, Maugham passed the examination in 'materia medica', which allowed him into the wards and the out-patient departments of the hospital. Many of the patients he now began to see were from the adjacent Lambeth slums. Philip Carey, the medical-student hero of *Of Human Bondage*, 'found an interest in just looking at them. . . . You saw . . . human nature taken by surprise, and often the mask of custom was torn off rudely, showing you the soul all raw . . . There was neither good nor bad there. There were just facts. It was life.' Maugham took his turn in the emergency rooms. Later he would say that the men were better patients than the women. He was beginning to dislike women; his lifelong misogyny was starting to show. But the main significance of these years was his growing tendency to equate 'life' with 'facts'. Maugham is sometimes categorised as a romantic novelist, perhaps because his settings are often exotic and his characters picturesque. But like most of the major English novelists who started writing in the last decades of the nineteenth century, his early work borders on naturalism, and his later work, in its language and subject matter, rarely leaves the realm of the plausible. Maugham as a novelist is among other things famous for his unshockableness. We can see that aspect of his sensibility starting to form here.

The partiality he noted in himself for the company of men, especially good-looking young men, made the Oscar Wilde scandal of 1895 especially nerve-wracking for Maugham, always aware of that policeman round the corner. The affair taught him at least two things: keep your private life to yourself; and consider living abroad – for the Wilde trials sent much of the mobile homosexual population of England rushing for the boat train to Calais. Maugham would always do the former, and eventually he would do the latter. He was aware of 'the love that dare not speak its name' in himself, and grew more cautious. Nor did he speak out on the subject, then or ever; his shyness and dread of scandal could not be overcome, no matter how secure, how rich, how respectable, how famous, or how elderly he grew. There are hints here and there – as most readers know, Mildred in *Of Human Bondage* is drawn from one of Maugham's youthful boy-friends – but he kept the subject largely out of his fiction, though any reader can find passages of Maugham's in which women observe men and think of their bodies as other men do rather than as women do; there is a good deal of sublimation of this sort going on in *The Razor's Edge*. In two places only, as Mr Morgan has observed, does Maugham deal with homosexuality explicitly; these are in his assessments of El Greco and of Melville. He belittles both for their homosexuality, and argues that they would have been greater men had they been heterosexual. No doubt he thought the same thing of himself: deep down he always considered himself a failure. The passage on El Greco occurs in *Don Fernando* (1935; an unmemorable novel) and contains the following sentences, written to characterise the homosexual in general terms: 'He has vitality, brilliance, but seldom strength. He stands on the bank, aloof and ironical, and watches the river of life flow on.' Other attributes of the homosexual Maugham identifies here include cynicism, humour, insight, love of elegance, love of beauty, wilfulness, and interest in decoration. His characterisation of Melville as homosexual, in 'The Art of Fiction' (1954), is based on several passages in which young men are described and which the eighty-year-old Maugham quotes with apparent unselfconsciousness. And yet some of his own fictional young men – the title character in the story 'Red' (1950), to take just one example – are drawn with unmasked sexual avidity. But Maugham the writer rarely lets his guard down. In his private life no pretensions were made about his sexual preferences. He lived with a succession of younger men at Cap Ferrat, and visited England without them.

When he was twenty-one Maugham went to Capri with his first lover, Ellingham Brooks. He was now working on several short stories with Ibsenesque themes, and a novel. Capri was an early gay mecca; Maugham found he could work there comfortably. Back in London he went on writing, largely in the evenings. 'A Bad Example', the first of hundreds of stories, suggests that a truly good man is always at a disadvantage due to the corruption of society, a theme Maugham would often return to. The second story, 'Daisy', is set in 'Blackstable' and London and focuses on another type to which Maugham often had recourse: the beautiful, sensual, kindhearted but amoral girl. 'Daisy' touches on adultery, prostitution, and the hypocrisy of respectable families. Maugham sent both to T. Fisher Unwin, who published Conrad's early books and several of Gissing's later ones. Edward Garnett, who had urged Unwin to publish Conrad when the latter was unknown, was the reader, and he now advised Unwin not to publish Maugham, at least not yet. He found the stories gratuitously contemptuous of social conventions – the same criticism that kept Hardy's earliest fiction out of print. Mid-Victorian readers were evaluating late Victorian manuscripts; there was a generation gap. Garnett to his credit did suggest that Maugham compose something longer and 'more important' and send it in.

In possession of his first rejection slips and his first professional literary advice, the young author turned to his novel and went on with it in earnest. It grew out of his experience in the obstetric wards at St Thomas's. Medical studies, as Mr Morgan has argued, provided Maugham not only with much of what he knew about human nature at this point in his life, but also with the subject matter and the cast of characters of his first book – as well as the clinical, detached attitude required to write it. Now twenty-two, Maugham was working as an obstetric 'clerk' in the Lambeth slums and delivering an average of three babies a day. On these visits he heard a good deal of Cockney speech. During the latter half of 1896 we find him completing the short novel that would make him famous at twenty-three (as Dickens was), *Liza of Lambeth*. It was submitted to Unwin on 14 January 1897, along with the author's summary, a brief note which read as follows:

> This is the story of a nine-day wonder in a Lambeth slum. It shows that those queer folk the poor live and love and die in very much the same way as their neighbours of Brixton and Belgravia, and that hatred, malice, and all uncharitableness are not the peculiar attributes of the glorious British Middle Class, and finally it shows that in this world nothing much matters, and that in Vere Street, Lambeth, nothing matters at all.

Thus the cynical novelist on his first offspring.

Gissing's *The Nether World* (1889) and slum life novels of the early Nineties such as Arthur Morrison's *Tales of Mean Streets* (1894) and some of Kipling's early tales of working-class life inspired Maugham to take copious notes during his forays into Lambeth on how the people there lived and spoke. *Liza of Lambeth* is about the courting days of a girl of the slums, with a sub-plot touching upon adultery. As such it gave Unwin and his advisers pause. 'It was still impossible to interest the public in the lower classes,' Maugham claims, with a good deal of poetic licence, in *The Summing Up* – for that particular trail had already been blazed not only by Gissing, Morrison, and Kipling, but also by George Moore, whose popular novels led almost directly to the relaxation of the circulating libraries' stranglehold on British publishing in the Nineties, which in turn made possible publication of such short tales as *Liza of Lambeth*. Maugham goes on, in his memoir, to say this:

> In *Liza of Lambeth* I described without addition or exaggeration the people I had met in the Out-Patients' Department at the Hospital and in the District during my service as an Obstetric Clerk, the incidents that had struck me when I went from house to house as the work called, or, when I had nothing to do, had seen on my idle saunterings. My lack of imagination (for imagination grows by exercise and contrary to common belief is more powerful in the mature than in the young) obliged me to set down quite straightforwardly what I had seen with my own eyes and heard with my own ears.

Though not a particularly good novel, *Liza* did have a vogue, due in part to Maugham's unblinking examination of sexual and social mores among a particular class of people, and his emphasis on the idea that physical desire rarely outlasts its satisfaction (Hardy and Gissing, as we know, had the same idea). These themes would be expanded to embrace other classes in Maugham's later books. In *Liza*, as in his subsequent fiction, there was no moral indignation – only an attempt to portray a portion of life accurately.

Unwin worried about bringing out a work so clinically realistic, but he reasoned that if he did not publish *Liza* somebody else would. And the recent triumphs of Moore and the abrupt demise, in 1894, of the traditional three-decker novel so beloved of the Victorian circulating libraries and the substitution in its place of single-volume 'cheap' editions, selling for six shillings or less, encouraged the publisher to try the book with the public. So did Edward Garnett. The decision to publish was made, and the novel appeared in September 1897.

Maugham sent presentation copies to his brothers, and was hurt but not surprised when both Charles and Frederic expressed their distaste, finding *Liza* too 'unpleasant'. The vicar of Whitstable died shortly after receiving his copy, leaving it unclear whether his instant demise should be considered a critical response. The first edition of two thousand copies was sold out in a few weeks, due in large part to Unwin's practised skill in extracting notices from almost everyone.

Maugham was pleased with the success of his first publication and delighted to be earning money from it. Indeed, he decided instantly to give up medicine. He passed his final examinations in October 1897 and was awarded diplomas as a licensed physician and surgeon. But his unswerving belief in himself as a writer now began to seem justified, and he was determined to live by his pen. His decision not to practise medicine moved one of the senior surgeons at St Thomas's who admired Maugham's medical abilities to comment years later on the novelist's career: 'Very sad. One of our failures, I'm afraid.' It would be another decade before Maugham could live comfortably on his earnings as a writer, but he persevered, vowing to take no other jobs to supplement his income. 'I was determined,' he wrote later, 'to stamp myself upon the age.' And so he did.

Maugham never denied, as we know, that he put a great deal of himself into his fiction, and in his non-fiction he argues that anyone who puts pen to paper must do the same. But among his fellow craftsmen he was notably insistent on the autobiographical content of fiction; only Conrad was as hectoring on this theme. The artist, Maugham argues in *The Summing Up* – as Conrad had done in *A Personal Record* – no matter which of the arts he practises, cannot help but draw in his work 'a complete picture of himself'. In *Ten Novels and Their Authors* (1954), Maugham declares that the novelist is always at the mercy of his own 'bias . . . Whatever he writes is the expression of his personality and it is the manifestation of his innate instincts, his feelings and his experience. However hard he tries to be objective, he remains the slave of his idiosyncrasies':

> What is it that must be combined with the creative instinct to make it possible for a writer to produce a work of value? . . . it is personality. It may be a pleasant or an unpleasant one; that doesn't matter. What matters is that, by some idiosyncrasy of nature, the writer is enabled to see in a manner peculiar to himself.

The little French boy traumatised by his mother's death followed by transplantation in a new country where everyone seemed to dislike him is everywhere in his work. The desperately unhappy childhood became part of the writer's permanent mental baggage. He carried his private melancholy everywhere: through a disastrous marriage, a series of affairs with unsavoury men, an amount of foreign travel (fuelled by a continuous and continuing desire to 'escape') that can only be called obsessive; all the while his deepest thoughts and feelings went into his work. He was a bereaved man, and understood this: thus all those comments about the autobiographical nature of fiction. He knew why he wrote. Within the large Maugham family in later years the famous and wealthy novelist was known familiarly to one and all as 'poor Willie'. The adjective was always there. No amount of success, no amount of money, could calm his fierce restlessness, the bouts of self-hatred, the constant searching for peace and happiness. When he spoke to the family of his childhood, which he never got over, it was still, it was always, of Paris and the beauty of his mother and the love she inspired: it was never of the English years. So Maugham's daughter, now Lady Glendevon, told the present writer. The novelist's craving for fame, for popularity, for approval – driving forces throughout his life – stemmed at least in part from the feeling of rejection that overtook him when he was suddenly transformed from a French son to an English nephew, an experience from which he never recovered. Once he achieved fame his secretiveness about his life, both present and past, became as obsessive as his travelling. He was now W. Somerset Maugham. In part, no doubt, to justify his unloved existence, he worked very hard. Everything about him eventually became, on the surface at least, almost exaggeratedly *comme il faut*, as one of his nieces has said. What was hidden beneath was nobody's business. But Maugham's submerged or 'secret' life exists in his books, as he himself suggests. Four of his major novels are especially revealing in this respect: *Of Human Bondage, The Moon and Sixpence, Cakes and Ale*, and *The Razor's Edge*.

Except for its final sections, *Of Human Bondage* is largely autobiography. Though we hardly need his testimony – the plot of the novel and the facts of the life speak for themselves – *Of Human Bondage*, Maugham admits in *The Summing Up*, is 'an autobiographical novel; fact and fiction are inextricably mingled; the emotions are my own.' He goes on to say something far more interesting: 'The book did for me what I wanted, and when it was issued to the world ... I found myself free for ever from those pains and unhappy recollections.' He speaks of the novel as if it were a confession, something he had to disgorge before he could move on, a cathartic purging of the soul – though one may reasonably doubt that, having published the story of his youth to the world, suitably fictionalised, he remained 'free for ever from those pains and unhappy recollections' of his early life (indeed, his love for others was always obsessive and the pain of rejection always acute). But he did his best to unload them; and the power to move *Of Human Bondage* still has stems largely from this.

Some additional comments on this powerful story of pain and endurance. The school Philip attends is (somewhat brazenly) called King's, though Canterbury is changed to Tercanbury. Philip, who 'would gladly have changed places with the dullest boy in the school who was whole of limb', decides that 'Oxford would be little better than a continuation of his life at school. He wished immensely to be his own master. Besides he . . . wanted to get away from [his old schoolfellows] . . . He felt that his life at school had been a failure. He wanted to start fresh.' Thus he goes to Germany rather than to Oxford. There he learns, among other things, that in England freedom neither of thought nor of action can exist: 'You're ground down by convention. You can't think as you like and you can't act as you like.' Once he is in Germany, away from his uncle, Philip gives up his faith without hesitation.

> The fact was that he had ceased to believe not for this reason or the other, but because he had not the religious temperament. Faith had been forced upon him from the outside. It was a matter of environment and example. A new environment and a new example gave him the opportunity to find himself. He put off the faith of his childhood quite simply, like a cloak that he no longer needed.

The novel also articulates the young Maugham's hunger for 'experience' and his contempt for the 'teachings' of his youth.

> He yearned above all things for experience and felt himself ridiculous because at his age he had not enjoyed that which all fiction taught him was the most important thing in life; but he had the unfortunate gift of seeing things as they were, and the reality which was offered him differed too terribly from the ideal of his dreams . . . It was an illusion that youth is happy, an

illusion of those who have lost it; but the young know they are wretched, for they are full of the truthless ideals which have been instilled into them, and each time they come in contact with the real they are bruised and wounded ... They must discover for themselves that all they have read and all they have been told are lies, lies, lies; and each discovery is another nail driven into the body on the cross of life.

Throughout his early years Philip, in his wretchedness, is always imagining that he is somebody else, and what that might be like. The artist in him is born as he subjects himself to the discipline of subduing his own personality in order to get inside other skins; and he has 'the unfortunate gift of seeing things as they were'. As Maugham was to do, after his medical studies Philip goes to Paris to study painting, and learns what Maugham learned: 'How the devil is one to get the intention of the soul except by painting exactly what one sees?' Maugham had obviously been reading Browning.

In Paris, the artist Clutton speaks for Maugham when he tells Philip, 'if you want to be a gentleman you must give up being an artist. They've got nothing to do with one another.' Artists and gentlemen inhabit different worlds: *The Moon and Sixpence* presents this lesson in greater detail. After all, Philip finds it difficult to 'wrench out of his nature the instincts of the middle-class from which he came'. Maugham's ultimate decision to break with everything 'familiar' – country, family, professional training – could come only after the same sort of struggle. Wishing desperately to succeed as an artist, he saw his respectable middle-class background as a barrier to this goal, as Strickland the painter does in *The Moon and Sixpence*. Art is not practised by people who go to an office: both novels argue this. Art is life's work, all-consuming.

Philip's medical education proved to him that he was 'more interested in people than in anything else in the world.' As a medical student he had observed 'humanity ... in the rough, [using] the materials the artist worked [with] ... he was in the position of the artist and the patients were like clay in his hands.' Philip's experience as a medical student enables him, in the words of the novel, to 'cast away' the 'degrading bondage' of Christianity, of everything his uncle taught him. His medical studies help him, as Maugham's helped him, to unshackle the moral and cultural bondage of his uncle and his class.

Philip exulted, as he had exulted in his boyhood when the weight of a belief in God was lifted from his shoulders: it seemed to him that the last burden of responsibility was taken from him; and for the first time he was utterly free. His insignificance was turned to power, and he felt himself suddenly equal with the cruel fate which had seemed to persecute him; for if life was meaningless, the world was robbed of its cruelty.

So there is no point in actively pursuing 'happiness'; to cease to do so is to cast aside one's last illusions, to see that it doesn't matter whether you are 'happy' or not, just as it doesn't matter whether you are alive or not. Maugham shows us here how as a young man he found a refuge from hope in cynicism. And yet as his later novels (especially *The Razor's Edge*) show, something in him never entirely gave up the quest for happiness, even when he 'knew' that it did not matter whether he was happy or not, and that in any case the thing was beyond his control. And so he threw himself obsessively into work, the one item he *could* control, the one thing he could make turn out as he liked. His 'experience of life' led to his cynicism, and his cynicism gave him, as a writer, a subject: the 'facts' of life. Thus Philip learns that 'Life was not so horrible if it was meaningless,' and so he is able to 'face it with a strange sense of power.' Putting to use what he had seen and learned as a student and a surgeon, Maugham wrote novels as if he were dissecting a corpse; and this perhaps helps account for the unmistakable ring of truth we hear in his fiction, even when improbabilities in it occur. In one way or another, it is always about real life.

Philip 'had heard people speak contemptuously of money: he wondered if they had ever tried to do without it,' as he and his author had done. Lack of means, Philip decides, 'made a man petty, mean, grasping; it distorted his character and caused him to view the world from a vulgar angle; when you had to consider every penny, money became of grotesque importance.' All the unhappy lessons of Maugham's youth seem to find their way into *Of Human Bondage*. 'No work, no dinner', the novel reminds us. At the end, Philip sees that without 'experience,' without suffering, without his bondage to the values of others, he could never have understood enough of life to depict it accurately as an artist.

And thinking over the long pilgrimage of his past he accepted it joyfully. He accepted the deformity which had made life so hard

230

for him; he knew that it had warped his character, but now he saw also that by reason of it he had acquired that power of introspection which had given him so much delight. Without it he would never have had his keen appreciation of beauty, his passion for art and literature, and his interest in the varied spectacle of life.

It is no accident, then, that Maugham's greatest novel is about a man who must give up everything – his health, his humanity, ultimately his life – to become an artist. In outline, of course, the story of Strickland in *The Moon and Sixpence* resembles the story of Gauguin, but in fact at many points there is no resemblance whatsoever between the two, and that is because the novel is not about either man: it is about Maugham.

No matter how hard critics of *The Moon and Sixpence* have tried to avoid seeing this, the author's sympathies are with the artist rather than the family and the 'civilization' he abandons. Maugham makes Strickland hateful because he wants to show that art comes not out of conventional thought and action but rather out of the unusual, the tragic, the sordid. Artists are not 'gentlemen'. Happy, well-adjusted, ordinary people, he believed, do not produce great works of art. Maugham's own life furnished some proof of this. Among other things, Strickland's career is a justification of Maugham's own actions – most specifically leaving his wife and daughter and going abroad to live. Maugham is the artist the novel is about. Its argument is an extension of his idea that the artist is justified in *any* line of conduct so long as he *is* an artist, for what he produces benefits everybody – everybody, that is, except himself, since the artist, morally and socially, must lead a relentlessly and ruthlessly monotonous life in order to be productive. 'The true artist will let his wife starve, his children go barefoot, his mother drudge for his living at seventy,' remarks a character in Shaw's *Man and Superman*, 'sooner than work at anything but his art.'

When Mme Gauguin read *The Moon and Sixpence* she remarked that in Strickland she could not find a single trait of her late husband. The story, which is not Gauguin's, demonstrates one of Maugham's favourite maxims: seeing the faults of great artists dramatised makes art that much more accessible to all of us. We perceive that artists are human beings, like ourselves, and that flawless work can be produced by flawed persons. We see that human beings can turn their weaknesses to account as well as their strengths. And the novel helps explain its author to its readers. Maugham may not consciously have intended this in *The Moon and Sixpence*, though he admits in the opening paragraph that the artist, in everything he does, 'lays before you also the greater gift of himself.' Even more explicit, later, is this: 'A man's work reveals him ... in his book or picture the real man delivers himself defenceless ... To the acute observer no one can produce the most casual work without disclosing the innermost secrets of his soul.' Again Maugham says here about his work what Conrad said about his. The social man may assume masks, but as soon as he puts pen to paper and pretends to be someone else he can speak of nothing but himself; thus, fiction never lies.

The society Strickland leaves – and by the time the novel appeared Maugham had long since left his for 'exile' in France – is portrayed as conventional and dull. Its values are expressed in Mrs Strickland's announcement that her husband left her for a dancer. This society understands that men sometimes abandon women for 'romance'; it cannot conceive of a man leaving a woman for a mere *idea*. Such a thing cannot be admitted in Mrs Strickland's circle because it cannot be explained there. Maugham attacks the philistinism of the English. 'My father made me go into business because he said there was no money in art,' Strickland remarks. In a way, Maugham's whole career was designed to refute the values of his Uncle Henry and Victorian Whitstable.

Though Strickland is a nasty creature, the reader of *The Moon and Sixpence* is forced to sympathise with him – with his escape from his conventional surroundings and with his desire to paint. The novel argues that the artist must be forgiven his sins, and the argument is utterly convincing. 'The writer,' Maugham declares here, 'is more concerned to know than to judge,' and the reader, despite the inimical nature of Strickland – perhaps because of it – is led over barriers to feel, ultimately, the same way. From first to last the book is a defence of unconventionality, an obsession of Maugham's.

A major chord of the novel is struck by the painter Dirk Stroeve:

'Why should you think that beauty, which is the most precious thing in the world, lies like a stone on the beach for the careless passer-by to pick up idly? Beauty is something wonderful and strange that the artist fashions out of the chaos of the world in the torment of his soul. And when he has made it, it is not given to all to know it. To recognize it you must repeat the adventure of the artist. It is a melody that he sings to you, and to hear it again in your own heart you want knowledge and sensitiveness and imagination.'

An aspect of Strickland that may remind us of Maugham is his cynicism about love. Gerald Haxton, for many years Maugham's lover, used to say that until the novelist's daily stint of work was done he did not care whether anyone lived or died. Something of this ruthlessness in 'romantic' matters is depicted in Strickland, who says: 'I can't overcome my desire, but I hate it; it imprisons my spirit; I look forward to the time when I shall be free from all desires and can give myself without hindrance to my work ... Love is a disease.' Maugham comments comfortably: 'he hated the instincts that robbed him of his self-possession.' What is known of Maugham's life in France suggests that he created a climate around himself in which the reciprocal love he claimed he missed was impossible, thus the expectations of it would always be disappointed. Certainly *The Moon and Sixpence*, like many great novels, was written by a very unhappy man.

According to Maugham, Strickland 'had become aware of the soul of the universe and [felt] compelled to express it ... His real life consisted of dreams and of tremendously hard work.' So did his own. The final summing-up of Strickland's nature has an autobiographical ring to it: 'It seems strange even to myself when I have described a man who was cruel, selfish, brutal, and sensual, to say that he was a great idealist ... He was single-hearted in his aim, and to pursue it he was willing to sacrifice not only himself – many can do that – but others. He had a vision.' He was both 'odious' and 'great.' The suggestion is that he had to be odious in order to be great. After all, as the narrator says at the end of *The Moon and Sixpence*, 'a man is not what he wants to be, but what he must be.'

Everyone knows that Alroy Kear in *Cakes and Ale* – 'no one among my contemporaries ... had achieved so considerable a position on so little talent' – is based on Hugh Walpole, and that Edward Driffield, 'the greatest novelist of our day' and the 'last of the Victorians', is drawn from Thomas Hardy. Maugham, who had never been invited to Max Gate – he calls it 'Ferne Court' – nevertheless gave such a mercilessly intuitive portrait of Hardy's second wife ('Amy Driffield') that Florence Emily Hardy, out of embarrassment and chagrin, stopped making public appearances – indeed, was rarely seen outside of Max Gate after the book's publication. Some said the novel, which shows her exploiting her husband's fame both before and after his death (and trying to turn him into a respectable old man while he was still alive), killed her. What is indisputable is that she died shortly after its appearance – reminiscent of the response of Henry Maugham to publication of *Liza of Lambeth*.

Driffield in his eighties is characterised in *Cakes and Ale* as 'rather shy ... and quiet, very well-mannered ... but a little dry' and unsophisticated. Florence is portrayed as 'dreadfully common'; she had been his secretary, but in the novel is described as 'a barmaid' or worse who manages to become 'an admirable amanuensis.' This is devastating but not quite fair. 'The dullness of their lives was almost incredible,' the narrator says.

Generally it is agreed that the novel's picture of Hardy in his last years, a not unsympathetic sketch, is accurate in many particulars. The inveterate hostess Lady Hodmarsh, 'the clever and handsome American wife of a sporting baronet with no intelligence and charming manners', is probably Lady St Helier. Mrs Barton Trafford may be based on Hardy's friend Florence Henniker. Blackstable and Tercanbury are again brought in as the settings for several scenes; Maugham's continuing hatred of Whitstable, into his fifties, is reflected in the town's verdict on Driffield: '"when you consider what he came from it's wonderful that he writes at all" ... was the manner in which he was generally spoken of at Blackstable.'

That Driffield is Hardy cannot really be disputed, though some have tried. 'He was for long thought to write very bad English ... his style was laboured, an uneasy mixture of classical and slangy.' Condemned for coarseness in his early years, he lived long enough to become respectable and to hear himself eulogised by another generation for his frankness. 'There are descriptive passages in his works that have found their way into all the anthologies of English prose.' At first he was thought 'too boldly realistic' and had trouble with the critics and the libraries, until it was 'discovered that his ... peasants were Shakespearean.' His strength as a writer lay 'in his depiction of the class he knew best, farmers and farm labourers. ... When he introduces a character belonging to a higher station in life even his warmest admirers ... must experience a certain malaise.' He is described as 'keen on architecture' – and also as a frequenter of local pubs, which Hardy certainly was in his later years. 'Of course the old man had written all his great books before he ever set eyes on' his second wife; the 'great books' were composed while he was living with his first wife – 'a very unfortunate marriage.'

Amy Driffield is said to have a hard time with the old man. 'Driffield had some queer ways and she had to use a good deal of tact to get him to behave decently.' Driffield also shares with Hardy a healthy suspicion of indoor plumbing; and both are childless. The second Mrs Driffield cannot understand why the great man wants to go on living 'in a place where everyone knew all about his origins' and knew as well that he spoke about them untruthfully.

Driffield is said to have brought a critical storm down upon his head by writing a novel called *The Cup of Life* (*Jude the Obscure*) which contains among other things 'the scene of [a] child's death, terrible and heart-rending, but written without slop or sickliness': 'Of all Driffield's books it is the only one I should like to have written,' says the narrator of *Cakes and Ale*. Why? Because 'to be shocked by it was to confess yourself a philistine'. Maugham was twenty when *Jude the Obscure* was published, and undoubtedly he and the vicar of Whitstable thought differently about the novel.

For Driffield 'longevity is genius', and after years on the shelf he becomes, at eighty, the Grand Old Man of English Letters. In early photographs he wears a moustache; in later years he is clean-shaven, his face seeming to grow thinner and more lined. 'The stubborn commonplace of the early portraits melted gradually into a weary refinement.' Respectability gives Driffield some added confidence, including the courage to remark of Henry James that he 'had turned his back on one of the great events of the world's history, the rise of the United States, in order to report tittle-tattle at tea-parties in English country houses.' Alroy Kear, writing a life of Driffield, says he can't repeat that: 'I'd have the Henry James gang down on me like a thousand of bricks.' The young Walpole had been an intimate friend of the elderly James, and Hardy in old age is on record as thinking of James as 'the only other' great living novelist. The view of James one gets in *Cakes and Ale* is Maugham's; putting it into the mouths of Hardy and Walpole is one of the novel's few false literary notes.

One can see that there is a good deal of Maugham in this famous novel 'about' Hardy, just as there was a good deal of him in the novel 'about' Gauguin. 'The reader cannot have failed to observe that I accepted the conventions of my class as if they were the laws of Nature,' the narrator, called 'Willie', observes sadly of his younger self. It is those bourgeois conventions, here embraced by Blackstable, that the novel attacks. The novel contains some other literary opinions of Maugham's, including this one on authorship:

> I began to meditate upon the writer's life. It is full of tribulation. First he must endure poverty and the world's indifference; then, having achieved a measure of success, he must submit with a good grace to its hazards. He depends on a fickle public . . . But he has one compensation. Whenever he has anything on his mind, whether it be a harassing reflection, grief at the death of a friend, unrequited love, wounded pride, anger at the treachery of someone to whom he has shown kindness, in short any emotion or any perplexing thought, he has only to put it down in black and white, using it as a theme of a story or the decoration of an essay, to forget all about it. He is the only free man.

This is one of the most autobiographical passages in Maugham's fiction. Needless to say, he used the 'one compensation' freely and avidly.

Finally there is the question of Rosie, the first Mrs Driffield, who bears no resemblance whatever to Emma Lavinia Hardy, either in her person as described in the novel or in her biography. The narrator of *Cakes and Ale* is quite taken with her; yet her identity has remained a mystery to commentators since the book's appearance sixty years ago. There has been some speculation recently that Rosie, like Mildred in *Of Human Bondage*, was drawn from one of Maugham's male lovers, but this is unlikely. Maugham's daughter has revealed to the present writer a possible persona for the mysterious Rosie. According to Lady Glendevon, Rosie is based on Maugham's first great love, an actress whom he met before the Great War – before, that is, he ever set eyes on Syrie Wellcome, the woman he married, and before any of his subsequent long-term male lovers appeared on the scene. Maugham and the young lady planned to marry, he bought her a ring – and at the last moment she ran off with, and married instead, the son of an Irish peer. The latter had made her an offer she couldn't refuse; Maugham never forgot how relative poverty and lack of position could contribute, in ways even he had never dreamed of before then, to a sense of insecurity and personal worthlessness.

At the end of *Cakes and Ale* the narrator sees Rosie again, now an elderly woman, in New York. This event too has an analogue in Maugham's life. The famous story of Dickens and his youthful love Maria Beadnell is repeated in that of Maugham and his first love, whom he saw again many years later and was shocked to find not only elderly but fat, a commodious embodiment of the anti-climax of the years. But unlike Dickens's Flora Finching in *Little Dorrit*, Maugham's Rosie in *Cakes and Ale* is treated respectfully. In fact she is given the novel's last line. Asked what she saw in Edward Driffield, she replies: 'He was always such a perfect gentleman.' Maugham, who had as a youth rarely been treated gently and never got over it, may have had in mind his beautiful mother's explanation of why she so adored his ugly father: 'Because he has never hurt my feelings.'

We come now to *The Razor's Edge*, Maugham's last important statement in fiction. Generally it has been regarded as evidence that the novelist went on writing too long: he was seventy when it was published. It is nonetheless a powerful and interesting book, as well as being, along with *Of Human Bondage*, one of the most directly autobiographical statements Maugham ever made. If he put into the earlier novel 'everything [he] then knew', one might say that he put into the later one everything he had learned since.

In 1896 the twenty-two-year-old Maugham recorded the following Notebook entry while on a visit to Capri:

> I wander about alone, forever asking myself the same questions: What is the meaning of life? Has it any object or end? Is there such a thing as morality? How ought one to conduct oneself in life? What guide is there? Is there one road better than another? . . . I could make nothing out of it all; it seemed to me one big tangle. In desperation, I cried out: I can't understand it. I don't know, I don't know.

That Maugham's search for 'meaning' and with it peace had not come to an end two decades later may be seen in *The Moon and Sixpence*, perhaps most specifically in Strickland's dilemma: his 'passion to create beauty . . . gave him no peace. It urged him hither and thither. He was eternally a pilgrim, haunted by a divine nostalgia, and the demon within him was ruthless.'

Maugham's 'divine nostalgia', his restlessness and dissatisfaction, his unending search for something satisfying and final, went on to the end of his life and may be seen in *The Razor's Edge*, whose main character, like Strickland, decamps from his stockbroker's office in mid-career in search of some sort of spiritual or inner peace, never fully defined. It is tempting to say simply that Maugham wasn't happy and that happiness is what he was still searching for. In that case: what could make him happy, and where might he find it?

Maugham was always the victim of a large, unfocused restlessness – feeling, like a Henry James or an Edith Wharton character, that there was something he had missed. Love, perhaps: he had sought it, and by his own testimony failed to find it, ever since his eighth birthday, the day his mother died. He had never made his peace with the critics, or they with him, and he had won few literary prizes. But he could count on a huge reading audience, and that pleased him. 'Genius is an infinite capacity for taking pains,' *Of Human Bondage* tells us. 'The only thing is to peg away.' He had pegged away for nearly half a century when he wrote *The Razor's Edge*, which reflects a private rather than a social or a political malaise. Was it his homosexuality, his essential solitariness – even when surrounded by friends at his French villa he would complain of loneliness – the failure of his marriage, separation from his family, expatriation from England? Maugham in old age, a 'cunning' novelist now retired, confortable, cosseted, still seeking respectability and spiritually miserable, a man who knows that 'actuality sometimes plays into the hands of art', is instantly recognisable as the speaker of the brilliant opening sentence of Anthony Burgess's novel *Earthly Powers* (1980): 'It was the afternoon of my eight-first birthday, and I was in bed with my catamite when Ali announced that the archbishop had come to see me.'

One of Maugham's nieces told the present writer that *The Razor's Edge* is the 'key' to the novelist's life – even more so than *Of Human Bondage*, the earlier book being merely an account of the time before its publication, the later one being a true chronicle of Maugham's disposition as well as his lifelong search for spiritual peace, the peace he was writing about in Capri in 1896, the peace that had always eluded him. The effects of his early trauma and bereavement were ceaseless and unexpiring, according to the late Clarissa Farrell, a daughter of Maugham's eldest brother Charles. The novelist, she said, was an unhappy soul who could find belief and faith nowhere, and yet constantly sought them as a step towards the spiritual peace he felt was missing in his life. He became something of a mystic. The Maugham family generally believes that Larry Darrell, the protagonist of *The Razor's Edge*, is more enduringly and comprehensively Somerset Maugham than *Of Human Bondage*'s Philip Carey.

'The sharp edge of a razor is difficult to pass over; thus the wise say the path to Salvation is hard.' If some sort of 'salvation' is what Maugham was looking for, *The Razor's Edge* among other things shows that he was never quite as successful at finding it as his hero Darrell, who does acquire some spiritual peace by the end of the book. Thrown off stride by fighting in the Great War, Darrell doubts he can 'ever find peace until I make up my mind about things ... It's hard not to ask yourself what life is all about and whether there's any sense to it or whether it's all a tragic blunder of blind fate.' These are the questions he gives up his job to try to answer – questions that had plagued Maugham for years. Was Schopenhauer wrong, and was there in fact some 'meaning' to things he had missed? How should he go about finding it? Other characters in the novel suspect that Darrell is just an idler, afraid of hard work. He tells his fiancée Isabel that what he seeks is 'The acquisition of knowledge.' When she presses him to be more specific, he replies: 'I want to know whether I have an immortal soul or whether when I die it's the end.' This of course is Maugham's question; he had gone all over the world, even to a guru's ashram in southern India, to try to find the answer. At seventy he had put aside his Schopenhauer, a young man's philosopher, and was still looking for that answer. The conventional people in *The Razor's Edge* who think Darrell is a fake are treated harshly by the novelist; we may be certain that he sympathises with Darrell's quest, as he sympathised with Strickland's.

The novel makes a point of underlining the emptiness of Isabel's life (which it also follows) in comparison with Larry's. He is the free spirit, tied to no one and to no place. He is freedom-from-convention personified, an allegorical figure of wish-fulfilment. Maugham characterises Larry's quest as 'a disinterested desire for knowledge' and suggests that 'merely to know' things is a 'sufficient satisfaction ... as it's a sufficient satisfaction to an artist to produce a work of art.' In fact, Larry's is the old idea of making one's life a work of art, given sufficient money, time, and ruthlessness in personal relations.

Near the end of the novel, asked what he has gained from his travels and his experiments in life, Larry replies with a single word:

'peace'. He seems detached from the concerns of ordinary people, and at ease with himself. He is, in a word provided by Maugham, 'disinterested'. Baffled, his friends conclude either that he is a crank or that he has somehow managed to achieve happiness 'without love' – that he has learned how to do without it. At the time *The Razor's Edge* was composed Maugham had felt unloved for sixty years and was just beginning to see, apparently, that it didn't matter. The novel's narrator, called 'Maugham', declares:

> Passion is destructive . . . And if it doesn't destroy it dies. It may be then that one is faced with the desolation of knowing that one has wasted the years of one's life, that one's brought disgrace upon oneself, endured the frightful pang of jealousy, swallowed every bitter mortification, that one's expended all one's tenderness, poured out all the riches of one's soul on a poor drab, a fool, a peg on which one hung one's dreams, who wasn't worth a stick of chewing-gum.

Among others, Elliott Templeton, who lives only for society, is compared to Larry, and we see Templeton fail the 'peace' test at the end of his life, when he seems equally afraid of living and of dying. Whatever the opposite of peace is, this addict of 'Society' has achieved it. At the end he weeps like a child because he has not been asked to a party given by a princess. 'The old bitch' are his last words.

Larry Darrell, seeking 'a rule of life that'll satisfy both his head and his heart', is the opposite of a social adventurer. Like Strickland, he is more like a social dropout, one of the twentieth century's first flower children. 'I wanted to make something of my life, but I didn't know what,' Larry says. 'I couldn't understand why there was evil in the world.' His studies and travels have given him faith that life can be useful rather than meaningless. When Maugham the narrator confesses to Larry that the happiest days of his own life were those he spent as a student at Heidelberg, when he had no money and no position and no responsibilities but plenty of freedom, Larry replies – it is like two Maughams, the saved and the unsaved, speaking to one another – that 'the distance that separates you [that is, Maugham the narrator] from faith is no greater than the thickness of a cigarette paper.'

Perhaps Maugham the man felt this himself, and created an alter-ego who could exist on the other side of that thin membrane of faith. He would not have been the first author to follow in the footsteps of one of his characters, or to wish to do so. One of the many oddities of *The Razor's Edge* is that it is doubly autobiographical in containing a character called 'Maugham' who resembles the biographical author, and a character called Darrell who seems to embody many of the fantasies the novelist entertained throughout the course of his life. The successes of 'Maugham' are treated lightly by the author; the tortuous, sinuous triumphs of Larry, spiritual in nature, are treated with awe and envy. Nowhere else does Maugham the man show so plainly how disappointing he found his own life in comparison with other possible lives. He was always wanting to be some other boy.

It is primarily through Hinduism that Larry learns 'God is within me or nowhere,' and thus that all 'exterior' searches for God are bound to fail. This is the 'knowledge', the 'reality', he comes to. Maugham seems to envy his final understanding and conviction 'that it is not essential to salvation to retire from the world, but only to renounce the self.' Larry reaches 'peace' down this road. 'It's damned lucky for you that you have a private income,' the narrator snaps at him; no doubt the author was recalling his own impecunious youth, when earning an income necessarily was high on his list of priorities. Of his private income, Larry says: 'It's given me what I value more than anything else in life – independence.' Maugham must have felt a little of that; when he said that the writer is the only free man, he did not mean the failed writer. At any rate, the two 'Maughams' seem to approach one another at the end of the novel. 'You can't think what a comfort it's been to me to think that if I wanted to I could tell anyone in the world to go to hell,' says Larry, speaking for all three of them.

On the last page of *The Razor's Edge* the author, talking directly to the reader, declares that he 'can only admire the radiance of such a rare creature [as Larry], I cannot step into his shoes and enter his innermost heart as I sometimes think I can do with persons more nearly allied to the common run of men.' Though Larry is his own creation, he cannot become him. He understands, Maugham says, 'that ultimate satisfaction can only be found in the life of the spirit,' but he also understands that he himself cannot achieve the sort of life he has given his hero, a life which exists only in the pages of a novel. For him it is too late. All he can do, as he has told us earlier in the book, is 'use convention as an instrument of its own purpose'; only then can 'Art' be 'triumphant'. Thus Maugham's own reluctant but persistent surface conventionality, the *comme il faut* side of him, is used as a foil in *The Razor's Edge* to the alternative life he is now too old to find. It is a remarkable novel, candid and courageous, a very personal confession from beginning to end.

In the Preface to *A Writer's Notebook*, Maugham declares his enormous admiration for the works of Jules Renard, especially his novel *Poil de Carotte*.

> It is the story of his own childhood, the story of a little uncouth boy whose harsh and unnatural mother leads him a wretched life. Renard's method of writing, without ornament, without emphasis, heightens the pathos of the dreadful tale, and the poor lad's sufferings, mitigated by no pale ray of hope, are heart-rending. You laugh wryly at his clumsy efforts to ingratiate himself with that demon of a woman and you feel his humiliations, you resent his unmerited punishments, as though they were your own. It would be an ill-conditioned person who did not feel his blood boil at the inflation of such malignant cruelty. It is not a book you can easily forget.

Maugham wrote this passage in his seventy-fifth year. He forgot little – certainly not his own boyhood nor the constant hope of his earliest years to be loved and accepted by others after the death of his mother (who was anything but harsh and unnatural) robbed him of the only secure foundation he had ever stood on. The effect upon him of his early struggles was indelible.

'You will hear people say that poverty is the best spur to the artist,' he wrote in *Of Human Bondage*. 'They have never felt the iron of it in their flesh.'

Works Consulted

Chapter One

F. W. Dupee, *Henry James*, 1951.

Leon Edel, *Henry James: The Untried Years 1843–1870*, 1952.

Howard M. Feinstein, *Becoming William James*, 1984.

Henry James, *Henry James: Letters, Vol. I, 1853–1875*, ed. Leon Edel, 1974.

Henry James, *The Complete Notebooks of Henry James*, ed. Leon Edel and Lyall H. Powers, 1987.

Henry James, *A Small Boy and Others*, 1913.

Henry James, *Notes of A Son and Brother*, 1914.

Henry James, *The Middle Years*, 1917.

Chapter Two

Robert Gittings, *Young Thomas Hardy*, 1975.

Robert Gittings, *The Older Hardy*, 1978.

F. E. Hardy, *The Life of Thomas Hardy: 1840–1928*, 1928, 1930, 1962.

Thomas Hardy, *Collected Letters of Thomas Hardy, Vol. I, 1840–1892*, ed. R. L. Purdy and Michael Millgate, 1978.

Michael Millgate, *Thomas Hardy: A Biography*, 1982.

Chapter Three

Pierre Coustillas, 'George Gissing: The Dynamics of Frustration' (unpublished).

George Gissing, *London and the Life of Literature in Late Victorian England: The Diary of George Gissing, Novelist*, ed. Pierre Coustillas, 1978.

John Halperin, *Gissing: A Life in Books*, 1982; 1987, 1988.
Jacob Korg, *George Gissing: A Critical Biography*, 1963.
Morley Roberts, *The Private Life of Henry Maitland*, 1912.
Gillian Tindall, *The Born Exile: George Gissing*, 1974.

Chapter Four

Jocelyn Baines, *Joseph Conrad: A Critical Biography*, 1960.
John Conrad, *Joseph Conrad: Times Remembered*, 1981.
Joseph Conrad, *The Collected Letters of Joseph Conrad, Vol. I, 1861–1897*, ed. Frederick Karl and Laurence Davies, 1983.
Joseph Conrad, *A Personal Record*, 1912.
Frederick C. Crews, *Skeptical Engagements*, 1987.
Zdzislaw Najder, *Joseph Conrad: A Chronicle*, 1983.
Elsa Nettels, *James and Conrad*, 1977.
Edward Said, *Joseph Conrad and the Fiction of Autobiography*, 1966.
Ian Watt, *Conrad in the Nineteenth Century*, 1979.

Chapter Five

Irving Howe (ed.), *Edith Wharton: A Collection of Critical Essays*, 1962.
R. W. B. Lewis, *Edith Wharton: A Biography*, 1975.
Blake Nevius, *Edith Wharton: A Study of Her Fiction*, 1953.
Edith Wharton, *A Backward Glance*, 1934.
Edith Wharton, *The Writing of Fiction*, 1925.
Cynthia Griffin Wolff, *A Feast of Words: The Triumph of Edith Wharton*, 1977.

Chapter Six

Anthony Curtis, *The Pattern of Maugham: A Critical Portrait*, 1974.
Anthony Curtis, *Somerset Maugham*, 1977.
W. Somerset Maugham, *The Summing Up*, 1938.
W. Somerset Maugham, *Ten Novels and Their Authors*, 1943.
W. Somerset Maugham, *A Writer's Notebook*, 1949.
Ted Morgan, *Maugham: A Biography*, 1979.

Index

Index

journalism, 69; witnesses public hangings, 69; and death, 69–70; studies Greek, 69–70; religious doubts, 70; decides against university education, 70–1, 77; life in London, 71–7; interest in opera, 72; wins architectural prizes, 72; embarks on literary career, 73–4; use of memory, 73; poetry, 74–7; pessimism, 74, 85, 94; studies Shakespeare, 76; acting, 76; unhappy love affair, 77; attitude to fiction, 77–8; returns to Dorset, 78, 85; uses name 'Wessex', 84; works for Crickmay in Weymouth, 86–7; and lesbianism, 92; as novelist-biographer, 127; literary style, 137; Edith Wharton reads, 187–8; on impermanence of desire, 225; in Maugham's *Cakes and Ale*, 233–5

WORKS

'Annabel' (poem), 75
'At a Bridal' (poem), 77
'At a Seaside Town in 1869' (poem), 86
'At Waking' (poem), 86
'The Bride-Night Fire' (poem), 75
'Concerning Agnes' (poem), 67
'A Confession to a Friend in Trouble' (poem), 76
'The Dawn after the Dance' (poem), 87
Desperate Remedies, 69, 71, 75–6, 81–4, 86–94
'Discouragement' (poem), 75
'Domicilium' (poem), 70
The Dynasts, 65
Far from the Madding Crowd, 61, 84, 86, 92–3
'Hap' (poem), 75
'Heiress and Architect' (poem), 76
'Her Dilemma' (poem), 76
'Her Reproach' (poem), 76
'How I Built Myself a House' (essay), 74

'In Vision I Roamed' (poem), 76
'An Indiscretion in the Life of an Heiress' (story; extract from 'The Poor Man and the Lady'), 78, 81–5, 88–9
Jude the Obscure, 63, 67, 70, 75, 93–4, 152, 188; publicly burned, 183; in Maugham's *Cakes and Ale*, 235
A Laodicean, 70, 75
'Louisa in the Lane' (poem), 67
The Mayor of Casterbridge, 63, 68
'The Musing Maiden' (poem), 75
'Neutral Tones' (poem), 76
'1967' (poem), 75
'On the Application of Coloured Bricks and Terra Cotta to Modern Architecture' (essay), 72
'One We Knew' (poem), 69
A Pair of Blue Eyes, 71, 78
'The Poor Man and the Lady' (lost novel), 71, 76, 78–82, 84–5, 88
'Postponement' (poem), 77
The Return of the Native, 64, 66, 79, 91, 93
'Revulsion' (poem), 77
'The Ruined Maid' (poem), 75
'She, to Him' (poem), 76
Tess of the d'Urbervilles, 60–1, 64, 67, 69–70, 83
'To an Impersonator of Rosalind' (poem), 76
'To Lizbie Browne' (poem), 67
The Trumpet Major, 65, 73, 86
Under the Greenwood Tree, 66, 78, 80
The Well-Beloved, 66, 68, 75
'Wessex Heights' (poem), 64
Winter Words, 67
'The Withered Arm' (story), 62
The Woodlanders, 83, 86
Harper's (magazine), 180
Harrison, Frederic, 105
Harrison, Nell *see* Gissing, Marianne Helen

251

Index